DIVIDED

ALSO BY DAVID CAY JOHNSTON

*The Fine Print: How Big Companies Use
"Plain English" to Rob You Blind*

*Free Lunch: How the Wealthiest Americans
Enrich Themselves at Government Expense
and Stick You with the Bill*

*Perfectly Legal: The Covert Campaign to Rig
Our Tax System to Benefit the Super-Rich
—and Cheat Everybody Else*

*Temples of Chance: How America Inc.
Bought Out Murder Inc. to Win Control
of the Casino Business*

DIVIDED

THE PERILS OF OUR
GROWING INEQUALITY

EDITED BY

DAVID CAY JOHNSTON

THE NEW PRESS

NEW YORK
LONDON

Source notes for previously published material appear at the end of all relevant chapters. Chapters without source notes were written especially for this volume.

Requests for permission to reproduce selections from this book should be mailed to: Permissions Department, The New Press, 120 Wall Street, 31st floor, New York, NY 10005.

Published in the United States by The New Press, New York, 2014
Distributed by Perseus Distribution

LIBRARY OF CONGRESS CATALOGING-IN-PUBLICATION DATA

Divided : the perils of our growing inequality / edited by David Cay Johnston.
    pages cm
    ISBN 978-1-59558-923-1 (hardback) -- ISBN 978-1-59558-944-6 (e-book) 1. Equality--United States. 2. Income distribution--United States. 3. United States--Social policy--21st century. I. Johnston, David, 1948- editor of compilation.
HM821.D585 2014
305--dc23

                                    2013041718

The New Press publishes books that promote and enrich public discussion and understanding of the issues vital to our democracy and to a more equitable world. These books are made possible by the enthusiasm of our readers; the support of a committed group of donors, large and small; the collaboration of our many partners in the independent media and the not-for-profit sector; booksellers, who often hand-sell New Press books; librarians; and above all by our authors.

www.thenewpress.com

Book design and composition by Bookbright Media
This book was set in Minion Pro

Printed in the United States of America

10 9 8 7 6 5 4 3 2

CONTENTS

EDUCATION

HEALTH CARE INEQUALITY

INTRODUCTION

David Cay Johnston

In 2001, soon after George W. Bush was inaugurated, I called the White House press office for comment on the latest IRS income data. The deputy spokesperson expressed disbelief at the official figures I read, so much so that I asked, "What do you think is the median income shown on tax returns in America?" The answer: $250,000. The actual figure at the time: $28,000.

Misperceptions about affluence and poverty continue to infect our politics, even as the massive chasm that divides the very richest Americans from everyone else has become the defining story of our time. No natural forces determine income, wealth, and the quality of human life. We make the decisions about who will prosper and who will not—or we let other people make them for us. In societies with democratically elected governments, we are the captains of our fate, because when we elect politicians we choose their policies as carried out by presidents and governors, Congress and legislatures, and those they appoint as judges and regulators. For now, what we have chosen is extreme inequality, the worst by far of any nation with a modern economy.

In choosing inequality, we have opted to give up a broad and strong middle class with rising expectations, growing incomes, broadening home ownership, and access to higher education. In choosing health care inequality, we have decided to dampen millions of spirits, deny a chance at success to millions of children, and

turn many hardworking taxpayers into people who become perma-
nently disabled and thus a burden on society, simply because they
cannot get corrective surgery or drugs to control their conditions
and return to productive lives. We have created a society in which
all the nation's economic gains flow to the top and the vast majority
sees income stagnation or decline. We have embraced bankruptcy,
debt, long bouts of joblessness, and flat or shrinking paychecks as
the new normal. And we have lavished cash, tax cuts, and subtle
subsidies on the richest among us, whose prosperity continues to
blossom.

It was not always this way.

From the end of World War II until the early 1970s, the vast
majority of Americans enjoyed steadily improving lives. Wages
increased and a growing share of workers benefited from steady employment with fringe benefits such as health care, paid vacations,
and pensions. The number of jobs grew steadily, especially for work
requiring a college education or advanced degrees, as taxpayer investments in basic research produced tangible products and life-
extending services. Many more people became home owners, often
finding that their monthly outlay was less than when they rented.
Poverty remained a problem, but it was in decline, especially for
older Americans. For most families with children one income was
enough. Americans had debts, but they grew in tandem with the
economy. Cars were typically bought on three-year loans, not the
five-, six-, and seven-year loans common today. The real income reported on federal tax returns by the vast majority of Americans, the
90 percent, doubled between the end of the war and 1973.

Then the lives of the vast majority stopped getting better and,
after a few years, began a long and painful slide backward. Unions
dwindled, shifting the power to set pay from organized groups of
workers with advice from market experts to individual employees
negotiating, or more often just accepting, pay set by employers. The
rising costs of health care diverted more compensation from cash
wages to insurance premiums. Trade rules that often favored other
nations destroyed many well-paying manufacturing jobs, including
more than 50,000 factories and 2.8 million jobs offshored to China.

As a result, the vast majority's average income rose above the 1973
level only four times—in 1999, 2000, 2001, and 2007—and even then

added only the equivalent of one additional week's income to each year. By 2012 the average income of the vast majority had shrunk to the equivalent of 45 weeks of 1973 income—a 13 percent decline to $30,997 from $35,584 in 1973, expressed in 2012 dollars.

Between 1998 and 2011, the median weekly wage—half make more, half less—stagnated between $533 and $546 in 2012 dollars, then dropped in 2012 to $529 and change, or $27,519 for the year. Almost a third of the 153.6 million Americans with a job at any time in 2012 made less than $15,000, averaging just $6,100.

In recent years nearly all of the income growth has been in jobs paying more than $75,000—about one in every eight jobs. At the top, pay soared. In 2012 the number of people whose jobs paid cash wages of $5 million or more grew by 27 percent to 8,982 workers while their inflation-adjusted combined pay increased by 40 percent over 2011.

Very highly paid jobs have grown to such a degree that, in 1994, the Social Security Administration changed its top compensation category from "more than $5 million" to "more than $20 million." In 1997 it lifted the top level again, to "more than $50 million."

As wage growth slowed and then stopped—or even fell back—for millions of workers and the 90 percent's average total income shrank, debts rose and bankruptcies grew much faster than population. Since 1980, there have been 32 million personal bankruptcy filings in a nation with an average of about 100 million households, meaning that one in roughly three households has sought refuge from creditors.

At the top it was an entirely different story. Here we do not find the storied captains of industry who risk their capital to create jobs so much as executives, entertainers (from baseball players to pop singers), and other working wealthy, often salaried. The top 1 percent's average income certainly grew between the end of the war and 1973 along with everyone else's, but while the vast majority's income doubled, the top 1 percent's income grew by only a third. In contrast, from 1973 until 2012, the years when the vast majority saw their incomes slip, the top 1 percent saw their average income more than double, rising 153 percent to more than $1 million. The top 1 percent made almost thirteen times the average of the 90 percent in 1973, but by 2012 the ratio was 41 to 1.

While the average income of the vast majority in 2012 fell back to the level of 1966 (actually, $9 less than in 1966), the news got only better for the top 1 percent. They saw their average incomes rise from nearly $441,000 to $1,264,000, a real increase that nearly tripled their pretax incomes. At the very, *very top*, the news was nothing short of fantastic. The top 1 percent of the top 1 percent, or one in every 10,000 households, saw their average income sky-rocket from $5.4 million in 1966 to almost $30.8 million in 2012. That means that for every $1 in 1966 income, each household at the top reported $5.67 in 2012. Most of these are not the same people, but the figures tell us how, as a group, America rewarded its wealthiest, while the vast majority (also not all the same people, forty-six years later) saw their incomes wither.

The resulting growth at the top has become so concentrated that between 2009, when the Great Recession ended, and 2012 just 16,000 households collected 31 percent of all the increased income in all of America with its 315 million people. That money went to the 1 percent of the 1 percent. The top 1 percent enjoyed 94.8 percent of all the increased income, with the small remainder going to the rest of the top 10 percent.

And the vast majority, the bottom 90 percent? Analysis of tax returns by renowned economists Emmanuel Saez and Thomas Piketty showed that during this same period, from 2009 through 2012, their average incomes shrank by 15.7 percent.

We have also chosen to let the rich keep more of their increased income. Federal tax burdens at the top have fallen dramatically, while rising slightly for the 90 percent. Between 1961 and 2011 the share of their income that the nation's 400 top taxpayers paid in federal income taxes fell 60 percent. During the same years the income tax burden on the 90 percent declined only 20 percent. Add in higher Social Security and Medicare taxes and the top 400 data remain the same, but the tax burden of the 90 percent actually increases slightly. This means that the burden of government has been pushed down the income ladder.

Signs of modern inequality abound. Small jets have replaced the private piston-engine plane of the 1960s. In the past decade, we have seen a growing fleet of private jumbo jets such as Boeing 767s and 747s. We see ever more private boxes at sports stadia (built primarily with tax dollars) that are reached through private entry and exit ramps. More than 7 million Americans live in gated communities. In this and myriad other ways, the superrich separate themselves from society physically, culturally, and psychologically. These trends help explain how the Bush White House's deputy press secretary could believe that half of Americans made more than $250,000, when fewer than one in fifty actually did.

Meanwhile, poverty is worsening. Among developed countries only Romania has a larger share of its children in poverty. In any recent year, more than one in five American children lived in a home without enough food for everyone at all times. Black and Hispanic children are five times more likely than children overall to live in households with what our government euphemistically calls "very low food security." Food banks report that their shelves often go bare before the lines of people are served and that most of their new customers since 2008 are married couples with children who used to have two jobs and now have none. To people accustomed to a pantry full of food and a refrigerator with not enough shelf space for everything that comes home from the grocery store, this may be hard to grasp. Yet one in every fifty-two people you meet today, statistically, has no income except food stamps.

In reality, however, it is possible to live a lifetime and not know any one of the 6 million Americans who now depend entirely on food stamps to survive, because we are so economically segregated.

In the late eighteenth century, the French kings lived in blissful ignorance of the poverty around them. One of them even built a private château for his mistress, in which he planned to have a massive dining table rise from the kitchen below so that the nobility would never have to see the servants, a project that had not been done by the time his son, the last French king, lost his head. Similarly, it is easy for the affluent in America to turn a blind eye to the poor and to surround themselves with the similarly wealthy. Without deep and continual contact with the society as a whole, those at the top begin to view themselves in ways that deny the reality of what is going on around them. When that happens, the policies they seek from government— purchased with campaign donations, free rides on private jets, and jobs for politicians' friends and families—distort the economy even more, tilting the playing field in their favor and against everyone else.

It need not remain this way. Change is more than possible. We can choose to restore broad prosperity, instead of promoting highly concentrated prosperity and deepening poverty, especially child poverty. We can build a better America, one that reduces poverty and strife and weakens the power of demagogues. Changing our policies, however, first of all requires knowledge, like the data on incomes about which a top Bush administration spokeswoman was blissfully ignorant. But even facts are useless without understanding the causes of extreme inequality, the levers that effect change. Change also requires organized action at the grassroots level, because in America reform has always come from the bottom up.

A society is defined by its rules. Inequality is the product of rules put in place by those we elected or, if we did not vote, let our fellow Americans elect. Those rules determine in good measure who prospers and who does not, who benefits from our tax system and who bears the burden. America began with a constitution that enshrined in law the ownership of human beings, yet we abolished slavery, the most extreme form of inequality. Women won back the right to vote thanks to decades of determined effort by Susan B. Anthony, Elizabeth Cady Stanton, and many, many others. The first child labor laws required half a century of effort, and more than a century passed before minimum ages and maximum hours for children at work were made law through the 1938 Fair Labor Standards Act. Some states have now weakened these laws and some Republicans in Congress say they should be repealed.

We have laws that allow unions to organize and negotiate for better pay and working conditions, though they have been greatly weakened in the past three decades. We also have strong environmental laws, but they are also under attack. These victories, achieved at great cost, have produced a comparatively healthier, wealthier, more engaged, and overall better society. In the same way, we can build a much better society if we choose.

Full employment is one of the twin duties Congress, by law, places on the Federal Reserve, our nation's central bank. The other duty, which normally gets the most official and press attention, is curbing inflation.

The lack of jobs for young adults, especially those with college and advanced degrees, will be a serious drag on our economy for decades unless we change course and focus on jobs. In late 2013 the economy was operating at only 93 percent of its potential, meaning that about one trillion dollars of additional economic activity was entirely within reach, but for our policies. In good part that shortfall between actual and potential existed because America was short between 9 million and 11 million jobs based on historic performance and population growth. We remain adrift in the economic doldrums because we choose to be there.

Pope Francis I, denouncing "an economy of exclusion," has made inequality a centerpiece of his reign:

> Just as the commandment "Thou shalt not kill" sets a clear limit in order to safeguard the value of human life, today we also have to say "thou shalt not" to an economy of exclusion and inequality. Such an economy kills. How can it be that it is not a news item when an elderly homeless person dies of exposure, but it is news when the stock market loses two points?
>
> Today everything comes under the laws of competition and the survival of the fittest, where the powerful feed upon the powerless. As a consequence, masses of people find themselves excluded and marginalized: without work, without possibilities, without any means of escape.
>
> Human beings are themselves considered consumer goods to be used and then discarded. We have created a "throw away" culture which is now spreading. It is no longer simply about exploitation and oppression, but something new. Exclusion ultimately has to do with what it means to be a part of the society in which we live; those excluded are no longer society's underside or its fringes or its disenfranchised—they are no longer even a part of it. The excluded are not the "exploited" but the outcast, the "leftovers."

***

I selected the following chapters from a much larger field of speeches, academic studies, essays, and books by a wide range of Americans who care about the durability of our nation and are respected by their peers for their expertise.

We will look first at incomes and wealth, including across generations, because they are the broadest and the best-documented measures, including a compelling speech by President Obama on why inequality matters. Health care comes next because of its enormous slice of our economy—currently 18 percent on its way over 20 percent—and its central role in well-being, the ability to be productive, and in creating inequality. Further contributions explore debt and poverty, including policies that criminalize debt and worsen hunger, which have received little attention in the news and thus remain a mostly hidden scandal.

Policies that promote both equality and inequality are the subject of the next section, providing an understanding of the powerful, but subtle, ways in which laws and rules shape individual economic well-being. Here, too, criminal law plays a powerful role. Pieces on the central role of family follow, showing how government policies affect families, as well as education, the key for many, including me, to a better life and a richer, safer, and happier world through new knowledge.

With the approval of those whose work is presented here, I have deleted outdated or arcane language, footnotes, and other details so the general reader can extract the greatest meaning from each piece. Over the years, I have heard frequently from readers and from audiences attending my public lectures about what struck them as new or valuable insights. In selecting the contributions I focused on what these audiences have told me they longed to know, what they were surprised to learn, and what they worried received too little attention from the press, from politicians, and even from me.

As you read the pieces, keep in mind that inequality is about much more than just incomes or wealth, which I have used as a lens to focus on the easiest-to-grasp measures. Inequality is also about access and opportunity, which are much harder to measure. Education, health care, and exposure to environmental hazards all shape society, affecting who gets a shot at success and who gets success handed to them; who can overcome obstacles and who has those obstacles cleared away for them.

The single most important point of *Divided* is: keep in mind who benefits and who does not. It's our choice. We decide. And we are free to make better choices that will strengthen our society so that America, and the liberties of the people, will endure.

INSIGHTS ON INEQUALITY

"Any city, however small, is in fact divided into two, one the city of the poor, the other of the rich; these are at war with one another."
—*Plato, Greek philosopher and economist, 427–347* B.C.E.

"An imbalance between rich and poor is the oldest and most fatal ailment of all republics."
—*Plutarch, Greco-Roman historian, 46–120* C.E.

"Jesus said unto him, If thou wilt be perfect, go and sell that thou hast, and give to the poor, and thou shalt have treasure in heaven: and come and follow me. But when the young man heard that saying, he went away sorrowful: for he had great possessions. Then said Jesus unto his disciples, Verily I say unto you, That a rich man shall hardly enter into the kingdom of heaven. And again I say unto you, It is easier for a camel to go through the eye of a needle, than for a rich man to enter into the kingdom of God."
—*Matthew 19:21–24*

"Wherever there is great property there is great inequality. For one very rich man there must be at least five hundred poor, and the affluence of the few supposes the indigence of the many."
—*Adam Smith in* The Wealth of Nations *(1776)*

"The disposition to admire, and almost to worship, the rich and the powerful, and to despise, or, at least, to neglect persons of poor and mean condition is the great and most universal cause of the corruption of our moral sentiments."

—*Adam Smith, father of market economics,*
1723–1790, in The Theory of Moral
Sentiments *(1759)*

"The causes which destroyed the ancient republics were numerous; but in Rome, one principal cause was the vast inequality of fortunes."

—*Noah Webster, American editor, 1758–1843*

"No person, I think, ever saw a herd of buffalo, of which a few were fat and the great majority lean. No person ever saw a flock of birds, of which two or three were swimming in grease, and the others all skin and bone."

—*Henry George, American reformer, 1839–1897*

"The man of great wealth owes a peculiar obligation to the state because he derives special advantages from the mere existence of government."

—*Theodore Roosevelt, U.S. president, 1858–1919*

"We can either have democracy in this country or we can have great wealth concentrated in the hands of a few, but we can't have both."

—*Louis Brandeis, Supreme Court justice, 1856–1941*

"The preferential treatment that the rich get from the government came into sharp focus with the compensation for the families of the victims of the 9/11 attack. Wealthy families received substantially higher compensations than poor families did, even though the former were better equipped to absorb the loss than the latter. It is clear that what's missing is a principle that would govern the redistribution of income by the government. Without it, the government spends taxes to shore up the existing distribution of income, no matter how unequal it is."

—*Moshe Adler, American economist, 1948–*

"Some people continue to defend trickle-down theories which assume that economic growth, encouraged by a free market, will inevitably succeed in bringing about greater justice and inclusiveness in the world. This opinion, which has never been confirmed by the facts, expresses a crude and naïve trust in the goodness of those wielding economic power and in the sacralized workings of the prevailing economic system."

—*Pope Francis I, 1936–*

"Poverty is not natural. It is man-made and it can be overcome and eradicated by the actions of human beings."

—*Nelson Mandela, 1918–2013*

"The distribution of wealth is not determined by nature. It is determined by policy."

—*Eric Schneiderman, New York State attorney general, 1954–*

"American inequality didn't just happen. It was created."

—*Joseph Stiglitz, Nobel Prize–winning economist, 1943–*

OVERVIEW

INEQUALITY AND DEMOCRACY

President Barack Obama

*President Barack Obama explains how inequality of income com-
bined with the rules that govern the economy created the 2008
economic collapse, reaching back more than a century to explain how to build a robust economy. President Obama delivered
these remarks on December 6, 2011, at Osawatomie High School
in Osawatomie, Kansas. The official transcript has been edited to remove extraneous remarks, such as comments to those on the dais,
and the frequent applause that punctuated these remarks.*

My grandparents served during World War II. He was a sol-
dier in Patton's Army; she was a worker on a bomber assembly line. And together, they shared the optimism of a nation that
triumphed over the Great Depression and over fascism. They believed in an America where hard work paid off, and responsibility
was rewarded, and anyone could make it if they tried—no matter
who you were, no matter where you came from, no matter how you
started out.

And these values gave rise to the largest middle class and the
strongest economy that the world has ever known. It was here in
America that the most productive workers, the most innovative
companies turned out the best products on Earth. And you know
what? Every American shared in that pride and in that success—

from those in the executive suites to those in middle management to those on the factory floor. So you could have some confidence that if you gave it your all, you'd take enough home to raise your family and send your kids to school and have your health care covered, put a little away for retirement.

Today, we're still home to the world's most productive workers. We're still home to the world's most innovative companies. But for most Americans, the basic bargain that made this country great has eroded. Long before the recession hit, hard work stopped paying off for too many people. Fewer and fewer of the folks who contributed to the success of our economy actually benefited from that success. Those at the very top grew wealthier from their incomes and their investments—wealthier than ever before. But everybody else struggled with costs that were growing and paychecks that weren't—and too many families found themselves racking up more and more debt just to keep up.

Now, for many years, credit cards and home equity loans papered over this harsh reality. But in 2008, the house of cards collapsed. We all know the story by now: mortgages sold to people who couldn't afford them, or even sometimes understand them. Banks and investors allowed to keep packaging the risk and selling it off. Huge bets—and huge bonuses—made with other people's money on the line. Regulators who were supposed to warn us about the dangers of all this, but looked the other way or didn't have the authority to look at all.

It was wrong. It combined the breathtaking greed of a few with irresponsibility all across the system. And it plunged our economy and the world into a crisis from which we're still fighting to recover. It claimed the jobs and the homes and the basic security of millions of people—innocent, hardworking Americans who had met their responsibilities but were still left holding the bag.

And ever since, there's been a raging debate over the best way to restore growth and prosperity, restore balance, restore fairness. Throughout the country, it's sparked protests and political movements—from the Tea Party to the people who've been occupying the streets of New York and other cities. It's left Washington in a near-constant state of gridlock. It's been the topic of heated and sometimes colorful discussion among the men and women running for president.

But, Osawatomie, this is not just another political debate. This is the defining issue of our time. This is a make-or-break moment for the middle class, and for all those who are fighting to get into the middle class. Because what's at stake is whether this will be a country where working people can earn enough to raise a family, build a modest savings, own a home, secure their retirement. Now, in the midst of this debate, there are some who seem to be suffering from a kind of collective amnesia. After all that's happened, after the worst economic crisis, the worst financial crisis since the Great Depression, they want to return to the same practices that got us into this mess. In fact, they want to go back to the same policies that stacked the deck against middle-class Americans for way too many years. And their philosophy is simple: we are better off when everybody is left to fend for themselves and play by their own rules.

A UNITED SOCIETY

I am here to say they are wrong. I'm here in Kansas to reaffirm my deep conviction that we're greater together than we are on our own. I believe that this country succeeds when everyone gets a fair shot, when everyone does their fair share, when everyone plays by the same rules. These aren't Democratic values or Republican values. These aren't 1 percent values or 99 percent values. They're American values. And we have to reclaim them.

You see, this isn't the first time America has faced this choice. At the turn of the last century, when a nation of farmers was transitioning to become the world's industrial giant, we had to decide: would we settle for a country where most of the new railroads and factories were being controlled by a few giant monopolies that kept prices high and wages low? Would we allow our citizens and even our children to work ungodly hours in conditions that were unsafe and unsanitary? Would we restrict education to the privileged few? Because there were people who thought massive inequality and exploitation of people was just the price you pay for progress.

Theodore Roosevelt disagreed. He was the Republican son of a wealthy family. He praised what the titans of industry had done to create jobs and grow the economy. He believed then what we know is true today, that the free market is the greatest force for economic progress in human history. It's led to a prosperity and a standard of living unmatched by the rest of the world.

But Roosevelt also knew that the free market has never been a free license to take whatever you can from whomever you can. He understood the free market only works when there are rules of the road that ensure competition is fair and open and honest. And so he busted up monopolies, forcing those companies to compete for consumers with better services and better prices. And today, they still must. He fought to make sure businesses couldn't profit by exploiting children or selling food or medicine that wasn't safe. And today, they still can't.

And in 1910, Teddy Roosevelt came here to Osawatomie and he laid out his vision for what he called a New Nationalism. "Our country," he said, ". . . means nothing unless it means the triumph of a real democracy . . . of an economic system under which each man shall be guaranteed the opportunity to show the best that there is in him."

Now, for this, Roosevelt was called a radical. He was called a socialist—even a communist. But today, we are a richer nation and a stronger democracy because of what he fought for in his last campaign: an eight-hour workday and a minimum wage for women; insurance for the unemployed and for the elderly, and those with disabilities; political reform and a progressive income tax.

ADAPTING TO CHANGING TIMES
Today, over one hundred years later, our economy has gone through another transformation. Over the last few decades, huge advances in technology have allowed businesses to do more with less, and it's made it easier for them to set up shop and hire workers anywhere they want in the world. And many of you know firsthand the painful disruptions this has caused for a lot of Americans.

Factories where people thought they would retire suddenly picked up and went overseas, where workers were cheaper. Steel mills that needed one thousand employees are now able to do the same work with 100 employees, so layoffs too often became permanent, not just a temporary part of the business cycle. And these changes didn't just affect blue-collar workers. If you were a bank teller or a phone operator or a travel agent, you saw many in your profession replaced by ATMs and the Internet.

Today, even higher-skilled jobs, like accountants and middle management, can be outsourced to countries like China or India. And if you're somebody whose job can be done cheaper by a computer or someone in another country, you don't have a lot of leverage with your employer when it comes to asking for better wages or better benefits, especially since fewer Americans today are part of a union.

Now, just as there was in Teddy Roosevelt's time, there is a certain crowd in Washington who, for the last few decades, have said, let's respond to this economic challenge with the same old tune. "The market will take care of everything," they tell us. If we just cut more regulations and cut more taxes—especially for the wealthy— our economy will grow stronger. Sure, they say, there will be winners and losers. But if the winners do really well, then jobs and prosperity will eventually trickle down to everybody else. And, they argue, even if prosperity doesn't trickle down, well, that's the price of liberty.

Now, it's a simple theory. And we have to admit, it's one that speaks to our rugged individualism and our healthy skepticism of too much government. That's in America's DNA. And that theory fits well on a bumper sticker. But here's the problem: it doesn't work. It has never worked. It didn't work when it was tried in the decade before the Great Depression. It's not what led to the incredible postwar booms of the '50s and '60s. And it didn't work when we tried it during the last decade. I mean, understand, it's not as if we haven't tried this theory.

Remember in those years, in 2001 and 2003, Congress passed two of the most expensive tax cuts for the wealthy in history. And what did it get us? The slowest job growth in half a century. Massive deficits that have made it much harder to pay for the investments that built this country and provided the basic security that helped millions of Americans reach and stay in the middle class—things like education and infrastructure, science and technology, Medicare and Social Security.

Remember that in those same years, thanks to some of the same folks who are now running Congress, we had weak regulation, we had little oversight, and what did it get us? Insurance companies that jacked up people's premiums with impunity and denied care to patients who were sick, mortgage lenders that tricked families into buying homes they couldn't afford, a financial sector where irresponsibility and lack of basic oversight nearly destroyed our entire economy.

We simply cannot return to this brand of "you're on your own" economics if we're serious about rebuilding the middle class in this country. We know that it doesn't result in a strong economy. It results in an economy that invests too little in its people and in its future. We know it doesn't result in a prosperity that trickles down. It results in a prosperity that's enjoyed by fewer and fewer of our citizens.

INEQUALITY DISTORTS OUR DEMOCRACY

Look at the statistics. In the last few decades, the average income of the top 1 percent has gone up by more than 250 percent to $1.2 million per year. I'm not talking about millionaires, people who have a million dollars. I'm saying people who make a million dollars every single year. For the top one-hundredth of 1 percent, the average income is now $27 million per year. The typical CEO who used to earn about 30 times more than his or her worker now earns 110 times more. And yet, over the last decade the incomes of most Americans have actually fallen by about 6 percent.

Now, this kind of inequality—a level that we haven't seen since the Great Depression—hurts us all. When middle-class families can no longer afford to buy the goods and services that businesses are selling, when people are slipping out of the middle class, it drags down the entire economy from top to bottom. America was built on the idea of broad-based prosperity, of strong consumers all across the country. That's why a CEO like Henry Ford made it his mission to pay his workers enough so that they could buy the cars he made. It's also why a recent study showed that countries with less inequality tend to have stronger and steadier economic growth over the long run.

Inequality also distorts our democracy. It gives an outsized voice to the few who can afford high-priced lobbyists and unlimited campaign contributions, and it runs the risk of selling out our democracy to the highest bidder. It leaves everyone else rightly suspicious that the system in Washington is rigged against them, that our elected representatives aren't looking out for the interests of most Americans.

But there's an even more fundamental issue at stake. This kind of gaping inequality gives lie to the promise that's at the very heart of America: that this is a place where you can make it if you try. We tell people—we tell our kids—that in this country, even if you're born with nothing, work hard and you can get into the middle class. We tell them that your children will have a chance to do even better than you do. That's why immigrants from around the world historically have flocked to our shores.

And yet, over the last few decades, the rungs on the ladder of opportunity have grown farther and farther apart, and the middle class has shrunk. You know, a few years after World War II, a child who was born into poverty had a slightly better than 50-50 chance of becoming middle class as an adult. By 1980, that chance had fallen to around 40 percent. And if the trend of rising inequality over the last few decades continues, it's estimated that a child born today will only have a one-in-three chance of making it to the middle class—33 percent.

It's heartbreaking enough that there are millions of working families in this country who are now forced to take their children to food banks for a decent meal. But the idea that those children might not have a chance to climb out of that situation and back into the middle class, no matter how hard they work? That's inexcusable. It is wrong. It flies in the face of everything that we stand for.

Now, fortunately, that's not a future that we have to accept, because there's another view about how we build a strong middle class in this country—a view that's truer to our history, a vision that's been embraced in the past by people of both parties for more than 200 years. It's not a view that we should somehow turn back technology or put up walls around America. It's not a view that says we should punish profit or success or pretend that government knows how to fix all of society's problems. It is a view that says in America we are greater together—when everyone engages in fair play and everybody gets a fair shot and everybody does their fair share.

So what does that mean for restoring middle-class security in today's economy? Well, it starts by making sure that everyone in America gets a fair shot at success. The truth is we'll never be able to compete with other countries when it comes to who's best at letting their businesses pay the lowest wages, who's best at busting unions, who's best at letting companies pollute as much as they want. That's a race to the bottom that we can't win, and we shouldn't want to win that race. Those countries don't have a strong middle class. They don't have our standard of living.

The race we want to win, the race we can win is a race to the top—the race for good jobs that pay well and offer middle-class security. Businesses will create those jobs in countries with the highest-skilled, highest-educated workers, the most advanced transportation and communication, the strongest commitment to research and technology.

BUILDING A PROSPEROUS FUTURE

The world is shifting to an innovation economy and nobody does innovation better than America. Nobody does it better. No one has better colleges. Nobody has better universities. Nobody has a greater diversity of talent and ingenuity. No one's workers or entrepreneurs are more driven or more daring. The things that have always been our strengths match up perfectly with the demands of the moment.

But we need to meet the moment. We've got to up our game. We need to remember that we can only do that together. It starts by making education a national mission—*a national mission*. Government and businesses, parents and citizens. In this economy, a higher education is the surest route to the middle class. The unemployment rate for Americans with a college degree or more is about half the national average. And their incomes are twice as high as those who don't have a high school diploma. Which means we shouldn't be laying off good teachers right now—we should be hiring them. We shouldn't be expecting less of our schools—we should be demanding more. We shouldn't be making it harder to afford college—we should be a country where everyone has a chance to go and doesn't rack up $100,000 of debt just because they went.

In today's innovation economy, we also need a world-class commitment to science and research, the next generation of high-tech manufacturing. Our factories and our workers shouldn't be idle. We should be giving people the chance to get new skills and training at community colleges so they can learn how to make wind turbines and semiconductors and high-powered batteries. And by the way, if we don't have an economy that's built on bubbles and financial speculation, our best and brightest won't all gravitate towards careers in banking and finance. Because if we want an economy that's built to last, we need more of those young people in science and engineering. This country should not be known for bad debt and phony profits. We should be known for creating and selling products all around the world that are stamped with three proud words: Made in America.

Today, manufacturers and other companies are setting up shop in the places with the best infrastructure to ship their products, move their workers, communicate with the rest of the world. And that's why the over one million construction workers who lost their jobs when the housing market collapsed shouldn't be sitting at home with nothing to do. They should be rebuilding our roads and our bridges, laying down faster railroads and broadband, modernizing our schools—all the things other countries are already doing to attract good jobs and businesses to their shores.

Yes, business, and not government, will always be the primary generator of good jobs with incomes that lift people into the middle class and keep them there. But as a nation, we've always come together, through our government, to help create the conditions where both workers and businesses can succeed. And historically, that hasn't been a partisan idea. Franklin Roosevelt worked with Democrats and Republicans to give veterans of World War II—including my grandfather Stanley Dunham—the chance to go to college on the GI Bill. It was a Republican president, Dwight Eisenhower, a proud son of Kansas, who started the Interstate Highway System and doubled down on science and research to stay ahead of the Soviets.

Of course, those productive investments cost money. They're not free. And so we've also paid for these investments by asking everybody to do their fair share. Look, if we had unlimited resources, no one would ever have to pay any taxes and we would never have to cut any spending. But we don't have unlimited resources. And so we have to set priorities. If we want a strong middle class, then our tax code must reflect our values. We have to make choices.

Today that choice is very clear. To reduce our deficit, I've already signed nearly $1 trillion of spending cuts into law and I've proposed trillions more, including reforms that would lower the cost of Medicare and Medicaid.

But in order to structurally close the deficit, get our fiscal house in order, we have to decide what our priorities are. Now, most immediately, short term, we need to extend a payroll tax cut that's set to expire at the end of this month. If we don't do that, 160 million Americans, including most of the people here, will see their taxes go up by an average of $1,000 starting in January and it would badly weaken our recovery. That's the short term.

THE ROLE OF TAXES

In the long term, we have to rethink our tax system more fundamentally. We have to ask ourselves: do we want to make the investments we need in things like education and research and high-tech manufacturing—all those things that helped make us an economic superpower? Or do we want to keep in place the tax breaks for the wealthiest Americans in our country? Because we can't afford to do both. That is not politics. That's just math.

Now, so far, most of my Republican friends in Washington have refused under any circumstance to ask the wealthiest Americans to go to the same tax rate they were paying when Bill Clinton was president. So let's just do a trip down memory lane here.

Keep in mind, when President Clinton first proposed these tax increases, folks in Congress predicted they would kill jobs and lead to another recession. Instead, our economy created nearly 23 million jobs and we eliminated the deficit. Today, the wealthiest Americans are paying the lowest taxes in over half a century. This isn't like in the early '50s, when the top tax rate was over 90 percent. This isn't even like the early '80s, when the top tax rate was about 70 percent. Under President Clinton, the top rate was only about 39 percent. Today, thanks to loopholes and shelters, a quarter of all millionaires now pay lower tax rates than millions of you, millions of middle-class families. Some billionaires have a tax rate as low as 1 percent. One percent.

That is the height of unfairness. It is wrong. It's wrong that in the United States of America, a teacher or a nurse or a construction worker, maybe earns $50,000 a year, should pay a higher tax rate than somebody raking in $50 million. It's wrong for Warren Buffett's secretary to pay a higher tax rate than Warren Buffett. And by the way, Warren Buffett agrees with me. So do most Americans—Democrats, independents, and Republicans. And I know that many of our wealthiest citizens would agree to contribute a little more if it meant reducing the deficit and strengthening the economy that made their success possible.

This isn't about class warfare. This is about the nation's welfare. It's about making choices that benefit not just the people who've done fantastically well over the last few decades, but that benefits the middle class, and those fighting to get into the middle class, and the economy as a whole.

Finally, a strong middle class can only exist in an economy where everyone plays by the same rules, from Wall Street to Main Street. As infuriating as it was for all of us, we rescued our major banks from collapse, not only because a full-blown financial meltdown would have sent us into a second depression, but because we need a strong, healthy financial sector in this country.

But part of the deal was that we wouldn't go back to business as usual. And that's why last year we put in place new rules of the road that refocus the financial sector on what should be their core purpose: getting capital to the entrepreneurs with the best ideas and financing millions of families who want to buy a home or send their kids to college.

Now, we're not all the way there yet, and the banks are fighting us every inch of the way. But already, some of these reforms are being implemented.

If you're a big bank or risky financial institution, you now have to write out a "living will" that details exactly how you'll pay the bills if you fail, so that taxpayers are never again on the hook for Wall Street's mistakes. There are also limits on the size of banks and new abilities for regulators to dismantle a firm that is going under. The new law bans banks from making risky bets with their customers' deposits, and it takes away big bonuses and paydays from failed CEOs, while giving shareholders a say on executive salaries.

This is the law that we passed. We are in the process of implementing it now. All of this is being put in place as we speak. Now, unless you're a financial institution whose business model is built on breaking the law, cheating consumers, and making risky bets that could damage the entire economy, you should have nothing to fear from these new rules.

Some of you may know, my grandmother worked as a banker for most of her life—worked her way up, started as a secretary, ended up being a vice president of a bank. And I know from her, and I know from all the people that I've come in contact with, that the vast majority of bankers and financial service professionals, they want to do right by their customers. They want to have rules in place that don't put them at a disadvantage for doing the right thing. And yet, Republicans in Congress are fighting as hard as they can to make sure that these rules aren't enforced.

LOOKING OUT FOR CONSUMERS

I'll give you a specific example. For the first time in history, the reforms that we passed put in place a consumer watchdog who is charged with protecting everyday Americans from being taken advantage of by mortgage lenders or payday lenders or debt collectors. And the man we nominated for the post, Richard Cordray, is a former attorney general of Ohio who has the support of most attorney generals, both Democrat and Republican, throughout the country. Nobody claims he's not qualified.

But the Republicans in the Senate refuse to confirm him for the job; they refuse to let him do his job. Why? Does anybody here think that the problem that led to our financial crisis was too much oversight of mortgage lenders or debt collectors?

Of course not. Every day we go without a consumer watchdog is another day when a student, or a senior citizen, or a member of our Armed Forces—because they are very vulnerable to some of this stuff—could be tricked into a loan that they can't afford— something that happens all the time. And the fact is that financial institutions have plenty of lobbyists looking out for their interests. Consumers deserve to have someone whose job it is to look out for them. And I intend to make sure they do. And I want you to hear me, Kansas: I will veto any effort to delay or defund or dismantle the new rules that we put in place.

We shouldn't be weakening oversight and accountability. We should be strengthening oversight and accountability. I'll give you another example. Too often, we've seen Wall Street firms violating major antifraud laws because the penalties are too weak and there's no price for being a repeat offender. No more. I'll be calling for legislation that makes those penalties count so that firms don't see punishment for breaking the law as just the price of doing business.

The fact is this crisis has left a huge deficit of trust between Main Street and Wall Street. And major banks that were rescued by the taxpayers have an obligation to go the extra mile in helping to close that deficit of trust. At minimum, they should be remedying past mortgage abuses that led to the financial crisis. They should be working to keep responsible home owners in their home. We're going to keep pushing them to provide more time for unemployed home owners to look for work without having to worry about immediately losing their house.

The big banks should increase access to refinancing opportunities to borrowers who haven't yet benefited from historically low interest rates. And the big banks should recognize that precisely because these steps are in the interest of middle-class families and the broader economy, it will also be in the banks' own long-term financial interest. What will be good for consumers over the long term will be good for the banks.

THE ROLE OF CITIZENS, PARENTS, AND BUSINESS LEADERS
Investing in things like education that give everybody a chance to succeed. A tax code that makes sure everybody pays their fair share. And laws that make sure everybody follows the rules. That's what will transform our economy. That's what will grow our middle class again. In the end, rebuilding this economy based on fair play, a fair shot, and a fair share will require all of us to see that we have a stake in each other's success. And it will require all of us to take some responsibility.

It will require parents to get more involved in their children's education. It will require students to study harder. It will require some workers to start studying all over again. It will require greater responsibility from home owners not to take out mortgages they can't afford. They need to remember that if something seems too good to be true, it probably is.

It will require those of us in public service to make government more efficient and more effective, more consumer friendly, more responsive to people's needs. That's why we're cutting programs that we don't need to pay for those we do. That's why we've made hundreds of regulatory reforms that will save businesses billions of dollars. That's why we're not just throwing money at education, we're challenging schools to come up with the most innovative reforms and the best results.

And it will require American business leaders to understand that their obligations don't just end with their shareholders. Andy Grove, the legendary former CEO of Intel, put it best. He said, "There is another obligation I feel personally, given that everything I've achieved in my career, and a lot of what Intel has achieved . . . were made possible by a climate of democracy, an economic climate and investment climate provided by the United States."

This broader obligation can take many forms. At a time when the cost of hiring workers in China is rising rapidly, it should mean more CEOs deciding that it's time to bring jobs back to the United States—not just because it's good for business, but because it's good for the country that made their business and their personal success possible.

I think about the Big Three auto companies who, during recent negotiations, agreed to create more jobs and cars here in America, and then decided to give bonuses not just to their executives, but to all their employees, so that everyone was invested in the company's success.

I think about a company based in Warroad, Minnesota. It's called Marvin Windows and Doors. During the recession, Marvin's competitors closed dozens of plants, let hundreds of workers go. But Marvin's did not lay off a single one of their four thousand or so employees—not one. In fact, they've only laid off workers once in over a hundred years. Mr. Marvin's grandfather even kept his eight employees during the Great Depression.

Now, at Marvin's when times get tough, the workers agree to give up some perks and some pay, and so do the owners. As one owner said, "You can't grow if you're cutting your lifeblood—and that's the skills and experience your workforce delivers." For the CEO of Marvin's, it's about the community. He said, "These are people we went to school with. We go to church with them. We see them in the same restaurants. Indeed, a lot of us have married local girls and boys. We could be anywhere, but we are in Warroad."

That's how America was built. That's why we're the greatest nation on Earth. That's what our greatest companies understand. Our success has never just been about survival of the fittest. It's about building a nation where we're all better off. We pull together. We pitch in. We do our part. We believe that hard work will pay off, that responsibility will be rewarded, and that our children will inherit a nation where those values live on.

And it is that belief that rallied thousands of Americans to Osawatomie—maybe even some of your ancestors—on a rain-soaked day more than a century ago. By train, by wagon, on buggy, bicycle, on foot, they came to hear the vision of a man who loved this country and was determined to perfect it.

"We are all Americans," Teddy Roosevelt told them that day. "Our common interests are as broad as the continent." In the final years of his life, Roosevelt took that same message all across this country, from tiny Osawatomie to the heart of New York City, believing that no matter where he went, no matter who he was talking to, everybody would benefit from a country in which everyone gets a fair chance.

And well into our third century as a nation, we have grown and we've changed in many ways since Roosevelt's time. The world is faster and the playing field is larger and the challenges are more complex. But what hasn't changed—what can never change—are the values that got us this far. We still have a stake in each other's success. We still believe that this should be a place where you can make it if you try. And we still believe, in the words of the man who called for a New Nationalism all those years ago: "The fundamental rule of our national life," he said, "the rule which underlies all others—is that, on the whole, and in the long run, we shall go up or down together." And I believe America is on the way up.

Barack Obama was elected president of the United States in 2008 and 2012.

THE VANISHING MIDDLE CLASS

Elizabeth Warren

Elizabeth Warren, now the senior United States senator from Massachusetts, wrote this in 2004 to make the case for creating a Financial Product Safety Commission (FPSC) on the model of the Consumer Product Safety Commission to protect consumers from abusive banking practices. Her idea became law as the Consumer Financial Protection Bureau, which Professor Warren helped set up in 2010–2011.

A strong middle class is the best ally of the poor.
The issues of poverty are typically framed around the poor themselves—the causes of their problems and the help they need. But lifting the poor out of poverty means finding a place for them in the middle.

A middle class that is rich with opportunity opens the paths out of poverty. A middle class that is financially strong can support the programs needed to give the poor a helping hand. A middle class that is prosperous provides the model for how education and hard work pay off. And a middle class that is secure provides the kind of political stability that wards off xenophobia and embraces the pluralism that is critical for the economic and social integration of the poor into mainstream America.

The best ally of the poor is a strong middle class, but America's

middle class is under attack economically. Multiple forces are pushing those families closer to the financial brink. What is bad for the
middle class is ultimately disastrous for the poor.

MAKING IT TO THE MIDDLE

What is the middle class? Whatever it is, most Americans believe
that they are in it. When asked in an open-ended question to identify their class membership, more than 91 percent of the adult
population of the United States volunteer an identification with
"working" or "middle" class. Although there are people who call
themselves upper class and others who call themselves lower class,
these identifications are numerically somewhat rare.

Although the U.S. government has defined the poverty level,
no government agency defines the middle class. One reason is
that class status is not a function merely of money or other easily
counted characteristics. The running joke of *The Beverly Hillbillies*
was that money did not change the social class of the Clampetts.
On the other side, people from "good families" who have fallen on
hard times might be described as "high class," but their status is not
a matter of current income.

Careful studies of the American population show that Americans
determine class identification using many variables, including education, occupational status, cultural factors, lifestyle, beliefs and
feelings, income, wealth, and more. Political scientists Kenneth
Dolbeare and Janette Hubbell assert, "Middle-class values are by
definition those of the American mainstream."

HIGH INCOMES, BUT AT A PRICE

Over the past generation new economic forces have reshaped the
middle class. The most profound changes have taken place in family income. Today the two-parent family right in the middle was
earning about $66,000 in 2005 [$77,600 in 2012 dollars].

But notice what has happened to the wages of a fully employed
male over the same time period. The answer is that the typical man
working full-time, after adjusting for inflation, earns about $800
less than his father earned in the early 1970s. After decades of rising incomes earlier in the twentieth century, about thirty years ago
wages for middle-class men flatlined.

How did family incomes rise? Mothers of minor children went back to work in record numbers. In the early 1970s, the median family lived on one paycheck. Today the family in the middle brings home two paychecks.

The shift from one income to two has had seismic implications for families across America. It means that all the growth in family income came from adding a second earner. Among two-paycheck families, median income is now $76,500, but the middle one-paycheck family now earns only $42,300. This means that one-income households—whether they are couples where one works and one stays at home or households with only one parent—have fallen sharply behind. A generation ago a one-earner family was squarely in the middle, but now that average one-earner family has slipped down the economic ladder. Over the past generation critical economic divisions within the middle class have begun to emerge.

SAVINGS AND DEBT

While not every family brought home two paychecks, by the 2000s a substantial majority of families sent both parents into the work-force. For those families, it would seem that the economic picture would be rosy. Not so. In the early 1970s the typical one-income family was putting away about 11 percent of its take-home pay in savings. That family carried a mortgage, and it also carried credit cards and other revolving debt that, on average, equaled about 1.3 percent of its annual income.

By 2004 that picture had shifted dramatically. The national savings rate dropped below zero. Revolving debt—largely credit cards—ballooned, topping 12 percent of the average family's income.

In a single generation the family had picked up a second earner, but it had spent every dollar of that second paycheck. Worse yet, it had also spent the money it once saved, and it had borrowed more besides. By the most obvious financial measures, the middle-class American family has sunk financially.

OVERCONSUMPTION—THE STANDARD STORY

There is no shortage of experts who are willing to explain exactly where the money went. The story is all about overconsumption, about families spending their money on things they do not really need. Economist Juliet Schor blames "the new consumerism," complete with "designer clothes, a microwave, restaurant meals, home and automobile air conditioning, and, of course, Michael Jordan's ubiquitous athletic shoes, about which children and adults both display near-obsession." Sociologist Robert Frank claims that America's newfound "luxury fever" forces middle-class families "to finance their consumption increases largely by reduced savings and increased debt." John de Graaf* and his co-authors claim that the "urge to splurge" is an affliction affecting millions of Americans who simply have no willpower. The distinction is critical: overconsumption is not about medical care or basic housing, and it is not about buying a few goodies with extra income. It is about going deep into debt to finance consumer purchases that sensible people could do without.

The beauty of the overconsumption story is that it squares neatly with many of our own intuitions. We see the malls packed with shoppers. We receive catalogs filled with outrageously expensive gadgets. We think of that overpriced summer dress that hangs in the back of the closet or those new soccer shoes gathering dust there.

The conclusion seems indisputable: the "urge to splurge" is driving folks to spend, spend, spend like never before. But is it true? Deep in the recesses of federal archives is detailed information on Americans' spending patterns going back for more than a century. It is possible to analyze data about typical families from the early 1970s, carefully sorting spending categories and family size. If today's families really are blowing their paychecks on designer clothes and restaurant meals, then the expenditure data should show that they are spending more on these frivolous items than their parents did a generation earlier. But the numbers point in a very different direction.

Start with clothing. Everyone talks about expensive sneakers, designer outfits, and the latest fashions. But how much more is today's typical family of four spending on clothing than the same

---

*Journalist and documentary producer who wrote *Affluenza: The All-Consuming Epidemic.*

family spent in the early 1970s? They are spending less, a whopping 32 percent less today than they spent a generation ago. The differences have to do with how people dress (fewer suits and leather shoes, more T-shirts and shorts), where they shop (more discount stores), and where the clothes are manufactured (overseas). Compared with families a generation ago, today's median earners are downright thrifty.

How about food? People eat out now more than ever before, and bottled water turns something that was once free into a $2 purchase. So how much more is today's family of four spending on food (including eating out) than the same family in the early 1970s? Once again, they are spending less, about 18 percent less. The reasons are that people eat differently (less meat, more pasta) and shop differently (big discount supercenters instead of corner grocery stores), and agribusiness has improved the efficiency of food production.

What about appliances? Families today have microwave ovens, espresso machines, and fancy washers and dryers. But those appliances are not putting a big dent in their pocketbooks. Today's family spends about 52 percent less each year on appliances than their counterparts of a generation ago. Today's appliances are better made and last longer, and they cost less to buy.

Cars? Surely, luxury vehicles are making a difference. Not for the median family. The per car cost of owning a car (purchase, repairs, insurance, gas) was on average about 24 percent lower in 2004 than in the early 1970s.

That is not to say that middle-class families never fritter away any money. A generation ago no one had cable, big-screen televisions were a novelty reserved for the very rich, and DVD and TiVo were meaningless strings of letters. Families are spending about 23 percent more on electronics, an extra $225 annually. Computers add another $300 to the annual family budget. But the extra money spent on cable, electronics, and computers is more than offset by families' savings on major appliances and household furnishings alone.

The same balancing act holds true in other areas. The average family spends more on airline travel than it did a generation ago, but it spends less on dry cleaning; more on telephone services, but less on tobacco; more on pets, but less on carpets. And, when it is all added up, increases in one category are pretty much offset by decreases in another. In other words, there seems to be about as much frivolous spending today as there was a generation ago.

WHERE DID THE MONEY GO?

Consumer expenses are down, but the big fixed expenses are up—way up. Start at home. It is fun to think about McMansions, granite countertops, and media rooms. But today's median family buys a three-bedroom, one-bath home—statistically speaking, about 6.1 rooms altogether. This is a little bigger than the 5.8 rooms the median family lived in during the early 1970s. But the price tag and the resulting mortgage payment are much bigger. In 2004 the median home owner was forking over a mortgage payment that was 76 percent larger than a generation earlier. The family's single biggest expense—the home mortgage—had ballooned from $485 a month to $854 [$1,038 in 2012 dollars].

Increases in the cost of health insurance have also hit families hard. Today's family spends 74 percent more on health insurance than its earlier counterparts—if it is lucky enough to get it at all. Costs are so high that forty-eight million working-age Americans simply went without coverage in 2005.

The per car cost of transportation is down, but the total number of cars is up. Today's family has two people in the workforce, and that means two cars to get to work. Besides, with more families living in the suburbs, even a one-earner family needs a second car for the stay-at-home parent to get to the grocery store and doctor appointments. Overall transportation costs for the family of four have increased by 52 percent.

Another consequence of sending two people into the workforce is the need for child care. Because the median 1970s family had someone at home full-time, there were no child-care expenses for comparison. But today's family with one preschooler and one child in elementary school lays out an average of $1,048 a month for care for the children.

Taxes also took a bigger bite from the two-income family of 2004. Because their second income is taxed on top of their first income, the average tax rate was 25 percent higher for a two-income family in 2004 than it was for a one-income family in 1972.

The ups and downs in family spending over the past generation are summarized in the following figure. Notice that the biggest items in the family budget—the mortgage, taxes, health insurance, child care—are on the up side. The down side—food, clothing, and appliances—represents relatively smaller purchases.

Also notice that the items that went down were more flexible, the

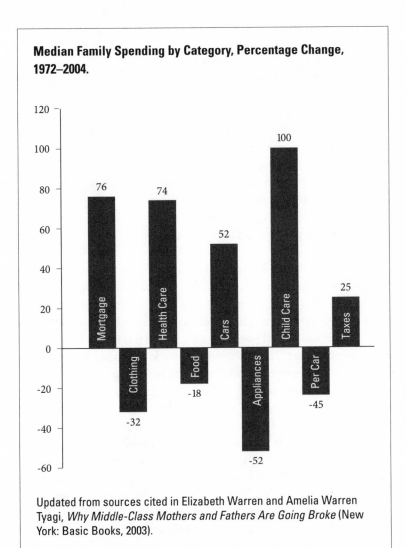

Median Family Spending by Category, Percentage Change, 1972–2004.

Updated from sources cited in Elizabeth Warren and Amelia Warren Tyagi, *Why Middle-Class Mothers and Fathers Are Going Broke* (New York: Basic Books, 2003).

sorts of things that families could spend a little less on one month and a little more the next. If someone lost a job or if the family got hit with a big medical bill, they might squeeze back on these expenses for a while. But the items that increased were all fixed. It is not possible to sell off a bedroom or skip the health insurance payment for a couple of months. If both parents are looking for work, child-care costs will go on even during a job search.

When it is all added up, the family at the beginning of the twenty-first century has a budget that looks very different from that of its early 1970s counterpart. There is more income, but the relationship between income and fixed expenses has altered dramatically.

The family of the 1970s had about half its income committed to big fixed expenses. Moreover, it had a stay-at-home parent, someone who could go to work to earn extra income if something went wrong. By contrast, the family of 2004 has already put everyone to work, so there is no extra income to draw on if trouble hits. Worse yet, even with two people in the workforce, after they pay their basic expenses, today's two-income family has less cash left over than its one-income parents had a generation ago.

NEW RISKS FOR THE MIDDLE CLASS

The numbers make it clear that the cost of being middle class is rising quickly—much more quickly than wages. Many families have tried to cope by sending both parents into the workforce. But that change has helped push up costs, and it has increased the risks these families face. They now have no backup worker. Instead, they now need both parents working full-time just to make the mortgage payment and keep the health insurance. And when they need twice as many paychecks to survive, they face twice the risk that someone will get laid off or become too sick to work—and that the whole house of cards will come tumbling down.

The new two-income family faces other risks as well. In the 1970s, when a child was ill or Grandma broke her hip, there was a parent at home full-time to deal with the needed care, to administer medications, and to drive to doctors' appointments. But someone in the family with no parent at home must take off work whenever anyone else in the family has a serious problem. As a result, problems that were once part of the ordinary bumps of life today have serious income consequences.

New risks keep multiplying. A trip to the emergency room can cost $10,000. The cost of sending a child to college is rising rapidly, while a family's ability to save continues to fall. Retirement presents another risk as generous pensions disappear and even the Social Security backup system looks shaky.

Some will read these data and conclude that one parent should just stay home. Whatever the advantages and disadvantages of that idea from a social perspective, for median earners, it is clearly a losing proposition from an economic perspective. Look at what a fully employed male can earn (and remember that a fully employed female will earn even less). Then look at the big, fixed expenses. Sure, the family can save on child care, and taxes will be lower, but the house payment and the health insurance stay the same, and car expenses are unlikely to drop much. That leaves the median one-income family with a 71 percent drop in discretionary income compared with a one-income family a generation ago. In other words, the two-income family can barely afford the basics, and the median one-income family is simply out of luck.

What do these data say to one-parent families? These families get the worst of both worlds. They have no partner to provide child care every day and no backup earner when something goes wrong. In those ways they look like the typical two-income family—except that they do not have that second income either. A typical one-parent household cannot cover even the basic expenses that would put that family squarely in the middle of American economic life.

It is no surprise that an increasing number of middle-class families have turned to bankruptcy. From 1980 until federal law was changed in 2005, the number of households filing for bankruptcy quadrupled. By 2004 more children were living through their parents' bankruptcy than through divorce. In fact, households with children were about three times more likely to file for bankruptcy than their childless counterparts. What were the main reasons cited for these bankruptcies? About 90 percent of the families cited some combination of job loss, medical problems, and family breakup.

SOLUTIONS

The pressures on the middle class have come from many sources, which is both the good news and the bad news. It is bad in the sense that no single silver bullet will fix everything. But it is good in the sense that many different approaches can make things better— much better—for families across the economic spectrum.

Credit rules offer one option for innovation, providing better protection for the poor and the middle class at the same time. Americans are drowning in debt. Their difficulties are compounded by substantial changes in the credit market that have made debt instruments far riskier for consumers than they were a generation ago. The effective deregulation of interest rates, coupled with innovations in credit charges (e.g., teaser rates, negative amortization, increased use of fees, cross-default clauses, penalty interest rates), has turned ordinary purchases into complex financial undertakings.

In the mid-1980s the typical credit-card contract was about a page long; today it is more than thirty pages, often of dense legalese that even a lawyer cannot understand. Small loans that seem safe in the beginning are repeatedly rolled over in the payday loan industry, making the average effective interest rate more than 400 percent. Credit reports, the foundation of the modern credit system, have errors of fifty points or more in 31 percent of all files, and consumers have little help when they try to straighten out the tangle.

Aggressive marketing, almost nonexistent in the early 1970s, now shapes many consumer choices. Six billion credit-card applications were mailed out in 2005, in addition to on-campus, phone, flyer, in-store, and all sorts of other marketing. Aggressive lenders who line up at the front gates of military installations now have the Department of Defense concerned about combat readiness and the stability of military families. The Department of Defense explained how credit marketing works near military bases:

Predatory lenders seek out young and financially inexperienced borrowers who have bank accounts and steady jobs, but also have little in savings, flawed credit or have hit their credit limit. . . . Most of the predatory business models take advantage of borrowers' inability to pay the loan in full when due and encourage extensions through refinancing and loan flipping.

Consumer capacity—measured by both available time and

expertise—has not expanded to meet the demands of a far more dangerous and aggressive credit marketplace.

The rules governing borrowing and lending have a long history, dating back to English rules imported to the colonies in the 1600s.

Even the Bible has injunctions against usurious money lending, and the Koran forbids charging any interest at all. Since the founding of the Republic, the states have regulated interest, with detailed laws on usury (the maximum interest rate that a lender can charge on a loan) and other credit regulations. While the states still play some role, particularly in the regulation of real estate transactions, their primary tool—interest-rate regulation—has been effectively ended by federal legislation. Currently any lender that gets a federal bank charter can locate its operations in a state with very high usury rates (e.g., South Dakota or Delaware) and then export those interest rates to customers located all over the country. Even in states that cap interest rates at 18 percent, a credit card from a bank that set up its operations in South Dakota can charge 39 percent. Local state laws suffer from another problem: as credit markets have gone national, a plethora of state regulations drives up costs while creating a patchwork of regulation that is neither effective nor well considered.

The Department of Defense is so worried about the effects of out-of-control lenders that it has asked Congress to impose a national usury ceiling to protect military families. This would be a good first start, but why not give all Americans the same protection? Moreover, is it clear that direct usury regulation, as opposed to several other ways to deal with credit, is the best approach?

I propose that Congress establish a Financial Product Safety Commission (FPSC) on the model of the Consumer Product Safety Commission. This agency would be charged with responsibility to establish guidelines for consumer disclosure, to collect and report data about the uses of different financial products, to review new financial products for safety and to require modification of dangerous products before they can be marketed to the public, and to establish guidelines and monitor creditor behavior to protect consumer information and prevent identity theft. In effect, the Financial Product Safety Commission would evaluate credit products to eliminate the hidden tricks and traps and slipshod practices that make some credit products far more dangerous than others. No customer should be forced to read the fine print in more than thirty pages of legalese in credit-card contracts to determine whether the company claims that it will raise its interest rate by more than twenty points if the customer gets into a dispute with another creditor. Data privacy should not be governed by hidden terms in contracts, and identity theft should be the responsibility of the company that let the data slip rather than the victim who tries to clean up the mess.

With an FPSC, consumer credit companies would be free to innovate, but such innovation should be within the boundaries of clearly disclosed terms and open competition—not hidden terms designed to mislead consumers. Those hidden terms not only disadvantage customers, they also disadvantage honest competitors who do not inflate their profits by using such tactics.

The consumer financial services industry has grown to $3 trillion in annual business. Credit issuers employ thousands of lawyers, marketing agencies, statisticians, and business strategists to help them increase profits. In a rapidly changing market, customers need someone on their side to help make certain that the financial products they buy meet minimum safety standards. The Financial Product Safety Commission would help level the playing field.

This is just one new idea for uniting the interests of the poor and the middle class, making millions of American families stronger financially. There are more. But the best ideas are those that are aimed at hardworking Americans everywhere, whether they are poor today or not. These are the ideas of opportunity and safety for all Americans who want to work hard and accomplish something important.

CONCLUSION

The strain on the middle class is growing, and more families are struggling just to make it from payday to payday. That leaves less room for families to move up from poverty. It also means that the middle class can offer the poor less help in their climb.

America was once a world of three economic groups that shaded each into the other—a bottom, a middle, and a top—and economic security was the birthright of the latter two. Today the lines dividing Americans are changing. No longer is the division on economic security between the poor and everyone else. The division is between those who are prospering and those who are struggling, and much of the middle class is now on the struggling side.

The solutions to poverty do not lie with programs aimed only toward the poor. The solutions lie with reuniting America, led by a strong middle class that looks forward to an even brighter future.

NECESSARIES

Adam Smith

People who deny that inequality is a problem in America often observe that most poor people own a color television and many own cars. Defining what is necessary is cultural, as Adam Smith explained in his 1776 book An Inquiry into the Nature and Causes of the Wealth of Nations, *from which this is excerpted.*

By necessaries I understand not only the commodities which are indispensably necessary for the support of life, but whatever the custom of the country renders it indecent for creditable people, even of the lowest order, to be without.

A linen shirt, for example, is, strictly speaking, not a necessary of life. The Greeks and Romans lived, I suppose, very comfortably though they had no linen. But in the present times, through the greater part of Europe, a creditable day-laborer would be ashamed to appear in public without a linen shirt, the want of which would be supposed to denote that disgraceful degree of poverty which, it is presumed, nobody can well fall into without extreme bad conduct.

Custom, in the same manner, has rendered leather shoes a necessary of life in England. The poorest creditable person of either sex would be ashamed to appear in public without them. In Scotland, custom has rendered them a necessary of life to the lowest order of men; but not to the same order of women, who may, without any discredit, walk about barefooted. In France they are necessaries neither to men nor to women, the lowest rank of both sexes appearing there publicly, without any discredit, sometimes in wooden shoes, and sometimes barefooted.

Under necessaries, therefore, I comprehend not only those things which nature, but those things which the established rules of decency have rendered necessary to the lowest rank of people. All other things I call luxuries, without meaning by this appellation to throw the smallest degree of reproach upon the temperate use of them. Beer and ale, for example, in Great Britain, and wine, even in the wine countries, I call luxuries. A man of any rank may, without any reproach, abstain totally from tasting such liquors. Nature does not render them necessary for the support of life, and custom nowhere renders it indecent to live without them.

INCOME INEQUALITY

HOW GAINS AT THE TOP INJURE THE MIDDLE CLASS

Robert H. Frank

The modern effects of Adam Smith's words on "necessaries" are examined by a Cornell University economist renowned for explaining how income inequality distorts and damages the social fabric and individual lives.

Suppose you had to choose between two worlds: World A, where you earn $110,000 a year and everyone else earns $200,000, and World B, where you earn $100,000 and everyone else earns $85,000.

Most neoclassical economists would have an easy time deciding. Neoclassical economics, long the dominant wing of the profession, tends to equate personal well-being with absolute income, or purchasing power. By that standard, World A wins hands down: even as the low earner on the totem pole, you would be doing 10 percent better there than in World B. In other words, you could have 10 percent more food, clothes, housing, airplane travel, or whatever else you wanted.

And yet, when the choice is put to American survey respondents, many seem torn, and most actually end up opting for World B. Is this just an amusing example of human irrationality? Are people so preoccupied with status and rank that they lose sight of objective reality? Or could it be the neoclassical economists who have missed something?

For a glimpse of the possible downside of World A, it may help to consider Wendy Williams, a lanky, soft-spoken adolescent living in a trailer park in an upscale Illinois community during the boom years of the late 1990s. Every morning, according to reporter Dirk Johnson's account in the *New York Times*, Wendy shares a school bus ride with a group of more affluent classmates, who "strut past in designer clothes," while she sits silently, "wearing a cheap belt and rummage-sale slacks." She is known as Rabbit because of a slight overbite—"a humiliation she once begged her mother and father to avoid by sending her to an orthodontist."

Most children have been counseled not to measure their financial circumstances against the circumstances of others. That advice can sometimes be easier to dispense than to follow, however. Wendy Williams makes a game effort to bridge the socioeconomic gap. "That's a really awesome shirt," she tells one of the other girls on the bus. "Where did you get it?"

But teenagers can be cruel. "Why would you want to know?" the other girl replies with a laugh.

It is odd that economists who call themselves disciples of Adam Smith should be so reluctant to introduce the psychological costs of inequality into their discussions. Smith himself recognized such concerns as a basic component of human nature. Writing more than two centuries ago, he introduced the important idea that local consumption standards influence the goods and services that people consider essential—the "necessaries," as Smith called them.

The absolute standard of living in the United States today is of course vastly higher than it was in Adam Smith's eighteenth-century Scotland. And higher living standards create a whole new set of necessaries. For a teenager in an affluent suburb, it is no stretch to imagine that these might include straight teeth. Looking good is an irreducibly relative concept; but it is one, we all know, that sometimes has objective consequences. No one would accuse you of foolish vanity if you went to a job interview with IBM wearing your best suit and tie rather than a tank top and jeans. Impressions count.

And impressions are not the only reason to be conscious of other people's choices. Think about buying a car. Thirty years ago, a middle-class family with kids might have been content with a four-door sedan of modest size. Imagine the grown-up child of that family, with children of her own, facing the same decision. She might be tempted to say, "A 2,500-pound sedan was good enough for my mom, so it's good enough for me."

But on today's roads, surrounded by 6,000-pound Lincoln Navigators and 7,500-pound Ford Excursions, a 2,500-pound Honda Civic doesn't simply look a lot smaller and frailer than it did in 1975. It's objectively more dangerous. The odds of being killed in a collision rise roughly fivefold if you're driving such a vehicle and the other party sits at the helm of a Ford Excursion. In sheer self-defense, you might want a bulkier—and costlier—car than Mom's.

In the housing market, as in the automobile market, you don't have to be a spendthrift to feel pressured into overspending. Imagine a young couple who buy a house in a prosperous suburb, taking on mortgage payments that commit them to working nights and weekends and leave them with no margin of safety in the event of a health or professional setback. We might consider them reckless if they assumed these burdens just to get a few hundred extra square feet of floor space, a Jacuzzi, and the bragging rights that go with an address in Pinnacle Heights. But if, in addition to spacious houses, Pinnacle Heights offered an outstanding school system for their children, we would probably judge them less harshly.

The housing and car markets present two possible instances of what I have termed a "spending cascade," in which top earners—the people who have fared the best in the current economy—initiate a process that leads to increased expenditures on down the line, even among those whose incomes have not risen. Logic suggests that growing inequality of income and wealth might encourage additional spending in this way. Empirical evidence suggests it, too.

Two small midwestern cities, Danville, Indiana, and Mount Vernon, Illinois, make the case pretty clearly. The median income in Mount Vernon was more than $10,000 higher than it was in Danville in the year 2000, but Danville's incomes were much more

unequally distributed. In Danville, a family at the ninety-fifth per-
centile mark earned more than $141,000, while the equivalent fam-
ily in Mount Vernon earned just over $83,000. Despite its much
smaller median income, Danville's median house price was almost
$131,000—more than double the Mount Vernon median. It turns
out that Danville and Mount Vernon follow the pattern of other
American communities: median house prices depend not only on
median incomes, but also on income inequality.

The Danville–Mount Vernon story illustrates how the huge income gains accruing to top earners in the United States in recent
decades have imposed costs on those in the middle. Of course,
nobody is forced to buy an expensive house or car. But inequality
may be creating an increasing number of situations in which we are
forced to choose between unpleasant alternatives. And through a
series of decisions that make good sense for us individually, we appear to be moving in a direction that makes little sense for us as a
society.

The family that overspends on housing at the cost of heavy debt,
long working hours, financial anxiety, and a scarcity of family time
is not just a familiar anecdote, but also a fair description of where
middle-class America as a whole has been going. The median size
of a newly constructed house in the United States was 1,600 square
feet in 1980. By 2001, it was more than 2,100 square feet. Meanwhile,
commutes were getting longer and roads more congested, savings
rates were plummeting, personal bankruptcy filings were climbing
to an all-time high, and there was at least a widespread perception
of a sharp decline in employment security and autonomy.

Happiness is not as easy to measure as house size. Nevertheless,
there is evidence that house size doesn't do much for it. If you
move from a two-thousand- to a three-thousand-square-foot
house, you may be pleased, even excited, at first. In time, however,
you are likely to adapt and simply consider the larger house the
norm—especially if other houses have been growing, too. Yet the
sacrifices we make in order to pay for bigger houses often take a
lasting toll.

One strategy of cash-strapped families is to limit their mortgage payments by commuting from longer distances. Your adap-

tation to a long trip from home to work through heavy traffic will probably not be as complete as your adaptation to a bigger house. Even after a long period, most people experience long commutes as stressful. In this respect, the effect is similar to that of exposure to noise and other irritants. A large increase in background noise at a constant, steady level seems less intrusive as time passes; nonetheless, prolonged exposure produces lasting elevations in blood pressure. If the noise is not only loud but intermittent, people remain conscious of their heightened irritability even after extended periods, and their symptoms of central nervous system distress become more pronounced. This pattern has been seen, for example, in a study of people living next to a newly opened highway. Interviewed four months after the highway opened, 21 percent of the residents said they were not annoyed by the noise; that figure dropped to 16 percent when the same residents were interviewed a year later.

The prolonged experience of commuting stress is also known to suppress immune function and shorten longevity. Even daily spells in traffic as brief as fifteen minutes have been linked to significant elevations of blood glucose and cholesterol, and to declines in blood coagulation time—factors that are positively associated with cardiovascular disease.

Commuting by automobile is also linked with the incidence of various cancers, especially cancer of the lung (possibly because of heavier exposure to exhaust fumes). The incidence of these and other illnesses rises with the length of commute, and is significantly lower among those who commute by bus or rail, and lower still among noncommuters.

Finally, the risk of death and injury from accidents varies positively with the length of commute and is higher for those who commute by car than for those who use public transport.

Among rush-hour travelers, the amount of time wasted in stalled traffic increased from 16 hours to 62 hours per year between 1982 and 2000; the daily window of time during which travelers might experience congestion increased from 4.5 hours to 7 hours; and the volume of roadways where travel is congested grew from 34 percent to 58 percent.

If long commutes are so hazardous, why do people put up with them? It may be because they have unconsciously allowed their spending decisions to lean toward conspicuous consumption (in the form of larger houses) and away from what, for want of a better term, I call "inconspicuous consumption"—freedom from traffic congestion, time with family and friends, vacation time, and a variety of favorable job characteristics.

Can we attribute this to rising inequality? Although there is no simple way to prove or disprove the hypothesis, it is consistent with a substantial body of research. In a 2005 study, for example, Bjornulf Ostvik-White, Adam Levine, and I found that areas with higher inequality—specifically, with higher ratios between the income of households in the ninety-fifth and fiftieth percentiles—had significantly higher personal bankruptcy rates, divorce rates, and average commute times. Analyzing international data over time, Samuel Bowles and Yongjin Park found that total hours worked were positively associated with higher inequality.

The wealthy are spending more now simply because they have more money. But their spending has led others to spend more as well, including middle-income families. If the real incomes of middle-class families have grown only slightly, how have they financed this additional consumption? In part by working longer hours, but mainly by saving less and borrowing more. American families carry an average of more than $9,000 in credit card debt, and personal bankruptcy filings are occurring at seven times the 1980 rate. Medical expenses account for a significant share of that debt. Some forty-five million Americans have no health insurance—five million more than when Bill Clinton took office. The national personal savings rate was negative in several recent years, including a few of the peak years of the 1990s economic boom. Millions of Americans now face the prospect of retirement at sharply reduced living standards. Increased spending by top earners may not be the sole cause of financial distress among middle-income families. But it has clearly been an important contributor.

Spending cascades are also an indirect cause of the median voter's growing reluctance to support expenditures for what were once considered essential public goods and services. Nationwide, more than 50 percent of our major roads and highways are in "backlog," which means they will cost from two to five times as much to repair as those that are maintained on time. We face an $84 billion backlog in the repair and replacement of the nation's bridges. Between blown tires, damaged wheels and axles, bent frames, misaligned front ends, destroyed mufflers, twisted suspension systems, and other problems, potholes on American roads cause an average of $120 worth of damage per vehicle each year, and untold numbers of deaths and injuries.

Americans spend less than we once did to ensure the safety of the food we eat. Despite growing instances of contamination from E. coli 0157, listeria, and other highly toxic bacteria, the Food and Drug Administration had resources sufficient to conduct only five thousand inspections of meat-processing plants in 1997, down from twenty-one thousand in 1981. And although food imports have doubled since the 1980s, FDA inspections of imports have fallen by half. Exposure to E. coli alone causes an estimated twenty thousand infections a year, and between two hundred and five hundred deaths.

We have been woefully slow to upgrade our municipal water-supply systems. The century-old pipes in many systems are typically cast-iron fittings joined by lead solder. As these conduits age and rust, lead, manganese, and other toxic metals leach into our drinking water. According to one estimate, some forty-five million of us are currently served by water systems that deliver potentially dangerous levels of toxic metals, pesticides, and parasites.

We have grown reluctant to invest in cleaner air. The Environmental Protection Agency proposed a tightening of standards for concentrations of ozone and particulate matter that would prevent more than 140,000 cases of acute respiratory distress each year and save more than fifteen thousand lives. The EPA proposal drew intense and immediate political fire, and bills were introduced in both houses of Congress to repeal the new standards, which have yet to be implemented.

Although spending on public education has not declined relative to historical norms, here, too, important inputs have not kept pace. For example, the national average starting salary for primary- and secondary-school teachers fell from 118 percent of the average salary of college graduates in 1963 to only 97 percent in 1994, a period that saw a significant decline in the average SAT scores of people who chose public-school teaching as a profession. And although we know that children learn more effectively in small classes than in large ones, we have offered fiscal distress as the reason for allowing class sizes to grow steadily larger during that same period.

We have slashed funding not only for services that benefit middle- and upper-income families, but also for the Head Start program, the school lunch program, homeless shelters, inner-city hospitals, and a host of other low-overhead programs that make life more bearable for the poor. We cut these programs not because they did not work, not because they destroyed incentives, but because the median voter decided that he couldn't afford them. That perception was, in large part, a consequence of the growing income gap.

When we choose between conspicuous and inconspicuous consumption, we confront a conflict between individual and social welfare that is structurally identical to that of a military arms race. We become like the superpowers during the heyday of the Cold War, robotically obedient to the doctrine of mutually assured destruction (with its memorable acronym MAD). The person who stays at the office two hours longer each day to afford a house in a better school district has no conscious intention of making it more difficult for others to achieve the same goal. But that is an inescapable consequence of her action. The best response available to others may be to work longer hours as well, thereby preserving their current positions. Yet the ineluctable mathematical logic of musical chairs ensures that only 10 percent of all children can occupy top-decile school seats, no matter how many hours their parents work.

A family can choose how much of its own money to spend, but it cannot choose how much others spend. Buying a smaller-than-average vehicle means a greater risk of dying in an accident. Spending less on an interview suit means a greater risk of not landing the best job. Spending less than others on a house means a greater risk of sending your children to inferior schools. Yet when all spend more on heavier cars, more finely tailored suits, and larger houses, the results tend to be mutually offsetting, just as when all nations spend more on missiles and bombs. Spending less frees up money for other pressing uses, but only if everyone does it.

If it is hard for nations to unwind from such a spiral, it is surely no easier for individuals. But the first steps are probably the same: We need to look at ourselves. We need to think about our actions in relation to their consequences. We need to talk.

Adapted from Inequality Matters: The Growing Economic Divide in America and Its Poisonous Consequences, *ed. James Lardner and David A. Smith.*

INEQUALITY IS HOLDING BACK THE RECOVERY

Joseph E. Stiglitz

The American economy could recover much faster from the Great Recession, and our young people could have a more prosperous future, if we understood better the effects of inequality and took steps to reduce it, a Nobel Prize–winning economist explains.

The reelection of President Obama was like a Rorschach test, subject to many interpretations. In this election, each side debated issues that deeply worry me: the long malaise into which the economy seems to be settling and the growing divide between the 1 percent and the rest—an inequality not only of outcomes but also of opportunity. To me, these problems are two sides of the same coin: with inequality at its highest level since before the Depression, a robust recovery will be difficult in the short term, and the American dream—a good life in exchange for hard work—is slowly dying.

Politicians typically talk about rising inequality and the sluggish recovery as separate phenomena, when they are in fact intertwined. Inequality stifles, restrains, and holds back our growth.

When even the free market–oriented *Economist* argues—as it did in a special feature in October 2012—that the magnitude and nature of the country's inequality represent a serious threat to America, we should know that something has gone horribly wrong. And yet, after four decades of widening inequality and the greatest economic downturn since the Depression, we haven't done anything about it.

FOUR FACTORS

There are four major reasons inequality is squelching our recovery.

The most immediate is that our middle class is too weak to support the consumer spending that has historically driven our economic growth. While the top 1 percent of income earners took home 93 percent of the growth in incomes in 2010, the households in the middle—who are most likely to spend their incomes rather than save them and who are, in a sense, the true job creators—have lower household incomes, adjusted for inflation, than they did in 1996. The growth in the decade before the crisis was unsustainable—it was reliant on the bottom 80 percent consuming about 110 percent of their income.

Second, the hollowing out of the middle class since the 1970s, a phenomenon interrupted only briefly in the 1990s, means that those families are unable to invest in their future, by educating themselves and their children and by starting or improving businesses.

Third, the weakness of the middle class is holding back tax receipts, especially because those at the top are so adroit in avoiding taxes and in getting Washington to give them tax breaks. The recent modest agreement to restore Clinton-level marginal income-tax rates for individuals making more than $400,000 and households making more than $450,000 did nothing to change this. Returns from Wall Street speculation are taxed at a far lower rate than other forms of income. Low tax receipts mean that the government cannot make the vital investments in infrastructure, education, research, and health that are crucial for restoring long-term economic strength.

Fourth, inequality is associated with more frequent and more severe boom-and-bust cycles that make our economy more volatile and vulnerable. Though inequality did not directly cause the crisis, it is no coincidence that the 1920s—the last time inequality of income and wealth in the United States was so high—ended with the Great Crash and the Depression. The International Monetary Fund has noted the systematic relationship between economic instability and economic inequality, but American leaders haven't absorbed the lesson.

Our skyrocketing inequality—so contrary to our meritocratic ideal of America as a place where anyone with hard work and talent can "make it"—means that those who are born to parents of limited means are likely never to live up to their potential. Children in other rich countries like Canada, France, Germany, and Sweden have a better chance of doing better than their parents did than American kids have. More than a fifth of our children live in poverty—the second worst of all the advanced economies, putting us behind countries like Bulgaria, Latvia, and Greece.

SQUANDERING OUR YOUNG

Our society is squandering its most valuable resource: our young. The dream of a better life that attracted immigrants to our shores is being crushed by an ever-widening chasm of income and wealth. Tocqueville, who in the 1830s found the egalitarian impulse to be the essence of the American character, is rolling in his grave.

Even were we able to ignore the economic imperative of fixing our inequality problem, the damage it is doing to our social fabric and political life should prompt us to worry. Economic inequality leads to political inequality and a broken decision-making process.

Despite Mr. Obama's stated commitment to helping all Americans, the recession and the lingering effects of the way it was handled have made matters much, much worse. While bailout money poured into the banks in 2009, unemployment soared to 10 percent that October. The rate in early 2013 (7.8 percent) appears better partly because so many people have dropped out of the labor force, or never entered it, or accepted part-time jobs because there was no full-time jobs for them.

High unemployment, of course, depresses wages. Adjusted for inflation, real wages have stagnated or fallen; a typical male worker's income in 2011 ($32,986) was lower than it was in 1968 ($33,880). Lower tax receipts, in turn, have forced state and local cutbacks in services vital to those at the bottom and middle.

Most Americans' most important asset is their home, and as home prices have plummeted, so has household wealth—especially since so many had borrowed so much on their homes. Large numbers are left with negative net worth, and median household wealth fell nearly 40 percent, to $77,300 in 2010 from $126,400 in 2007, and has rebounded only slightly. Since the Great Recession, most of the increase in the nation's wealth has gone to the very top.

SOARING TUITION AND DEBT

Meanwhile, as incomes have stagnated or fallen, tuition has soared. In the United States now, the principal way to get education—the only sure way to move up—is to borrow. In 2010, student debt, now $1 trillion, exceeded credit-card debt for the first time.

Student debt can almost never be wiped out, even in bankruptcy. A parent who co-signs a loan can't necessarily have the debt discharged even if his child dies. The debt can't be discharged even if the school—operated for profit and owned by exploitative financiers—provided an inadequate education, enticed the student with misleading promises, and failed to get her a decent job.

Instead of pouring money into the banks, we could have tried rebuilding the economy from the bottom up. We could have enabled home owners who were "underwater"—those who owe more money on their homes than the homes are worth—to get a fresh start, by writing down principal, in exchange for giving banks a share of the gains if and when home prices recovered.

We could have recognized that when young people are jobless, their skills atrophy. We could have made sure that every young person was either in school, in a training program, or on a job. Instead, we let youth unemployment rise to twice the national average. The children of the rich can stay in college or attend graduate school, without accumulating enormous debt, or take unpaid internships to beef up their résumés. Not so for those in the middle and bottom. We are sowing the seeds of ever more inequality in the coming years.

The Obama administration does not, of course, bear the sole blame. President George W. Bush's steep tax cuts in 2001 and 2003 and his multitrillion-dollar wars in Iraq and Afghanistan emptied the piggy bank while exacerbating the great divide. His party's newfound commitment to fiscal discipline—in the form of insisting on low taxes for the rich while slashing services for the poor—is the height of hypocrisy.

There are all kinds of excuses for inequality. Some say it's beyond our control, pointing to market forces like globalization, trade liberalization, the technological revolution, the "rise of the rest." Others assert that doing anything about it would make us all worse off, by stifling our already sputtering economic engine. These are self-serving, ignorant falsehoods.

Market forces don't exist in a vacuum—we shape them. Other countries, like fast-growing Brazil, have shaped them in ways that have lowered inequality while creating more opportunity and higher growth. Countries far poorer than ours have decided that all young people should have access to food, education, and health care so they can fulfill their aspirations.

Our legal framework and the way we enforce it has provided more scope here for abuses by the financial sector; for perverse compensation for chief executives; for monopolies' ability to take unjust advantage of their concentrated power.

Yes, the market values some skills more highly than others, and those who have those skills will do well. Yes, globalization and technological advances have led to the loss of good manufacturing jobs, which are not likely ever to come back. Global manufacturing employment is shrinking, simply because of enormous increases in productivity, and America is likely to get a shrinking share of the shrinking number of new jobs. If we do succeed in "saving" these jobs, it may be only by converting higher-paid jobs to lower-paid ones—hardly a long-term strategy.

Globalization, and the unbalanced way it has been pursued, has shifted bargaining power away from workers: firms can threaten to move elsewhere, especially when tax laws treat such overseas investments so favorably. This in turn has weakened unions, and though unions have sometimes been a source of rigidity, the countries that responded most effectively to the global financial crisis, like Germany and Sweden, have strong unions and strong systems of social protection.

As Mr. Obama's second term begins, we must all face the fact that our country cannot quickly, meaningfully recover without policies that directly address inequality. What's needed is a comprehensive response that should include, at least, significant investments in education, a more progressive tax system, and a tax on financial speculation.

The good news is that our thinking has been reframed: it used to be that we asked how much growth we would be willing to sacrifice for a little more equality and opportunity. Now we realize that we are paying a high price for our inequality and that alleviating it and promoting growth are intertwined, complementary goals. It will be up to all of us—our leaders included—to muster the courage and foresight to finally treat this beleaguering malady.

This piece originally appeared on the New York Times *Opinionator blog on January 19, 2013.*

WAGE THEFT

Kim Bobo

To people with middle-class or better jobs, the idea of not being paid in full for their work may seem odd. But for millions of workers in low-paying jobs, getting shorted on pay is a common occurrence, one that the writer of this piece shows is reduced when unions are strong.

> But the king of Egypt said, "Moses and Aaron, why are you taking the people away from their labor? Get back to your work!"
>
> —*Exodus 5:4*

Mercedes Herrerra is thirty-nine years old. She grew up in Veracruz, Mexico. She came from a hardworking family. As she says, "My mom instilled in me a desire to stand up for people." Herrerra and her husband have four children, one granddaughter, and one grandson "on the way."

Herrerra came to Houston in 1994. She first started cleaning houses in 1996. Then she moved to cleaning downtown buildings and sports facilities, working primarily for staffing agencies. She and her co-workers were frequently victims of wage theft.

She was never paid for overtime. Her employers would tell her, "There is no overtime. After forty hours you work for someone else." (This is not legal.)

After Hurricanes Katrina and Rita, Herrerra was hired by a cleaning firm contracted to clean the Reliant [Convention] Center. She was in charge of keeping the bathrooms clean. Her staffing agency charged her $100 per week for her shoes, gloves, masks, cleaning supplies, and shuttle rides to the center. She wasn't told when she was hired that such charges would be taken from her paycheck. As a result, her hourly wage fell significantly below minimum wage. (This is not legal.)

Frequently, employers would just not pay her for all the hours she worked. Herrerra would always complain and try to get all the wages she was owed, but most of her colleagues didn't feel comfortable standing up for themselves.

For lots of the cleaning firms around town, Friday was a rush day. Workers would be told they had to clean the same number of rooms they regularly did in four hours in only three, so that the managers could get off early. After three hours, the worker would be required to clock out and then finish the work on his or her own time. (Yes, this too is illegal.)

Perhaps worse for Herrerra than the wage theft was the treatment she received. Managers would scream at her and her colleagues. Some would tell workers they were old and worthless.

In 2008, Herrerra took a position cleaning buildings in the Galleria [Houston shopping mall] for ABM, a national janitorial firm. Although ABM always paid her, before the workers organized she only earned $5.15 an hour and she had no vacation days, no sick days, no health insurance or pension, and lots of work. She was only given four hours of work a day. She had to clean eighteen large restrooms in four hours per day.

When one of the organizers came to her door to talk about organizing a union, she knew it was right. Herrerra says, "I had so much anger built up from years of exploitation." First, she went to a rally at a building to support other janitors. Then she went to some meetings for training. Then she began talking with her co-workers about joining the union. She got people's names and addresses and tried to motivate them to get involved.

When she got involved, the organizing had already been going on about a year. It took almost two years total to win a union contract.

Things have changed a lot since the Service Employees International Union (SEIU) worked with the 5,300 janitors in Houston to negotiate a union contract. Herrerra started making $7.25 per hour and gets a raise every year. She gets one week of vacation after one year and two weeks after five years. She gets six paid holidays. Now she is getting five hours of work a day and next year she will get six. Even though she doesn't yet get paid for sick days, she doesn't fear losing her job because she takes a sick day. Next year, workers will get individual health coverage, and the union is building a health clinic. The workers want lots more in their contract (higher wages, family health care, pensions, paid sick days), but they know it will be difficult to win until more of Houston's janitors are represented by the union.

But wage theft has been wiped out for the unionized janitors. Anytime there is a problem on wages, workers call the union hotline and someone works out the problems.

Unions not only raise wages, benefits, and working conditions. They stop wage theft. Unions are one of the most effective wage-theft deterrents around.

Unions are critical institutions to support and strengthen in the overall campaign to stop wage theft in the nation. Particularly because so many younger people do not know much about unions, this chapter helps explain how unions help workers and improve society overall.

A LITTLE UNION HISTORY

A union is a formal, structured way for workers to collectively work together to address wages, benefits, and working conditions within a workplace. Workplace organizing is not new. Labor and community organizers claim that Moses was the first organizer. He probably wasn't—there were surely many organizers before him seeking justice in the workplace. Nonetheless, he clearly helped organize the Israelites to fight the oppression of the Egyptians against the slaves. Moses proposed a three-day strike, which infuriated the pharaoh. Organizing for better working conditions and even striking are not new.

The earliest unions in U.S. history were the craft guilds. During colonial times, groups of craftsmen (and sometimes women) organized themselves to share skills and make sure that they weren't competing with one another in driving down wages. The Carpenters Company of Philadelphia was founded in 1724 and set wages and working conditions for carpenters in the region. In 1741, the Journeymen Caulkers of Boston issued a statement about how they wanted to be paid. By the end of the century there were organized shoemakers, tailors, painters, printers, cabinetmakers, shipbuilders, and many others. These craft guilds were the forerunners of many of the building-trades' unions, such as the painters', roofers', and carpenters' unions.

The first factories in the United States were textile mills, which emerged in the early 1800s. These were soon followed by iron factories, which enabled the growth of machines for manufacturing and railroads. As factories expanded throughout the 1800s, so too did groups of workers within factories seeking to improve wages and working conditions, although through the first half of the century, the formal organizations of workers were still skilled craftspeople (mostly men). The second half of the century saw more formal unions organized in factory settings and many strikes and campaigns to improve wages and limit working hours. By the end of the century, unions were organizing themselves to function locally, by state, and nationally. Labor unions pushed not only for improved wages and benefits locally, but also for state and national standards on wages and limits on working hours.

Labor history is the story of workers organizing and their great struggle for recognition. Workers did not organize unions for some vague ideological belief in unions. Rather, they organized unions because they thought they would have a better chance to improve their working conditions if they joined with their colleagues than by doing things on their own. Most large employers, and certainly the captains of industry, vehemently opposed unions. Workers who stood up for their rights were often fired or beaten, and sometimes killed.

Relations between unions and employers became so contentious in the midst of the Great Depression that it was hard for the nation to prosper, which finally prompted Congress and President Roosevelt to intervene. In 1935, Congress passed the National Labor Relations Act, known as the Wagner Act, which outlined labor's rights to organize and bargain union contracts. The National

Labor Relations Board was established to make sure employers treated workers fairly when they tried to organize unions.

The passage of this law gave a huge boost to labor organizing. From 1935 to 1937, a total of 5 million workers (one in six) joined labor unions. The religious community supported this expansion of unions. From 1935 through 1955, Catholic parishes and orders ran nearly two hundred Catholic labor schools, which taught workers how to organize unions. An interesting article in *Time* from 1951 describes one such school in Manhattan:

> In his eleven years as director of Manhattan's Xavier Labor School, Father Philip Carey has become a familiar figure to thousands of working men and women. He is a mild and scholarly Jesuit whose students are electricians, scrubwomen, plumbers, bus drivers, pipe fitters, and wire lathers. The lesson Father Carey teaches them: how to build strong and effective unions.
>
> Last week, as the first term of the academic year ended at Xavier, 150 men and women were enrolled. But these were only a fraction of the school's real student body. When a New York's dock strike raged Xavier's assistant director, Father John Corridan, was devoting full time to a steady stream of longshoremen coming for advice. The school never takes sides in such disputes; its influence is felt only indirectly. But over the years, union men all over the East have come to realize that Jesuits Carey and Corridan are as wise about labor problems as any men alive.
>
> The school's formal course lasts two years, and students of every faith are welcome. Tuition (which is often waived): $5. There are night classes in public speaking and parliamentary procedure, labor ethics and law, in economics and trade union methods. Xavier's volunteer faculty (three lawyers, ten union officers, two business-men and the two priests) translates its subjects into down-to-earth problems. Students study contracts, sample constitutions, hold mock conventions and negotiation meetings. Sometimes, actual union problems

come before their "grievance clinics," with representatives of management on hand to talk things over with the union. Since 1936, Xavier has turned out 6,000 alumni from the big, sprawling school building on West 16th Street.

The Catholics weren't the only ones actively supporting workers organizing unions during this union expansion period. The Presbyterians organized the Labor Temple in New York City. The Methodists supported mine workers in their rural congregations. The Congregationalists trained, and the Episcopalians nurtured, Frances Perkins. The Jewish Workmen's Circle organized Labor Lyceums. African American ministers E.B. McKinney and Owen Whitfield led efforts to organize Mississippi Delta sharecroppers into the Southern Tenant Farmers Union (STFU).

The engagement of the religious community in supporting workers' efforts to organize unions extended to a broad range of religious bodies—Catholic, Protestant, Evangelical, Jewish, and others. Why did unions receive such extensive religious support? Unions were seen as effective vehicles through which workers could improve their wages, benefits, and working conditions. Unions were an effective way to stop wage theft and lift workers and their families out of poverty.

UNIONS STOP WAGE THEFT

Unions are still the best and most effective vehicle for stopping wage theft, for the following reasons:

Unions train workers about their rights in the workplace. Basic laws protecting workers are confusing, and consequently most workers are unsure about their rights and where to turn for help. Unions train local leaders about their rights in the workplace. When workers know the laws and their rights, they are much more vigorous advocates on their own behalf.

Unions have attorneys available to answer questions and file suits. Whenever questions about the legality of some payment arrangement arise, unionized workers can ask their union's attorneys to answer questions. If problems can't be resolved at the worksite, the attorneys help workers file claims, grievances, or suits.

Unions provide workers a structure for expressing concerns. With a union contract comes a structure for addressing problems in the workplace. Usually, each workplace has one or more shop stewards who support workers in addressing problems in their workplace. If workers aren't being paid correctly, the shop stewards will work with the workers to make sure problems are corrected through a grievance procedure.

Unions protect workers who complain. One reason many workers don't file complaints with government agencies about problems on the worksite, even if they know there is a legal violation, is that they are fearful that their employers will retaliate against them. Because union contracts outline clear procedures for how workers can't be fired and for how unions will challenge unfair practices, workers feel safe about raising concerns.

Unions create a counterbalance to management's control in the workplace. In most workplaces without a contract, workers have little real power to influence decisions made in the workplace. When employers steal wages, or are tempted to steal wages, unions challenge them and hold them accountable to paying workers based on both the labor laws and the contract. If situations aren't clear, they will usually get clarified in the next contract negotiations.

Unions maintain relationships with community allies and resources. Unions usually have relationships with newspaper reporters, social service agencies, religious organizations, politicians, and others who can join workers in pressuring their employers (if needed) to do the right thing.

Industries that have high percentages of workers represented by unions (referred to as high "union density") almost never have significant wage-theft problems. The unions aggressively enforce their contracts and enforce the nation's labor laws. Unions provide a strong "pushback" force against the forces that might be tempted to steal wages.

HOW ELSE DO UNIONS HELP WORKERS?

In addition to stopping wage theft, unions play important roles in improving working conditions for workers. Unions help workers secure the following:

Better wages. Workers in unions earn more money than
workers doing the exact same job in nonunionized workplaces. According to the Bureau of Labor Statistics, in 2006
the union pay advantage was 30 percent higher for all workers, and it is even larger for people of color and women.
Janitors in Chicago and janitors in Houston were doing the
same jobs for the same companies, but unionized janitors
earned twice as much.

Benefits. Unionized workers are more likely to have health
insurance. Union members are also more likely to have
health plans that include dental, prescriptions, and eyeglass
coverage. In 2006, 80 percent of union workers in the private sector had employer-provided medical care benefits,
compared with 49 percent of nonunion workers. Many
unions are fighting to preserve or establish affordable co-
payments for health insurance. Unionized workers are
more likely to have short-term disability benefits as well.
Janitors in Houston would never have had health care without the union.

Retirement benefits. Unionized workers are more likely to
have retirement benefits. Most union members, 68 percent,
have defined-benefit coverage plans, compared with only
14 percent of nonunion workers.

A voice in decisions. All workers want to be involved in decisions that affect their working lives, and yet many find
themselves and their suggestions routinely ignored or rejected. Workers want to do high-quality work, and they
often use their union contracts as a way to improve the
overall quality of work provided. The early labor guilds
were formed in order to improve members' quality of work,
and those values still hold in the building-trades' unions.
Teachers often bargain over ways to improve the quality
of teaching for children. Nurses bargain over patient care.
Public-sector workers bargain over how to serve their clients or the public better.

Workers want a voice in decisions about work, but many feel
that they are denied the right to talk and think when they

enter the workplace. Too often, management, which controls workers' basic livelihood, discourages workers' participation in the company decision-making process. This
is especially frustrating to workers when issues such as the
scheduling of hours, workloads, and ways to make the work
more effective are decided. Unions help workers have a
voice in the decisions.

Safe working environments. If you work in a place where
workers routinely get injured or some have even been
killed, you will probably want a union to help negotiate safe working conditions. Take the case of those whose
jobs involve working in trenches—working in manholes
or any confined space below ground level. Between 1985
and 1995, 522 workers in the United States were killed
in trench-related mishaps, only 60 of whom worked for
union shops. The other 462 were employed by nonunionized firms. Recent tragedies in nonunion coal mines also
highlight the stark difference in safety standards between
union and nonunion shops. In 2006, 12 miners died from
an explosion at the Sago mine, owned by the nonunion
firm, International Coal Group. The company was cited by
the Mine Safety Health Administration for multiple violations, but got away by paying just $24,000 in fines. A union
presence would have helped ensure that safety standards
were met.

Job security. As companies outsource, downsize, and shift
from permanent to contingent employees, workers have
grown concerned about their job security. People want
assurance that companies won't outsource their jobs to
some cheaper group, another state, or even another country. Unions can't guarantee complete job security, but
contracts negotiated by unions attempt to create some job
protections when at all possible. In addition, unions protect workers from bosses who fire workers without cause.
Most states in the nation are "at will" states, meaning that
workers can be fired for any reason that isn't protected
under various laws. So you can't be fired for being a certain faith or a certain race, but you can be fired because the

boss doesn't like your "attitude" or you didn't come to work when your child was sick, for example. Union contracts ensure that there is "just cause" and a fair process before firing someone.

Fairness. Workers want to know what the rules are, what the consequences are for breaking those rules, and what the appeal (grievance) process is for alleged rule violations. Some personnel policies clearly outline them. Most don't. Too often workers follow the policies while the employers do not. Without a personnel policy that acts as a binding contract, or a union contract that makes the rules and procedures clear, workers feel, and often are, vulnerable to the whims of supervisors. Promotions, raises, penalties, and dismissals often seem random and unfair. Minorities and women benefit from union contracts that enshrine nondiscrimination language and ensure that all union members, no matter their race or gender, are paid, promoted, and treated based on their abilities to do the job.

ARE UNIONS PERFECT?

I have never given a presentation about religion-labor partnerships or wage theft and not been asked a question about problems with unions. Let me share the typical questions and some of my responses.

Aren't unions corrupt? Unions, like religious bodies, are made up of human beings with all their flaws and frailties. There is some corruption in unions, as within religious institutions. And wherever corruption or greed is uncovered, it must be cleaned up. For that purpose, most unions have rigorous procedures to combat corruption. When a local union is found to be corrupt, the national leadership will take over control until it can be cleaned up and an election of new leaders held. As wrong as union corruption is, it is unfortunate that it receives so much front-page media attention in comparison to the important justice work done by unions to improve wages, benefits, and working conditions for workers in low-wage jobs. By the way, did you see the stories about the Presbyterian treasurer who stole money, or the Episcopal treasurer who stole $2 million, or the National Baptist president who stole

$102,000? Corruption is part of the human condition and is neither unique nor even particularly prevalent in unions.

The perception of unions as corrupt is reinforced by many mainstream newspapers that refer to union leaders as union "bosses," using a mob connotation, even though union leadership is mostly democratically elected by union members. Most of the union leaders I know are hardworking, ethical men and women who are seeking to improve conditions for their members and other workers in society. Corporate CEOs aren't called corporate bosses by the press, so why should union leaders be given that name?

Aren't unions violent? Unions advocate legal and peaceful means for achieving social gains. All national union leaders abhor violence and teach their members to practice and preach nonviolence. Nonetheless, when workers are locked out, their jobs are moved overseas, or their economic livelihood is threatened, a handful of workers may act out their anger in inappropriate ways. Unions do not condone or in any manner support the behavior of a handful of workers who may resort to violence. Despite knowing that unions don't condone violence, when union-busting consultants want to denigrate unions, they describe them as violent and show photos of violence on a picket line. Violence is wrong, whether it involves workers on a picket line, security guards harassing picketers, or companies causing economic violence (stealing wages) against workers.

Aren't unions racist or sexist? Like corruption, racism and sexism are sins shared by unions, the religious community, and the society at large. A key goal of the leadership of the AFL-CIO and Change to Win is ensuring full participation for all in work, in society, and in unions. Although work still needs to be done, the AFL-CIO has made significant progress in making its leadership more closely reflect its membership. Part of this may be due to a change the AFL-CIO made to its constitution, which was meant to significantly develop the race and gender diversity of its leadership. Upon its establishment in 2005, Change to Win instituted three positions on its leadership council specifically designed to further race and gender diversity on the council.

Don't unions drive companies overseas? Unions themselves do

not drive companies overseas. Nonetheless, it is true that companies often choose to move to other countries or other parts of the United States in search of lower wages and more vulnerable workers. Manufacturing firms that operate in the global economy often look for alternative production locations where labor or resource costs are lower. Unions are very sensitive to industry concerns about competitiveness because they want jobs to stay with their members. As a result, most unions are willing to bargain around ways to keep a company competitive, but the unions must also be convinced that the company is willing to invest in its workers and to invest in adequate research and product design.

WHY AREN'T UNIONS STRONGER?

Given the crisis of wage theft in the nation and the effective role unions play in stopping wage theft, one would think that unions would be growing by leaps and bounds. In fact, many workers would like to have a union in their workplace—53 percent of all working Americans who are not currently represented by unions would vote to join a union if they had the opportunity to do so without risking their jobs. However, many workers are afraid.

Whenever I am speaking with a group about unions, I always ask, "What would happen if you tried to organize a union at your workplace?" Every single time the response is the same: "I would get fired."

Whether or not it is true that someone would get fired, the collective wisdom and understanding in the society is that if you try to organize a union, you will get fired. Needless to say, this puts a decided chill on organizing. Who can afford to lose a job unexpectedly?

The weak laws alone are bad enough for those who choose to organize. Adding insult to injury, a sophisticated, multimillion-dollar industry has developed to consult and advise employers on how to oppose unions and frighten workers. More than 80 percent of companies faced with union organizing efforts hire these consultants and law firms to wage antiunion campaigns. No other industrialized nation has such a powerful union-busting industry or weaker labor protections.

U.S. labor law related to unions is mainly governed by the National Labor Relations Act (NLRA) and the Taft-Hartley amendments. The original National Labor Relations Act was passed in 1935 to improve workers' living standards by increasing the power of unions. Over the course of the next sixty-five years, the intent of the law has been changed through amendments to the act, and various judicial and administrative decisions have weakened the unions. The Taft-Hartley amendments to the NLRA, passed in 1947, increased managers' abilities to oppose unions. The amendments permitted the employers to campaign against union representation as long as there was "no threat of reprisal or force or promise of benefit." Workers repeatedly express feeling under attack when employers oppose unions.

WHAT HAPPENS TO WORKERS WHO ATTEMPT TO ORGANIZE?

1. Ninety-one percent of employers require employees to attend a one-on-one meeting with their supervisors where they are told why unions are bad and why they should vote against a union.
2. Fifty-one percent of employers illegally coerce union opposition through bribes and favors.
3. Thirty percent of employers illegally fire prounion employees.
4. Forty-nine percent of employers illegally threaten to eliminate all workers' jobs if they join a union.

Most of this antiunion activity occurs after the workers have signed cards indicating they want to be represented by a union and before the official NLRB-supervised election. If the point of an election is to determine what workers really want, then it would seem that both sides—union and management—should be able to present their cases fairly. But given the laws, the antiunion campaigns, and the control that employers have over workers' lives, the cases are not presented evenly. In effect, the time between signing union cards and holding an election appears to be a time to scare workers into voting against unions.

Antiunion activities have become so prevalent that an initiative was introduced in Congress in early 2006 to expand employees' freedom to choose and pursue union representation. The Employee Free Choice Act (EFCA), as the initiative is known, calls for stronger penalties for violations of the election process that occurs between union-card signing and the NLRB-supervised election, mediation and arbitration for stalled contract negotiations, and union formation through majority sign-up. Whether there is an NLRB-supervised election, card-check recognition, or a community-sponsored election, the principles of fairness and respect for one another must be maintained by all parties, employees and employers alike.

UNIONS ARE VITAL TO SOCIETY

Unions are vitally needed in U.S. society. When unions represent most workers in an industry, wage theft is virtually eliminated. Given the prevalence of wage theft, it would be useful if all workers in the garment industry, poultry plants, nursing homes, agriculture, restaurants, hotels, and retail stores were represented by unions. Many unions are focusing their organizing efforts on workers in these industries. Their campaigns are worthy of support.

Unions and collective bargaining contracts are one of the best ways to help U.S. families reach the American dream of middle-class wages, benefits, and working conditions. In the past, unions have turned low-paying, sweatshop jobs in manufacturing and construction into well-paying middle-class jobs. This effort is still needed in manufacturing and construction and must be extended to retail jobs as well. Unions help companies share their wealth with the workers who help create the wealth.

Unions also raise working conditions for large groups of workers by advocating laws that set national standards and by promoting the general welfare of all workers. Unions will be leading advocates for national health care, paid sick days, pension protections, and a host of other standards that would improve conditions for Americans.

The Israelites in Egypt needed to organize. Mercedes Herrerra in Houston needed a union. Millions of workers around the nation need protection against wage theft.

There is no better vehicle for protecting against wage theft than unions. If you want to fight poverty, encourage unions. If you want to improve your life at work, join unions. If you want to stop wage theft, support unions.

Adapted from Wage Theft in America: Why Millions of Working Americans Are Not Getting Paid—and What We Can Do About It.

HOME DEPOT'S CEO-SIZE TIP

Barbara Ehrenreich

Barbara Ehrenreich, who has a doctoral degree in chemistry, took low-paid work to experience the lives of those who often get shorted on pay, rely on tips that are often minimal and are abused by bosses for her book Nickled and Dimed: On (Not) Getting by in America. *Here she takes a satirical look at the other end of the pay scale.*

I'm not upset by the $210 million golden parachute CEO Robert Nardelli received in his 2007 send-off from Home Depot. Not at all. To those critics who see it as one more step in the slide from free-market capitalism to gluttonous free-for-all, I say: what do you really know about Nardelli's circumstances? Maybe he has a dozen high-maintenance ex–trophy wives to support, each with a brood of special-needs offspring. Ever think what that would cost?

Or he may have a rare disease that can be held at bay only by daily fusions of minced fresh gorilla liver. Just try purchasing a gorilla a day for purposes of personal consumption—or any other endangered species, for that matter. There are the poachers to pay, the smugglers, the doctors and vets. I'm just saying: don't start envisioning offshore bank accounts and 50,000 square-foot fourth homes until you know the whole story.

Another reason I'm not troubled by the $210 million payoff is that the Home Depot board may think of it as a kind of tip for its fired CEO, and, like me, they may not feel tips need to be linked to performance. I don't tip as a reward for good service; I give a tip because it's part of the tipped person's living. Waitstaff, for example, earn about $2 or $3 an hour—a bit more in certain states—so a tip is just my contribution to their wage. Sloppy waitress? Surly cabdriver? I'm not their supervisor—they get their 20–25 percent anyway.

So what if Home Depot stock fell from $50 to $41 on Nardelli's watch? Maybe the board should be commended for their generous tipping policies. Possibly they're trying to send a message to us stingy 20 percenters: that 300 percent (based on Nardelli's $64 million earnings over his six-year tenure) is more like it.

Or it could be that Home Depot has a more profound philosophical message to impart. The board may have decided to flout the very principle of capitalist exchange: that what you get paid should in some way reflect the work that you've done—or the "value-added," as they say in the business. Other companies are taking the same anti-market approach. Pfizer rewarded its failed CEO with an exit package of $200 million, and Merrill Lynch's Stan O'Neal got a $161.5 million retirement package after presiding over that company's $8.4 billion write-down of mortgage-related losses.

Picture the board members sitting cross-legged on the floor in a circle, munching s'mores and giggling about how cleverly they've undermined the basis of our capitalist economy. Home Depot sales clerks get about $8 to $10 an hour for lifting heavy objects and running around the floor all day; the CEO gets a total of almost $300 million for sinking the stock. We're not talking about a rational system of rewards—just random acts of kindness, vast sums of money alighting when and where they will, generally in the outstretched hands of those who already have far too much.

From Nickled and Dimed: On (Not) Getting by in America.

WHY DO SO MANY JOBS PAY SO BADLY?

Christopher Jencks

In 2012 dollars, the median wage in America has been stuck at slightly more than $500 per week since 1999, and the average income of the bottom 90 percent of Americans has been falling. In 2012 it fell back to the level of 1966 when Lyndon Johnson was president. A Harvard professor of social policy explains the reasons for these trends.

The American economy turned out $7.6 trillion worth of consumer goods and services in 2004—enough to provide every man, woman, and child with almost $26,000 worth of food, housing, transportation, medical care, and other things. If all that stuff had been divided equally, the typical household, which now has three members, would have gotten about $78,000 worth.

Yet as an abundance of recent research confirms—and as all can plainly see—many Americans had to scrape by on far less than that. About one American worker in six reported having been paid less than $8 an hour in 2003. That works out to less than $17,000 a year even for someone employed full-time. And many low-wage workers earned far less than $17,000 because they were unemployed part of the year, worked fewer than forty hours a week, or earned under $8 an hour.

Some of those low-wage workers were teenagers who didn't have to pay most of their own expenses, much less support anyone else.

For them, $8 an hour was a pretty good wage. But many of America's low-wage workers were single mothers trying to support a family. Others were married men whose wives stayed home with their children. These workers are eligible for the Earned Income Tax Credit, but most of them still find making ends meet a constant challenge.

Most Americans think these workers deserve a better deal and tell pollsters that the minimum wage (currently $5.15 an hour) should be raised. But a market economy is not designed to ensure that workers get paid what other people think they deserve. The logic of a market economy is that we should all be paid the smallest amount that will ensure that our work gets done, and that is what low-wage workers generally receive.

American economists and business leaders have long argued that the best way to improve low-income families' standards of living is to make the economy more productive. At times economic growth truly has benefited almost everyone. When World War II dragged the United States out of the Great Depression, unskilled workers and their families gained proportionately more than most other Americans. Even after the war ended, the rich and the poor enjoyed roughly similar percentage gains in income until the early 1970s. So when John F. Kennedy said "a rising tide lifts all boats," he was describing the experience of his generation. Since 1973, however, things have been very different. Productivity and national income have increased but wages have diverged.

Measuring changes in purchasing power is complicated and contentious, but the best historical measure is probably what the Commerce Department's Bureau of Economic Analysis calls the chain price index for personal consumption expenditure. Using this measure, the nation's output of consumer goods per worker rose 58 percent between 1973 and 2003. Yet if we use the same price index to measure the mean hourly earnings of nonsupervisory workers, we find that they rose only 6 percent.

Among men without any college education, real wages have actually fallen since 1973. Immigrants now do many of the jobs that native-born high school graduates would once have done, and this competition has driven down wages. As a result, male high school graduates and dropouts are having more trouble supporting a family.

Meanwhile, more women have entered the labor force, and their tolerance for men who cannot pay the bills has diminished, especially if these men are also hard to live with, as they often are. Marriage rates have fallen, and divorce rates exceed 50 percent among couples with below-average earning power. More than half of all mothers without college degrees now spend some time as a single parent. Most married couples now feel that they need two breadwinners rather than one. Partly for that reason, the number of workers has grown more than the adult population, while the number of children has grown less than the adult population.

The net result of all these changes is that while the economy grew dramatically between 1973 and 2004, most of the benefits went to those who needed them least: affluent, college-educated couples.

The best trend data on household income now come from the Congressional Budget Office (CBO), which pools data collected by the Census Bureau with data on similar individuals collected by the Internal Revenue Service. These figures, which are available from 1979 through 2000, allow the CBO to calculate households' total income, including capital gains and noncash benefits like food stamps, and also to subtract taxes.

Mean household income rose 40 percent between 1979 and 2000. But in sharp contrast to the situation between 1940 and 1973, more than a third of the total increase since 1979 has gone to the richest 1 percent of all households, and another third has gone to the next richest 19 percent. That hasn't left much for the bottom 80 percent. While the incomes of the top 1 percent tripled between 1979 and 2000, the income of the median household rose only 15 percent, and the incomes of those in the bottom quintile rose only 9 percent. The gains at the bottom almost all came between 1994 and 2000.

The moral of this story seems clear: while economic growth is almost always a necessary condition for improving the lives of those in the bottom half of the income distribution, America's experience over the past generation shows that growth alone is not sufficient.

So what makes the difference? Why are the benefits of growth sometimes widely shared and sometimes not? If you ask economists and business leaders why households in the bottom half of the distribution have benefited so little from economic growth since 1973, they tend to talk about impersonal forces like globalization, computers, and skill deficits. But if these explanations were sufficient, we would see the same pattern in every rich country, and we don't.

The Luxembourg Income Study (LIS) now provides roughly comparable measures of how household income is distributed in most wealthy democracies. Data on Britain, Canada, France, Germany, Sweden, and the United States are available back to the 1970s. Even then the United States was the most unequal of the six nations. Sweden was the most equal. But at that time, Canada, Britain, France, and Germany all looked more like the United States than like Sweden.

Since then the distribution of household income has grown substantially more unequal in both Britain and the United States, while hardly changing at all in Canada, France, Germany, or Sweden. The LIS has data going back to the 1980s on a number of other rich democracies. This body of evidence also tells a mixed story. Household income inequality increased somewhat in Australia, Austria, Belgium, Finland, and Norway, but it has hardly changed in Denmark, Ireland, or the Netherlands.

Today the United States is by far the most unequal rich democracy in the world.

Impersonal forces like globalization, computerization, and skill deficits are not promising explanations for these differences. Most of the countries with stable income distributions are even more dependent than the United States on the global economy. Computer use and sales spread faster in the United States than in most other countries, but by the end of the 1990s, computers had permeated every affluent society. Thus, if the skills required to use computers or interpret their output were in short supply, and if this explained the run-up in inequality, we should now see the same pattern in every technically advanced society.

The International Adult Literacy Survey does suggest that workers' reading and math skills are somewhat more unequal in the United States than in the other wealthy countries, but because the correlation between these skills and workers' earnings is quite modest, the distribution of such skills cannot explain why inequality is greater in the United States.

A somewhat more credible story points to faster growth in post-secondary school enrollment in Europe than in the United States, which could have kept the price of skilled labor lower in Europe. But European workers still have less schooling than their American counterparts, and educational change cannot easily explain why European workers' pay is more equal than ours.

So why do ordinary American workers get to keep less of what they produce than ordinary workers in other rich countries? And why is this form of American exceptionalism becoming more pronounced? The answer turns out be pretty simple: "It's politics, stupid." Political scientists have been churning out papers on this question for more than a decade, and while the details differ, they mostly tell a broadly similar story. At least in rich democracies, differences in income distribution seem to be traceable to differences in constitutional arrangements, electoral systems, and economic institutions. Those differences in turn affect the political balance between left and right, the level of spending on the welfare state, and a wide range of economic policies.

Economic inequality is less pronounced in countries where the constitutional system has few veto points, allowing the government of the day to make fundamental changes. Rules that favor a multiparty system rather than a two-party system also produce more equal economic outcomes. So does proportional representation. Such arrangements apparently make it more likely that a ruling coalition will seek to protect labor unions, raise the minimum wage, and centralize wage negotiations, all of which tend to reduce wage inequality. Such coalitions also tend to expand the welfare state.

If you think all of this sounds very different from the United States, you are right. The men who drafted the U.S. Constitution were property holders. Most of them worried about the possibility that democratic governments might be tempted to appropriate their property, or at least impose very high taxes in order to provide benefits to less affluent voters. The founders wanted a system of government that would make such populism easy to resist, and to a large extent they got what they wanted.

Despite the subsequent spread of cultural egalitarianism, both federal and state legislators have remained remarkably solicitous of property holders' rights. Legislators have also shown a persistent preference for relying on private markets rather than public institutions to make economic decisions.

These legislative priorities enjoy broad popular support. Americans are less likely than Europeans to tell pollsters that income differences are too large. Americans are also more suspicious of government than Europeans, which means that Americans are less likely to endorse policies for reducing wage inequality that involve government "meddling" in the marketplace. But these attitudes are not built into Americans' DNA, nor are they an inescapable legacy of our history. In part, of course, they reflect the public's tendency to endorse the institutional status quo, which most Americans think has served the nation well.

The promarket consensus also reflects the influence of journalists and political pundits, most of whom seem to be even more skeptical about government than about private enterprise or the current influence of the business elite. This consensus owes something to the absence of a political party that questions it. The absence of such a party derives both from rules that make third parties extremely difficult to organize and from a system of campaign finance that makes every party dependent on rich contributors.

But none of these obstacles to redistribution is insuperable. Americans are not as unhappy as Europeans about economic inequality, but most Americans still say that income differences are too large and, by a sizable majority, favor increasing the minimum wage. While there are certainly institutional obstacles to redistribution, most of those obstacles also existed between 1940 and 1970, when the distribution of income became more equal.

Low-wage America is a mosaic of occupations and industries. Many tightfisted employers face relentless competitive pressure to cut costs, and many are operating in fields where logistical considerations and other factors make it particularly easy to knock down wages domestically or ship work overseas.

In almost every line of business, though, executives turn out to have a good deal of discretion about how they structure and reward work. Some take the low road and squeeze their frontline workers, driving down wages and working people harder. Others take the high road, adopting new technologies that keep their operations competitive, upgrading workers' skills, and reorganizing the way work gets done.

You can find instances of both in the same sector of the economy. In retailing, for example, Walmart has been a Wall Street darling, in part because of its low wages and stingy benefits, which analysts and investors associate with high profits.

But Costco, whose warehouse sales outlets directly compete with Walmart's Sam's Club stores, has achieved similarly impressive results while paying its workers about 40 percent more in wages (an average of $15.97 an hour in 2004, compared to Walmart's $11.52) and providing much more generous and inclusive (and costly) health insurance. In return, Costco gets a remarkably productive and loyal workforce; only 6 percent of its employees leave after the first year, compared with 21 percent at Sam's. "I'm not a social engineer," says Costco CEO James D. Sinegal. "Paying good wages is simply good business."

You can find plenty of success stories along the high road. Indeed, it defies common sense as well as economic logic to believe that a poorly skilled and badly paid American workforce could, in anything but the very short run, be the key to global competitiveness (never mind an attractive society). Which road a firm chooses depends on the social context in which its managers operate. They are more likely to take the high road if they are connected to institutions, public and private, that promote such alternatives. The U.S. system for connecting highly skilled work to advanced technology, unfortunately, is rudimentary and fragmented. Managers are also more likely to choose the high road if they face a strong progressive union that can make abusing workers costly while simultaneously making collaborative efforts between workers and managers easier. But American business is almost uniquely hostile to unions.

The experience of other countries suggests that managers will also be more inclined to choose the high road if they have to pay a high minimum wage, forcing them to think more inventively about how to keep a firm competitive. Perhaps most important, managers will be more likely to take the high road if they are honored and rewarded for doing so. Too often, sadly, the honor and the rewards go to those who drive wages down instead of up.

Adapted from Inequality Matters: The Growing Economic Divide in America and Its Poisonous Consequences, *ed. James Lardner and David A. Smith.*

IN THE HEART OF OUR ECONOMY AND OUR LIVES

Beth Shulman

Workers in low-paying jobs are often seen as disposable, even though they play an indispensible role in our economy. A lawyer who helped the working poor listened to some of them tell about lives, their work, and their responsibilities.

Low-wage jobs and the workers in these jobs are intimately involved in every aspect of American life. The country's recent prosperity rests on the growing sectors of the economy in which they work. Yet in spite of their contributions, these jobs and the workers in these jobs are dismissed and undervalued. It is the part of our economy that remains invisible. It is time to take a closer look at these jobs and the many roles they play in all of our lives.

Contrary to the dominant myth that most low-wage jobs are the ones you see in your neighborhood McDonald's, fast-food jobs constitute less than 5 percent of all low-end jobs.

Then where do we find the people working in these low-wage, low-reward jobs? They are all around us: security guards, nurse's aides and home health care aides, child-care workers and educational assistants, maids and porters, 1-800 call-center workers, bank tellers, data-entry keyers, cooks, food-preparation workers, waiters and waitresses, cashiers and pharmacy assistants, hairdressers and manicurists, parking lot attendants, hotel receptionists and clerks, ambulance drivers, poultry, fish, and meat processors, sewing-machine operators, laundry and dry-cleaning operators, and agricultural workers.

These jobs require knowledge, patience, care, and communication skills. Most of them require constant interaction with people, whether a patient in a health care setting, a child in a day-care center, a guest in a hotel, a tenant in a commercial office building, or a customer in a department store.

Yet jobs requiring these human-relational skills continue to be viewed as less important than mechanical or technical skills that require little human contact.

As important as these jobs are, most of us do not even notice them. When we do so, it is almost always in a negative light. Low-wage jobs are lumped together and referred to as "hamburger flippers." This label insinuates a lack both of real skill and of social value. Even policy analysts and public officials refer to these jobs by the phrase "low-wage, low-skilled," as if the two terms were inseparable. This label mistakenly assumes that if a job pays poorly, it must be because it does not call for many skills. Many also erroneously equate the absence of a college education with the absence of job skills. These misguided assumptions preclude us from seeing the real demands and skills of these jobs. But first we need to see how these jobs fit into our overall economy.

LOW-WAGE JOBS IN THE SERVICE ECONOMY

Low-wage jobs are principally found in the service sector. This is no coincidence. In the last half of the twentieth century, the United States became a service economy rather than a manufacturing one. WalMart is the largest creator of jobs.

Less than forty years ago, one out of every three nonfarm jobs was in the manufacturing sector. As recently as the 1970s, it provided jobs to almost one-third of men between the ages of twenty-five and fifty-four who did not attend college. Entering the twenty-first century, however, manufacturing comprised only 16 percent of the total economy, or one out of every six jobs. As manufacturing has shrunk, so has the number of middle-income jobs. In 1983, these middle-income jobs constituted 44 percent of the workforce. By 2005 it was under 40 percent and has been falling since. Many of these middle-income jobs were in large-scale manufacturing, which provided workers an average yearly income of $34,500. This was especially true for jobs traditionally held by men.

Meanwhile, the service-producing sector has dramatically expanded. In 1947, service-sector industries accounted for only half of all hours of employment. A half century later, approximately 80 percent of the 134 million nonfarm jobs are in the service-producing industries: retail trade, transportation, telecommunications, utilities, wholesale trade, finance, insurance and real estate, federal, state, and local government, and services. The broad service category comprises health services, social services, administrative support services, personal services, entertainment and recreation services, and business services.

The media trumpeted the "new economy" and its creation of millions of well-paid, "knowledge" jobs, such as engineers, lawyers, social scientists, architects, professors, doctors, and writers, as well as a myriad of executive, administrative, and managerial occupations. High-end occupations, in fact, grew from 17 percent of the American workforce in 1950 to almost a third by 1995 and are expected to add another 7.7 million jobs in the next ten years.

Beyond these well-paying occupations, the service economy encompasses a middle sector of jobs in transportation, telecommunications and utilities, and public administration and education. The median wages in these industries are $12.50, $14.01, and over $20, respectively. This compares to $10 in the overall service sector and $11.47 in manufacturing. Not coincidentally, these three industries are the most highly unionized sectors of the service economy.

There is a third segment of the service economy that is the least publicized and least discussed. It is the low-wage sectors that account for nearly two-thirds of America's low-wage jobs and are concentrated in retail trade and health, social administrative support, personal, entertainment and recreation, and business services.

These low-end service and retail jobs produce 30 percent of the United States gross domestic product and are in industries whose profits doubled between 1993 and 1998. Yet their median wages are the lowest in the U.S. economy: $6.50 in retail trade and ranging from a high of $9.30 in business and repair services to a low of $6.50 in personal services. A full-time worker at $6.50 an hour earns a gross annual salary of $13,570. Even at the high end, a full-time worker would make less than $20,000 per year. But the harsh reality is that more than one-third of retail trade jobs and one-fourth of service jobs are only part-time. And working part-time, these same jobs provide an average annual income of only $6,962 in retail and $9,932 in services.

It is important to note that there are also millions of low-end jobs outside of the service sector: 7 million in manufacturing, principally in food processing, food packing, and food canning, textile and machine operations, and laborer occupations; and one million in agriculture, where workers are principally engaged in fruit and vegetable picking.

These millions of low-paying jobs in services, manufacturing, and agriculture have one thing in common—the lowest unionization rates in the United States. Less than 6 percent of the jobs that pay below $8.70 per hour are organized as contrasted with a 22 percent unionization rate for jobs that pay more than $15 an hour.

And what of the future? The service sector will not only remain the dominant source of employment in the first decade of the century, but it will also be the dominant source of economic output in the U.S. economy. Through 2010, it is projected that virtually all 22 million new jobs will be in the nonmanufacturing industries with retail trade and low-end services expected to account for the large majority. Similarly, nearly 60 percent of the output growth in the service-producing sector is projected to take place in these service industries.

Five of the ten occupations anticipated to have the largest real job growth between 2000 and 2010 are in the lowest pay occupations: food preparation and service workers, retail salespersons, cashiers, security guards, and waiters and waitresses. And of the next twenty occupations with the largest predicted job growth, more than half are in low-wage service jobs: janitors, home health aides, nursing aides, laborers, landscapers, teachers' assistants, receptionists and information clerks, child-care workers, packagers, medical assistants, and personal and home-care aides. Put another way, jobs that require no education and training beyond high school except on-the-job training will account for 57 percent of the job growth between 2000 and 2010. Only 27 percent of U.S. jobs will require a bachelor's degree or above.

As important as these numbers are in describing the realities of the new economy, we need to move beyond a quantitative picture to a qualitative one. We need to closely examine what these low-wage jobs are really all about. Many of the old stereotypes mask their diversity, their difficulty, and their importance. We must look more closely at these jobs.

1-800 CALL-CENTER WORKER

"Hello, this is Ellen speaking. Can I help you?" Another afternoon begins. Ellen Nelson works in an Arlington, Texas, airline reservation center. When Ellen was hired, she received two months of training on how to cancel reservations, rearrange travel plans, figure out the cost of different travel arrangements, use frequent-flier miles, take an infant or a pet on the plane, and deal with passenger emergencies. She had to learn the city and country codes worldwide. There is little in print, so workers must know how to find all the information on the computer to respond to a customer's question.

Ellen works the 3:00 to 11:30 shift from Sunday through Thursday. But she arrives forty-five minutes before her shift to get ready. She takes any vacant cubicle and wipes off the computer and keyboard before she turns it on. She got sick a lot before she started cleaning the computer. "There are always a lot of changes," she says, "especially on Monday." It takes her fifteen minutes just to read all the new airline information and changes in schedules and prices. This is time for which she doesn't get paid.

She then becomes available to take calls on her shift. The calls are fed continuously into her phone, and her employer monitors the number and length of the calls and listens to her conversations with the customers. If she exceeds five minutes per call, she can be disciplined. The time constraint makes it difficult for Ellen when she talks with travel agents who have many clients or with customers who need instructions on how to buy tickets over the Internet. Her employer also records how much time she spends off the phone, called slippage. When Ellen takes time to finish paperwork or go to the bathroom, it is slippage that is docked against her. Too much can lead to discipline or being fired. In order to avoid being penalized, she doesn't take her two fifteen-minute breaks. "It is a lot of pressure and stress. There is no downtime," she says.

It's very noisy inside the call center. It is a twenty-four-hour-a-day, seven-day-a-week operation. Built on two levels, the center houses 2,600 agents over a twenty-four-hour period. From the entrance, you can see all the workstations. The agents are seated row after row for the entire length of the building. Ellen sits in a bay abutting other workers on either side and in front and in back of her. She hears other agents' phone conversations from all directions. Because the center is so large, it is impossible to regulate the temperature. You burn up in one workstation and freeze in another.

"It is hard to get to know anyone at work," Ellen laments. There are no real attachments in there. Without permanent workstations, there is generally someone new sitting next to you each time you come onto your shift. You don't have time to stop and visit anyway. During breaks and lunch, everyone is rushing to go to the bathroom and to the cafeteria, order food, eat it, and get back to their stations on time.

"Some of the customers are nice. That is the redeeming factor. But others are insulting to you. They yell at us because their flights are cancelled or they can't change a flight on a nonrefundable ticket. It is difficult because regardless of how a customer treats you, you have to be pleasant. That is your job. It's nonstop. I am a modern-day factory worker making a product that is a reservation."

Ellen's job is one of the 3.3 million call-center jobs in the United States. With the advent of computerization, these jobs have become an integral part of our lives. These jobs have such titles as customer service representative, reservation agent, ticket and gate agent, account representative or executive representative, telemarketing representative, technical support representative, and eligibility and claims specialist. They are in industries as disparate as manufacturing, insurance, banking, travel, and retail. Many handle more than one hundred customers per day. They must be conversant with a variety of databases that collect and store the information required to perform the job.

Ellen's job is considered one of the best call-center jobs. It pays more than other centers because it is in the airline industry, which is highly unionized. The vast majority of call-center workers are in jobs that pay less than $8.50 an hour. Ellen's job is also a step up from workers who have to call out to people to try to sell them a product. Here, the customer comes to you. But all these jobs are high pressure and stressful. Workers are forced to balance service to the customer with employer pressure to meet a sales quota in an atmosphere of constant surveillance.

CHILD-CARE WORKER

Sharon Bright helps educate children at a day-care center for underprivileged children. During the summer months, when the children are not in school, she works from 12:00 to 7:00 and during the school year from 3:00, the time the center opens, until closing time at 7:00.

There are only four day-care workers for fifty children. Sharon evaluates each child's reading and math levels and works with them to improve their skills. She supervises arts and crafts, sports, and games, and takes the children on field trips to museums. "Many of the children use degrading language with each other. I try to improve their self-esteem and work to improve the respect they have for each other. It's a real challenge. A lot of kids just don't like themselves," she says. In many cases, Sharon acts like a surrogate parent. She is there when they need to talk, when they need a hug, when someone hurts their feelings.

During the summer, she also helps prepare lunch and dinner for the children. Many times these are the only meals the children will have that day. She tries to ensure a balanced diet, but it is difficult because money is short and she must rely on donated food. "It takes a long time to prepare food for fifty children," she says. "It is not like cooking at home."

Because the pay is low—Sharon makes $7.50 an hour—turnover is high. "But you have to build trust to be effective," Sharon says. "When you work with the same students every day, you understand them, their habits, and what they need. The day-care worker informs the parent about the child's developmental milestones, whether they see any problems, and whether there are emotional issues that need to be addressed. If there is a constant turnover of workers, it is hard to know a child's history.

"When you work with children there are no breaks," she says. "It is nonstop. It is not like working in an office where you can leave for thirty minutes and clear your head." Sharon is lucky if she gets a five-minute break. She can't leave the children alone, and there is no one to replace her.

The job requires a lot of patience. "You have to be willing to do whatever it takes to answer any questions the children ask. You have to like children and be active with them. It is not a sit-down job. A day-care worker must be able to relate to the children: the things going on in their neighborhoods, the music, the slang, their interests. You don't have to like what the children like, but you have to know about it and be able to screen what is inappropriate."

Educating and caring for young children pays low wages. Of the over 3 million child-care workers, including family child-care providers, more than 80 percent earn less than $8.50 an hour. One-third of the workers earn less than $5.75 an hour. The 1.2 million teacher's assistants do no better. And these occupations are expected to grow in the next ten years by over 400,000. This workforce—98 percent of whom are female—has a higher concentration of jobs that are paid below the official poverty line than almost any other occupation in the United States. These jobs are clearly important and the workers skilled and educated; indeed, these workers are better educated than the general population. Almost a third of the child-care workers and teacher's aides have a college or advanced degree, and 44 percent have some college. But because of the low pay, there is a 30–40 percent average annual turnover rate in the industry that hurts the quality of care provided to our children.

POULTRY-PROCESSING WORKER

The noise is deafening. The floors are slippery with chicken grease. The smell of chicken blood fills the air. Workers standing in pools of water, hang, slice, split, pull, and cut chickens at breakneck speeds of ninety-one birds per minute. Standing close together in their hair nets, gloves, coats, and boots, they wield knives in temperatures ranging from freezing to 120 degrees. The plant runs twenty-four hours a day, working three continuous shifts. Workers are on the line six days a week, sometimes seven. These are the jobs that put chicken on our tables.

Bob Butler, the Albertville, Alabama, poultry processor, has seen almost all the jobs in his plant. "The toughest and most dangerous job," he says, "is live hanging." The workers grab live chickens with their hands. While the chickens peck, scratch, claw, and defecate on them, the worker shackles the chicken by the legs. Feathers fly and the birds screech. The stench from the birds never leaves one's nostrils. Grabbing and shackling the chickens must be done at breathtaking speeds—one bird every two seconds.

Once the chickens are hung, a machine cuts their throats. But if the machine doesn't do it properly, a worker cuts the chicken's throat with a knife, sending chicken blood everywhere. The chickens then go through scalding water that removes their feathers. The next machines sever their heads and feet.

The hot chickens then fall onto a transfer table where four workers, two on either side of the table, rehang the chicken by grabbing their legs and flipping them onto shackles. The small work space and one-hundred-degree temperatures create a "nasty smell," Bob says. "The closest I can come is when an animal is killed on the side of the road and has been lying there for several days. It is worse than that."

Once the chickens are rehung, they continue on a conveyor belt where workers open the chicken with their thumbs and yank and twist out their guts with their hands. During this process, the workers must make sure the chicken's gall bag doesn't break. Otherwise the chicken will be ruined. The trimmer, who sits next to the U.S. Department of Agriculture inspector, checks the chickens for any bad areas and either cuts them off or takes the chickens off the line. A machine then cuts the heart and livers, but the workers determine whether they are edible. A worker then pulls out the gizzards with his hands while another worker ensures that the gizzards are clean and free of intestines and lungs. A trimmer then cuts off the neck bone.

After the evisceration line, the chickens are chilled for ten to fifteen minutes and dropped once again onto a table. The chiller hangers then grab the freezing chickens with their hands and flip them onto shackles. Next, workers in thirty- to forty-degree temperatures, standing elbow to elbow in water, slice the chicken into parts. It is so noisy from the machines that workers must wear earplugs to prevent hearing loss.

Twelve workers standing on a catwalk then grab the chicken breasts, thighs, drums, and wings and put them into a bag. They must pack seventy-five breasts a minute. Workers' hands swell from the constant grabbing motion, and tendonitis is common.

After the chicken is packed, a worker weighs it and sends it to a shaker table that vibrates the meat to settle it before the box is closed. A worker then tapes the boxes and sends them down a belt where a worker stacks thirty to forty boxes on a pallet, six to eight feet high. A shipping worker wraps the pallet with plastic and loads it on a truck or drives it to the freezer for storage. To avoid frostbite in the freezer, he wears a face mask and protective clothing.

There are more than 200,000 poultry-processing jobs in the United States. Because of strong consumer demand for chicken, it is one of the fastest-growing segments of the meat industry. Over the last ten years, the dollar value of poultry production has more than doubled from nearly $6 billion to $12 billion. Poultry production employs more workers than any other segment of the meat industry, growing from 19,000 workers in 1947 to today's 200,000 workers. Although an essential job, poultry-processing workers suffer poor wages (75 percent earn less than $8.50 an hour), minimal benefits, and harrowing working conditions. Their counterparts in the meat and fish industries face the same harsh conditions.

HOME HEALTH CARE AIDE

The phone call came in. Joann Morris's coordinator had a new client for her, a fifty-one-year-old woman with multiple sclerosis. Her name was Millie. She was incontinent and couldn't walk. Because her tremors were so forceful and continuous, she could rarely control her hands or arms, and her speech was slurred. That was six years ago.

Joann is a home health care aide. In addition to the training required to be state certified, she takes continuing in-service programs to maintain her certification. In a home-based setting, Joann provides personal and physical care for the elderly, disabled, patients with serious health problems, or those recovering from surgery.

Joann has been with the home health care agency for ten years. Her first patient was a woman with arthritis, diabetes, and cataracts. She was homebound and incapacitated. Her second client had a type of arthritis that caused her to bend over so far her hands almost touched the floor. Her third client had Parkinson's disease. She also cared for two homebound AIDS patients when a fellow aide was ill.

When Joann arrives at Millie's apartment at 8:30, she first sits and talks with her, washes her hands, and changes Millie's diaper. Joann then gives Millie a bed bath; a regular bath would be too dangerous. She gets the materials ready: a basin, water, soap, two washcloths, and towels. If Millie can do her own genitals, she encourages her to do it. "It gives her a feeling of being in charge of her own body and a sense of independence," Joann says. Millie's skin is very tender, so she has to be careful. After the bath, Joann applies powder or lotion.

After dressing Millie, she prepares breakfast and gives Millie her daily medications. Afterward, Joann moves her to a wheelchair with a mechanical lift. "It is good for her circulation and well-being for her to get up," Joann comments. "Bed-bound patients easily get bedsores. If untreated, they get deeper and deeper and can ultimately cause death."

She is very careful when she moves her. She rolls Millie on her side, straightens the lift pad, takes the S hook and connects it to the pad and makes sure it is locked in place, and then pumps the lift and guides her head and pushes the lift over the wheelchair and guides her down. She continually observes Millie to make sure she isn't dizzy or afraid. "One misstep could be a disaster," she says.

When Millie is in her wheelchair, Joann serves her lunch, a meal that she herself rarely has time to have. She helps with Millie's bills and letters and then changes the bed linens that get soaked with urine when Millie leaks through her diaper at night. She turns the mattress once a week and airs it out with a little Pine-Sol. Millie likes the smell. "Every patient is different in what they like," she says. "I try to buy colorful sheets instead of drab hospital colors. I try to make her life as bright and cheerful as I can."

She then sweeps, mops, and dusts the apartment and does Millie's laundry. If there is a doctor's appointment, Joann takes her. If Millie wants to nap, she uses the lift to get her back in bed. While she is asleep, Joann prepares her dinner, confers with the nurse about Millie's prescriptions, readies her nightly medications, and tidies up the kitchen and refrigerator.

Once Millie gets up, she changes her diaper and prepares her for dinner. Most of the time, Millie likes to eat in private. "Her shaking embarrasses her," so Joann leaves the room. Sometimes she needs to talk. She needs a shoulder. It is really hard for her. After dinner, Joann kisses her on the forehead. She tells her "God bless" and "Have a good evening," and then she leaves to go home at 5:00. After she leaves, she usually shops for Millie's groceries, clothes, and other household needs for the next day.

Home health care aides and nursing aides provide for the well-being of our elderly and disabled in individual homes and nursing home settings. Yet two-thirds of the home health aides and nursing aides are paid less than $8.50 an hour. Home health care work is often part-time, which exacerbates the already low wages. These poor wages result in turnover rates of 40–60 percent. And in nursing homes, the inadequate staffing on top of these meager wages produces turnover rates of 70–100 percent. With constant turnover, experienced aides bear a greater patient load, which produces an even greater burnout rate. This vicious cycle is found throughout the nursing home and home health care industries.

Home health care and nursing aide jobs are two of the fastest-growing occupations in the health care sector, a sector that accounts for half of the fastest-growing occupations in the U.S. economy. One out of five jobs created in the nonfarm economy since January 1988 has been in health services. As patients shifted from hospitals to less expensive alternatives such as nursing homes and home settings, there was an explosion of home health care and nursing aide jobs. The number of home health aide workers, now over 600,000, is expected to increase by 300,000 in the next decade. During that same period, the field of nursing aides, orderlies, and attendants, now at approximately 1.3 million, is also expected to add another 300,000 jobs.

PHARMACY TECHNICAL ASSISTANT

Judy Smithfield works in a superstore as a pharmacy technical assistant, a "pharmacy tech." Her 12:00–9:00 shift begins with a call from a nurse in a doctor's office dictating a prescription over the phone or a customer at the counter giving her a prescription. Once she has the information, she gives it to the pharmacist to process in the computer. Then it is Judy's responsibility to check that information and get the proper medication from the shelf. She counts the pills that are prescribed, puts them into the bottle, affixes the proper label to the medication, gives the filled prescription to the pharmacist for her review, and puts it in the proper bin for the customer to pick up.

Once the customer arrives, Judy must ensure that she has the right prescription and that the proper forms are filled out. She must ask the customer whether they understand the prescription, whether they want counseling or have any further questions. Their response must be put in writing.

Three times a week, Judy receives the drug orders that are delivered to the store. "They must be put in the place designated so there is no confusion in filling prescriptions," Judy emphasizes. "It is essential." The pharmacist must sign for controlled substances, but Judy fills these prescriptions.

It can get very busy at the pharmacy counter, especially during flu season. If someone has to wait twenty minutes for a prescription that they just brought in, they get angry. "They say, 'All you have to do is put pills in a bottle. What takes so long?' They don't understand that we must follow procedures to ensure accuracy," Judy says. When people get impatient and angry, Judy has learned to apologize a lot. But sometimes that doesn't work. "Sometimes they get real upset," she says.

There are two pharmacy techs and three pharmacists on Judy's shift that fill over four hundred prescriptions per day. If the pharmacy gets behind in the prescriptions, Judy stays late, sometimes until midnight. Many times she works six days a week because they don't have enough help. Her feet and back ache from standing all day.

Judy is part of the large retail sector. More than 21 million Americans, one out of every six workers, currently holds a retail job. From 1979 to 1995, the number of jobs in retail grew 39 percent, resulting in almost 6 million new employees. And another 2.3 million are expected to be added in the next five years. Retail workers serve customers at drugstores, department stores, rental counters, and grocery stores. They are salespersons, cashiers, stock clerks, counter and rental clerks, and pharmacy assistants. Many

perform some of the same functions as Judy, waiting on customers, stocking products, and answering customer questions. Her pay,
like the rest of the retail industry, is low. Three-fourths of the retail
jobs pay less than $8.50 an hour. Compounding the low pay is the
frequency of part-time schedules. Thirty-eight percent of retail employees work part-time. As a result, nearly two-thirds of the non-
managerial workers earn less than $12,500 per year.

RECEPTIONIST

Nancy Holland's day begins at 8:30 when she picks up and distributes faxes and the more than thirty Audix messages that have come
in after hours to the receptionist desk. She then opens the switch-
board to receive incoming calls. During the day, there is an average
of six hundred to seven hundred phone calls. "I try to be as helpful
as possible to them and talk very slowly and make sure I am directing them to someone who can assist them so they won't have to call
back," she says.

While Nancy is receiving calls, she opens the president's mail,
sends it to his office, and receives, sends, and distributes faxes. She
handles the general mail of the organization and marks it for distribution. She files, processes letters, works on the computer, and
assists shipping when they need help in mail-outs. She stuffs enve-
lopes, manages the chronological files for the president's secretary,
and fills in when secretaries are on medical or personal leave.

And every day she receives visitors to the organization. She says,
"When someone comes in, I put my best foot forward to be pleasant
and helpful. It is important to their overall view of the organization. I am a part of making people who come to our organization
feel good about the people they are going to see and potentially that
will help better our business.

"The toughest part of my job," says Nancy, "is being tied to a desk
all day. I can't get off the desk unless I have someone to relieve me. It
is very restrictive. There are people coming in all the time, so it has
to be covered continuously."

Nancy's job is one of the many jobs that support business operations. Her job is crucial to how outsiders view the company.
In many instances, if someone has a good impression, it is greatly
determined by how Nancy performs her job, whether she is polite

and friendly, whether she knows who has the information being requested by a caller or visitor, and whether she assists these people in a professional manner. Her job also facilitates internal operations by circulating information, performing clerical functions, and supporting other departments within the organization. Yet a majority of the 1.5 million receptionists earn less than $8.50 an hour. The number of jobs in this field is expected to increase by over 400,000 in the next five years.

These low-wage jobs are the backbone of the new economy. Yet just as Americans misunderstand and undervalue these low-wage jobs, they misconceive who works in these jobs. Their misconceptions help them dismiss the problems faced by these workers. It is important, therefore, to understand who these workers really are and who must reap the consequences of jobs that provide so few rewards.

Adapted from The Betrayal of Work: How Low-Wage Jobs Fail 30 Million Americans.

HOUSEHOLD WEALTH INEQUALITY

Edward N. Wolff

Wealth and income are related but not identical. Income refers to a stream of money, wealth to a pool, often held in paper more durable than dollar bills, such as stock and bond certificates and real estate titles. Professor Wolff, who has built a career studying trends in wealth, breaks down the data on who owns wealth in America. Note that wealth in pensions is temporary as payments end when the worker and spouse die.

Wealth inequality in the United States hit a seventy-year high in 1998, with the top 1 percent of wealth holders controlling 38 percent of total household wealth. Focusing more narrowly on financial wealth, which excludes the value of equity in homes, the richest 1 percent of households owned 47 percent of the total.

A household in the middle—the median household—had wealth of about $62,000 in 1998. That amount is not insignificant, but consider that the top 1 percent's average wealth is $12.5 million, more than two hundred times as much per household.

From 1989 to 1998, the top 1 percent's share of wealth remained virtually unchanged, Federal Reserve Survey of Consumer Finance data show. Then wealth held by the top 1 percent fell in the recession year of 2001 to 33.4 percent. By 2010, the first recovery year after the Great Recession of 2008–9, the top 1 percent's wealth rose to 35.4 percent of the national total.

How did this concentration of wealth come to pass? After the stock market crash of 1929, there ensued a gradual, if somewhat erratic, reduction in wealth inequality, which seems to have lasted until the late 1970s. Since then, inequality of wealth holdings, like that of income, has risen sharply.

If Social Security and other pension wealth are included ("augmented wealth"), the improvement between 1929 and 1979 appears greater, but the increase in inequality since 1980 is still sharply in evidence.

The rise in wealth inequality from 1983 to 1998 (a period for which there is comparable detailed household survey information) is particularly striking. The share of the top 1 percent of wealth holders rose by five percentage points. The wealth of the bottom 40 percent showed an absolute decline. Almost all the absolute gains in real wealth accrued to the top 20 percent of wealth holders.

CHANGES IN AVERAGE WEALTH HOLDINGS

Average wealth grew at a respectable pace from 1962 to 1983. It grew even faster from 1983 to 1989. By 1989, the average wealth of households was $244,000 (in 1998 dollars), almost two-thirds higher than in 1962. From 1989 to 1998, wealth growth slowed. In fact, mean marketable wealth grew only about half as fast between 1989 and 1998 as between 1962 and 1989 (1.2 versus 2.3 percent per year). Still, by 1998, average wealth had reached $270,000.

Average financial wealth grew faster than marketable wealth in the 1983–89 period (2.7 versus 2.3 percent per year), reflecting the increased importance of bank deposits, financial assets, equities, and small businesses in the overall household portfolio over this period. This reversed the relationship of the 1962–83 period, when financial wealth grew more slowly than marketable wealth (1.4 versus 1.8 percent per year). In the 1989–98 period, the gain in average financial wealth again outstripped net worth (1.7 versus 1.2 percent per year).

Average household income also grew faster in the 1983–89 period than in the 1962–83 period. Its annual growth accelerated from 1.5 percentage points to 2.7. Whereas in the first of the two periods, average income grew more slowly than average wealth (a 0.3 percentage point per year difference), in the latter it grew slightly faster (a 0.1 percentage point per year difference). However, in the 1989–98 period, income growth plummeted to 0.9 percent per year (0.2 percentage points per year lower than wealth growth).

The robust growth of average wealth disguises some changes in the distribution of that wealth. This becomes clear after examination of median (midpoint) rather than mean wealth.

Mean wealth is simply the average: total wealth divided by total number of households. If the wealth of only the top 20 percent of households increases (with nothing else changing), then mean wealth increases because total wealth increases.

In contrast, the median of the wealth distribution is defined as the level of wealth that divides the population of households into two equal-sized groups (those with more wealth than the median and those with less). Returning to the earlier example, if only the top quintile enjoys an increase in wealth, median wealth is unaffected even though mean wealth increases because all additional wealth accrues to people well above the median income. The median tracks what is happening in the middle of the wealth distribution.

When trends in the mean deviate from trends in the median, this is a signal that gains and losses are unevenly distributed.

The trend in median household wealth gives a contrasting picture to the growth of mean wealth. Median marketable wealth grew faster in the 1962–83 period than in the 1983–89 period (1.6 versus 1.1 percent per year). Median wealth also grew much more slowly than mean wealth in the latter period (a difference of 1.1 percentage points per year).

Overall, from 1983 to 1989, while mean wealth increased by 15 percent, median wealth grew by only 7 percent. This implies that the bulk of the gains were concentrated at the top of the distribution—a finding that implies rising wealth inequality. The

1989–98 period was a repeat of the preceding one. While mean wealth grew by 11 percent, median wealth increased by only 4 percent. That means inequality continued to increase.

RISING WEALTH INEQUALITY IN THE 1980S

Between 1983 and 1989 the most telling finding is that the share of marketable net worth held by the top 1 percent, which had fallen by ten percentage points between 1945 and 1976, rose to 37 percent in 1989, compared with 34 percent in 1983. Meanwhile, the share of wealth held by the bottom 80 percent fell by from 19 percent to 16 percent.

Between 1989 and 1998, inequality continued to rise, though at a more moderate pace. The share of wealth held by the top 1 percent increased by another percentage point (to 38 percent), though the share of the bottom 80 percent stabilized. That means there was a slight decline in the share held by the top fifth, except for the top 1 percent, who gained.

These trends are mirrored in financial net worth, which is distributed even more unequally than total household wealth. In 1998, the top 1 percent of families as ranked by financial wealth owned 47 percent of the total (in contrast to 38 percent of total net worth). The top quintile, or fifth, accounted for 91 percent of total financial wealth, and the second quintile accounted for nearly all the remainder. The bottom 60 percent of Americans had virtually no financial wealth.

The concentration of financial wealth increased to the same degree as that of marketable wealth between 1983 and 1989. The share of the top 1 percent of financial wealth holders increased by four percentage points, from 43 to 47 percent of total financial wealth. The share of the next 19 percent fell from 48 to 46 percent, while that of the bottom 80 percent declined from 9 to 7 percent. Between 1989 and 1998, the share of total financial wealth of the top 1 percent increased a bit more (by 0.4 percentage points) but the share of the bottom 80 percent recovered to where it was in 1983.

Income growth distribution, too, became more concentrated between 1983 and 1989. As with wealth, most of the relative income gain accrued to the top 1 percent of recipients, whose share of total household income grew by four percentage points, from 13 to 17 percent. The share of the next 19 percent remained unchanged at 39 percent. The bottom 80 percent of the income distribution sustained almost all of the (relative) loss in income. Their share of income fell from 48 to 44 percent.

Between 1989 and 1998, income inequality increased a bit more. While the share of the top 1 percent remained stable, the share of the next 19 percent rose by 0.6 percentage points and that of the bottom 80 percent correspondingly fell by 0.6 percentage points.

Another way to view rising wealth concentration is to look at how the increases in total wealth were divided over a specified period. This is calculated by dividing the increase in wealth of each group by the total increase in household wealth. The top 1 percent of wealth holders received 53 percent of the total gain in marketable wealth over the period from 1983 to 1998. The next 19 percent received 38 percent, while the bottom 80 percent received only 9 percent.

This pattern represents a distinct turnaround from the 1962–83 period, when every group enjoyed some share of the overall wealth growth and the gains were roughly in proportion to the share of wealth held by each in 1962. Over this period, the top 1 percent received 34 percent of the wealth gains; the next 19 percent claimed 48 percent. The bottom 80 percent got 18 percent, which is double their share of gains from 1983 to 1998.

Gains in the overall growth in financial wealth were also distributed unevenly, with 56 percent of the growth accruing to the top 1 percent and 36 percent to the next 19 percent from 1983 to 1998. The bottom 80 percent gained only 11 percent.

MEASURING WITH GINI

Finally, changes in wealth distribution can be assessed by looking at the Gini coefficient, a measure of inequality devised by the Italian sociologist Corrado Gini early in the twentieth century. This indicator is widely used to summarize data on the degree of inequality of income, wealth, or anything else of value. It ranges from 0 (exact equality) to 1 (one person owns everything); a higher Gini coefficient means greater inequality. This measure, like the others reviewed here, points to an increase in inequality: between 1983 and 1989 the Gini coefficient increased from 0.80 to 0.84. Between 1989 and 1998, the Gini coefficient remained at this high plateau.

This increase in wealth inequality recorded over the 1983–98 period—and particularly between 1983 and 1989—is almost unprecedented. The only other period in the twentieth century during which concentration of household wealth rose comparably was from 1922 to 1929. Then inequality was buoyed primarily by the excessive increase in stock values, which eventually crashed in 1929, leading to the Great Depression of the 1930s.

Despite the seemingly modest increase in overall wealth inequality during the 1990s, the decade witnessed a near explosion in the number of very rich households. The number of millionaires climbed by 54 percent between 1989 and 1998, the number of "pentamillionaires" ($5 million or more) more than doubled, and the number of "decamillionaires" ($10 million or more) almost quadrupled. Much of the growth occurred between 1995 and 1998 and was directly related to surging stock prices.

MORE RECENT DEVELOPMENTS: A POSTSCRIPT

The years from 1998 to 2007 saw rapid growth in both mean and median household wealth. Buoyed by large gains in both housing and stock prices, though particularly the former, median wealth climbed by 33 percent and mean wealth by 56 percent in real terms. Despite the fact that mean wealth grew faster than the median, wealth inequality remained relatively unchanged as measured by the Gini coefficient and by 2007 was almost exactly at the same point as in 1989. However, the ranks of the very rich continued to expand, with the number of millionaires climbing by 52 percent between 1998 and 2007 and the number of penta- and decamillionaires each growing by 94 percent.

Then the Great Recession hit in 2007, and house prices and stock prices plummeted by 24 and 26 percent in real terms, respectively. As a consequence, median wealth dropped by an astonishing

47 percent in real terms, while mean wealth was down by (only) 18 percent. Because median wealth fell much more than mean wealth, inequality surged over these years, with the Gini coefficient climbing from 0.84 to 0.87, about the same extent as it did from 1983 to 1989.

Adapted and updated from Top Heavy: The Increasing Inequality of Wealth in America and What Can Be Done About It. *Updates from "The Asset Price Meltdown and the Wealth of the Middle Class," NBER Working Paper No. 18559, November 2012.*

INEQUALITY ACROSS GENERATIONS

Jared Bernstein

The circumstances of birth, whether rich or poor, tend to persist in the United States, but new policies could remove barriers to poor strivers improving their lot, as this economics expert shows.

Research findings show that here in the United States, income, wealth, and opportunity are significantly correlated across generations.

A child of a low-income father has only a small chance of achieving very high earnings in adulthood. Almost two-thirds of children of low-income parents (those in the lowest quintile) will themselves have wealth levels that place them in the bottom two quintiles. And while there is some disagreement in the literature, some of the research shows that we have become considerably less mobile over time. This finding is important, because it means there has been no increase in mobility that might serve to offset the higher levels of cross-sectional inequality.

One of the most surprising findings of this research is that the United States has less mobility than other advanced economies, even those in Scandinavia. Certainly these results belie a simplistic story of a favorable trade-off between less regulation and social protection and greater mobility. These other countries manage to provide far more extensive safety nets, and families there appear to face fewer class barriers. An important question for future research is whether these two features are causally linked: do more elaborate social protections clear mobility pathways that are blocked in economies that operate in a freer market framework?

What should we do to diminish these correlations and boost mobility, especially among those who are disadvantaged at the starting line? It's an important question, because equal opportunity at the start is a core American value. We generally reject notions that support equality of outcomes; ours will always be an economy and a society with some degree of inequality. But if this inequality results not from a meritocracy wherein the most able "win the race," but from a rigged race where too many contestants are running with weights strapped on their backs, we sense that economic injustice is in play.

Thus, a primary concern of public policy in this area is to remove the weights—that is, lower the barriers created by economic, racial, or political differences that stand between people and their ultimate potential.

Obviously, education is key, and the fact that "smart" poor children access college at the same rate as lower-performing rich children suggests an economic barrier. Programs that identify high-performing students in low-income settings could help in this area, but thinking more broadly, perhaps any student who has the ability should be able to go to college. In other words, would it not make sense to promote full access to higher education for anyone who is interested and able? Costing out such a program is beyond the scope of this chapter, and, of course, budgetary trade-offs need to be considered. But given the role of college education in boosting economic mobility, this is worth considering.

Of course, educational disadvantages start way before college. State-based programs that provide access to college for disadvantaged but high-performing students have found that remediation is an important part of the process, because some of these students need extra services to help them adapt to college.

Better social safety nets and greater work supports—any work-related subsidy provided to low-income workers—are also part of the solution to raising mobility.

Especially in the low-wage U.S. labor market, there is a significant gap between what low-income workers earn and what they need to make ends meet. While such supports are associated with current consumption, and thus may sound less relevant regarding mobility, it is difficult for such persons to get ahead without these supports. Child care is a good example. Research has shown that the absence of affordable child care has led to either interruption in labor-market participation, inferior child-care provision, or both. Clearly, this dynamic works against building mobility-enhancing experience in the labor market and a head start for children.

Finally, the data suggest that the persistence of wealth across generations gives a leg up to the haves relative to the have-nots. Offsetting this mobility blocker is at the heart of the asset-building movement, a broad set of programs designed to increase wealth among the poor. Often, these programs have operated at too small a scale to make much of a dent in the historical persistence of wealth accumulation. But larger initiatives, such as sizable demo grants for all children, have also been proposed. In fact, the "college for all who are able" idea can be viewed in this light as well, as an ambitious investment in building human capital assets for the disadvantaged.

Adapted from All Things Being Equal: Instigating Opportunity in an Inequitable Time, *ed. Brian D. Smedley and Alan Jenkins.*

"I DIDN'T DO IT ALONE"

Chuck Collins and Felice Yeskel

No one who built a great fortune did it on their own. They benefited from the investments made by taxpayers in education, roads, civil justice, and science, as well as the contributions of those who taught them how to read and play games, and who helped keep them out of trouble as youths. Two leading advocates for a fairer economy explain all this in thoughtful detail.

Self made men, indeed! Why don't you tell me of the self-laid egg?
—*Francis Lieber*

During the political battle over preserving the federal estate tax, an interesting thing happened. Thousands of multimillionaires and billionaires signed a petition, sponsored by United for a Fair Economy's Responsible Wealth project, to maintain the estate tax.

The fact that many wealthy people would endorse paying a tax was news in itself. But underlying their support for a tax on accumulated wealth is a new way of looking at society's contribution to wealth creation and a reevaluation of the American success narrative.

Some commentators argued that this "billionaire backlash," as

Newsweek called it, was rooted in unselfishness or class betrayal. But for many of the individuals who signed the petition, it was a matter of simple accounting: "We owe something back to the society that created opportunities for us."

The notion that wealthy individuals might have an obligation to pay something back to society is a radical departure from the individualistic, antigovernment ethos. Many successful people view government and society as irrelevant to their good fortune, or worse, as a hindrance. They attribute their success solely to their own character, values, and performance.

A 2004 report published by Responsible Wealth took on this "great man theory of wealth creation." Relying on interviews with wealthy supporters of the estate tax, United for a Fair Economy published *I Didn't Do It Alone*. The report amplified the voices of individuals who countered the myth and reflected on the role of society, privilege, historical timing, and luck in their success, in addition to their own moxie, creativity, and hard work. Those profiled discussed such factors as the role of U.S. property law and patents, public investment in education and technology, orderly and regulated investment markets, and other factors in creating a fertile ground for their wealth creation.

Investor Warren Buffett observed that his skills are "disproportionately rewarded" in the U.S. marketplace. He reflected that if he were attempting to do business in another country, without our system of property laws and market mechanisms, he "would still be struggling thirty years later."

Amy Domini, founder and president of Domini Social Equity Fund, attributed her success in part to basic government-provided public infrastructure. "Getting my message out over the public airwaves has allowed me to be far more successful than if I had been born in another time and place," she said. "The mail runs on time, allowing me to communicate with existing and potential shareholders, and the rise of the publicly financed Internet has lowered the costs of these communications still further. I can fly safely—and most often conveniently—throughout the country, sharing my ideas and gaining new clients, again thanks to a publicly supported air-travel system."

Venture capitalist Jim Sherblom was the chief financial officer of biotech wonder company Genzyme when it went public in 1986. He estimated that the stock market, a socially financed and regulated institution that provides enormous liquidity for private companies, created 30 to 50 percent of the value of the company.

The stock market's liquidity and trust depend enormously on societal institutions that regulate, ensure transparency, and enforce fair transactions. If there is any doubt about this, consider how the accounting scandals behind Enron and WorldCom affected the value of dozens of publicly owned technology companies. Hundreds of billions of dollars in wealth vanished overnight. Cook the books, shake the public trust, and watch wealth disappear.

New York–based software designer Martin Rothenberg argued that his "wealth is not only a product of my own hard work, but resulted from a strong economy and lots of public investment in others and me." He credited his New York City public technical school for his early education, and the GI Bill and government-backed student loans for funding his university degree. Later, government investment directly supported the lab research that led to his establishing a company that he later sold for $30 million.

Our society needs a new narrative of success, one that shows a more complex reality: that societal forces are important in fostering success. This is no small challenge, for the American self-made success narrative is deeply rooted. But wider recognition of the social roots of wealth should lead to a deeper understanding of the need to pay taxes and invest in public goods and services.

The mythology of self-made success would not be such a problem if it were a matter of simple personal self-delusion. But this worldview, held by many who hold great power and influence in our society, has serious consequences for the kind of society we have, and for our commitment to equality of opportunity.

REDUCING THE ASSET AND WEALTH GAP

There are a variety of actions we can take to reduce the enormous gap in wealth ownership in America.

Asset-building policies have been an integral part of U.S. history.

The Homestead Act in the nineteenth century gave white settlers access to land—often land expropriated from Native Americans. During the years after World War II, the GI Bill enabled millions of Americans, primarily white men, to have a debt-free college education and access to low-interest mortgages.

Unfortunately, in recent years, our government has targeted its subsidies to those who don't need any help with asset building. An estimated $175 billion* in federal subsidies are directed to corporations in the form of tax loopholes, direct cash transfers, and subsidized access to public resources. This misdirected "corporate welfare" benefits large corporations and affluent individuals.

Government assistance should be focused on nonaffluent households, small businesses, family farms, and democratic enterprises such as cooperatives. Immediate reforms are needed to enable low- and moderate-income families to earn, save, and invest more money in order to build asset security.

Thoughtful Americans are advancing a variety of proposals that would narrow the wealth gap, ranging from expanding worker ownership to creating universal asset-building accounts. What follows is a brief survey of some of these initiatives.

Over the long run, we should make sure that tax policies encourage access to higher education and asset building by low- and middle-income Americans rather than disproportionately subsidizing wealthier Americans.

SOME SOLUTIONS TO CONSIDER

Individual Development Accounts (IDAs) are like Individual Retirement Accounts (IRAs), but are targeted to low- and moderate-income households to assist them in asset accumulation. Participants in IDAs may have their tax-free deposits matched by public or private dollars. A number of private charities have financed pilot IDA programs through community-based organizations. A publicly funded IDA program, with matching

---

*This estimate does not consider state and local subsidies, estimated in 2010 at $700 billion by Professor Kenneth Thomas of the University of Missouri–St. Louis, who studies financial incentives to business.—*Ed.*

funds based on income, would provide significant opportunities for asset-poor households to build wealth.

Participants could withdraw funds from IDAs to purchase a home, finance a small business, or invest in education or job training. Even small amounts of money can make a substantial difference in whether or not individuals get on the asset-building train.

Baby Bonds One interesting proposal to reverse inequality trends over generations would be to create a "kids savings account" for children when they are born. In 2003, the British Parliament created just such a program, which people refer to as the "baby bond."

The idea is to provide every American child with $1,000 at birth, plus $500 a year for children ages one to five, to be invested either until adulthood or until retirement. Through compound returns over time, the account would grow substantially, provide a significant supplement to Social Security and other retirement funds, and enable many more Americans to leave inheritances to their children. That would strengthen opportunities and asset building across generations.

Such universal accounts could be capitalized by a portion of estate-tax revenue levied on estates in excess of $10 million, redistributing a small portion of the largess of the 1 percent to address the generational inequalities of wealth.

No-Tax Threshold Progressive tax policies can enable working families to keep more money in their pockets. These include an expanded earned-income credit an increased personal exemption, and a higher no-tax threshold.

Affordable Housing Owning a home has long been considered a stepping-stone to building assets. Public policies that increase access to home ownership include subsidized mortgages and mortgage insurance, down-payment assistance funds, second-mortgage subsidy programs, and grants and low-interest loans for home improvements and weatherization. Stricter enforcement of fair housing and community reinvestment laws would remove barriers to asset building for people of color.

Home ownership is not the only tenure option that should be promoted, however, as it is not appropriate for all households at all stages of life. Nor should home ownership be considered the only "asset account" and "line of credit" for low- and moderate-income families, as it has many risks.

Access to decent and affordable cooperative and rental housing would enable many people to save and meet other financial security goals. Public subsidies should be targeted to "third sector" housing ownership that includes community land trusts, housing cooperatives, mutual housing, and other models that reduce housing costs and preserve long-term affordability.

A NEW GI BILL?

On June 22, 1944, President Franklin Roosevelt signed into law the Servicemen's Readjustment Act of 1944, known as the "GI Bill of Rights." Without the GI Bill, the American Dream would have never become real for millions of Americans. The GI Bill opened tremendous opportunities for veterans and their families and transformed America.

The GI Bill was one of the greatest investments made in our nation's history—and it almost didn't happen. Influential college presidents testified against it, complaining that millions of unschooled veterans would lower education standards and create millions of "educational hobos." Congressional conservatives tried to block it as too expensive and gave in only after concerted grassroots lobbying by the American Legion.

It's time to revitalize the American Dream and restore the foundation for a new century of progress. America needs a bold effort to expand opportunity, close the racial wealth divide, and ensure that college is affordable to all Americans.

Why can't we establish a GI Bill for the next generation? It should not be restricted only to those who served in the military. A universal fund would provide grants for college and subsidized mortgages for all those who need them. This opportunity fund could be capitalized by a reformed federal estate tax, our nation's only tax on accumulated wealth. Much of that wealth has appreciated tax-free over generations. A reformed estate tax, completely exempting the first $2.5 million in wealth for an individual and $5 million for a couple, would generate almost a trillion dollars in revenue over the next two decades. Unfortunately, Congress is considering abolishing the estate tax, even at a time of war, sacrifice, huge budget deficits, and widening gaps in opportunity.

What would be more American than for those who have accrued tremendous wealth in our country to pay a small portion of their accumulated wealth to capitalize a fund for opportunity for the next generation?

BROADENING EMPLOYEE OWNERSHIP
In *The Ownership Solution*, Jeff Gates urges us to look beyond wage and job policies and expand the ownership stake that workers and their communities have in private enterprise. There is a range of public policies that could promote broader ownership and reward companies that share the wealth with employees, consumers, and other stakeholders. These include encouraging employee ownership through government purchasing, licensing rights, public-pension-plan investments, loans and loan guarantee programs, and so on.

While the overall trend of wealth growth has been toward concentration, a significant exception is found among employee owners of businesses. As of 1998, nonmanagement employees owned more than 8 percent of total corporate equity, up from less than 2 percent in 1987. Newer figures are not available.

This ownership takes the form of Employee Stock Ownership Plans (ESOPs), profit-sharing plans, widely granted stock options, and other forms of broad ownership. In 2004, according to the National Center on Employee Ownership, the average ESOP had about $45,500 in corporate equity, disregarding what they were able to save from their paychecks. A second study of 102 ESOP companies in Washington State found that average employee-owned wealth was $32,000.

Many of the proposals described above are aimed at assisting people with very little savings and assets to increase their personal net worth. There will continue to be distortions, however, in who benefits from public policy unless we address the issue of the current overconcentration of wealth and power at the pinnacle of the population.

From Economic Apartheid in America: A Primer on Economic Inequality and Insecurity.

ARTHUR A. ROBERTSON AND THE 1929 CRASH

Studs Terkel

A legendary investor from the first half of the twentieth century told the oral historian and broadcaster known for collecting stories of common people what it was like when the stock market crashed in 1929, a story rich with lessons for the future of America.

Arthur A. Robertson's offices are on an upper floor of a New York skyscraper. On the walls are paintings and photographs. A portrait of President Lyndon Johnson is inscribed, "To my friend, a patriot who serves his country." Another, of Hubert Humphrey: "To my friend, Arthur Robertson, with all my good wishes." Also, a photograph of Dwight Eisenhower: "To my friend, Arthur Robertson." There are other mementos of appreciation from Americans in high places.

He recounts his early days as a war correspondent, advertising man, and engineer: "We built a section of the Sixth Avenue subway. I've had a peculiar kind of career. I'm an industrialist. I had been in Germany where I picked up a number of porcelain enamel plants. I had a hog's hair concession from the Russian government. I used to sell them to the outdoor advertising plants for brushes. With several associates, I bought a company nineteen years ago for $1,600,000. We're on the New York Stock Exchange now and recently turned

WAGE THEFT

Kim Bobo

To people with middle-class or better jobs, the idea of not being paid in full for their work may seem odd. But for millions of workers in low-paying jobs, getting shorted on pay is a common occurrence, one that the writer of this piece shows is reduced when unions are strong.

But the king of Egypt said, "Moses and Aaron, why are you taking the people away from their labor? Get back to your work!"

—*Exodus 5:4*

Mercedes Herrerra is thirty-nine years old. She grew up in Veracruz, Mexico. She came from a hardworking family. As she says, "My mom instilled in me a desire to stand up for people." Herrerra and her husband have four children, one granddaughter, and one grandson "on the way."

Herrerra came to Houston in 1994. She first started cleaning houses in 1996. Then she moved to cleaning downtown buildings and sports facilities, working primarily for staffing agencies. She and her co-workers were frequently victims of wage theft.

She was never paid for overtime. Her employers would tell her, "There is no overtime. After forty hours you work for someone else." (This is not legal.)

be that we asked how much growth we would be willing to sacrifice for a little more equality and opportunity. Now we realize that we are paying a high price for our inequality and that alleviating it and promoting growth are intertwined, complementary goals. It will be up to all of us—our leaders included—to muster the courage and foresight to finally treat this beleaguering malady.

This piece originally appeared on the New York Times *Opinionator blog on January 19, 2013.*

down $200 million for it. I'm chairman of the board, I control the company, I built it.

"I thought seriously of retiring in 1928 when I was thirty. I had seven figures [a million dollars, which in 1922 equaled about $14 million in 2013 money] by the time I was twenty-four.

"In 1929, it [Wall Street] was strictly a gambling casino with loaded dice. The few sharks taking advantage of the multitude of suckers. It was exchanging expensive dogs for expensive cats. There had been a recession in 1921. We came out of it about 1924. Then began the climb, the spurt, with no limit stakes. Frenzied finance that made Ponzi* look like an amateur. I saw shoeshine boys buying $50,000 worth of stock with $500 down. Everything was bought on hope.

"Today, if you want to buy $100 worth of stock, you have to put up $80 and the broker will put up $20. In those days, you could put up $8 or $10. That was really responsible for the collapse. The slightest shake-up caused calamity because people didn't have the money required to cover the other $90 or so. There were not the controls you have today.** They just sold you out: an unwilling seller to an unwilling buyer.

"A cigar stock at the time was selling for $115 a share. The market collapsed. I got a call from the company president. Could I loan him $200 million? I refused, because at the time I had to protect my own fences, including those of my closest friends. His $115 stock dropped to $2 and he jumped out of the window of his Wall Street office.

"There was a man who headed a company that had $17 million in cash. He was one of the leaders of his industry and controlled three or four situations that are today household words. When his stock began to drop, he began to protect it. When he came out of the second drop, the man was completely wiped out. He owed three banks a million dollars each.

"The banks were in the same position he was, except that the

---

*Charles Ponzi, a Boston financier, fleeced Americans in the 1920s by soliciting money for investments that seemed to earn fabulous returns. But the payouts came from new investors, attracted by the fantastical gains Ponzi clients talked about in what is now called a Ponzi scheme or a pyramid scheme. In 2013 money, Ponzi's investors lost nearly a quarter billion dollars.

**Modern hedge funds typically borrow $30 for each $1 of cash equity invested.

government came to their aid and saved them. Suddenly they became holier than thou, and took over the businesses of the companies that owed them money. They discharged the experts, who
had built the businesses, and put in their own men. I bought one
of these companies from the banks. They sold it to me in order to
stop their losses.

"The worst day-to-day operators of businesses are bankers. They
are great when it comes to scrutinizing a balance sheet. By training they're conservative, because they're loaning you other people's
money. Consequently, they do not take the calculated risks operating businesses requires. They were losing so much money that they
were tickled to get it off their backs. I recently sold it for $2 million.
I bought it in 1933 for $33,000.

"In the early thirties, I was known as a scavenger. I used to buy
broken-down businesses that banks took over. That was one of my
best eras of prosperity. The whole period was characterized by men
who were legends. When you talked about $1 million you were
talking about loose change. Three or four of these men would get
together, run up a stock to ridiculous prices and unload it on the
unsuspecting public. The minute you heard of a man like Durant
or Jesse Livermore buying stock, everybody followed. They knew
it was going to go up. The only problem was to get out before they
dumped it.

"Durant owned General Motors twice and lost it twice . . . was
worth way in excess of a billion dollars on paper, by present standards, four or five billion. He started his own automobile company,
and it went under. When the Crash came, he caved in, like the rest
of 'em. The last I heard of him I was told he ended up running a
bowling alley. It was all on paper. Everybody in those days expected
the sun to shine forever.

"October 29, 1929, yeah. A frenzy. I must have gotten calls from
a dozen and a half friends who were desperate. In each case, there
was no sense in loaning them the money that they would give the
broker. Tomorrow they'd be worse off than yesterday. Suicides, left
and right, made a terrific impression on me, of course. People I
knew. It was heartbreaking. One day you saw the prices at a hundred, the next day at $20, at $15.

"On Wall Street, the people walked around like zombies. It was like *Death Takes a Holiday*. It was very dark. You saw people who yesterday rode around in Cadillacs lucky now to have carfare.

"One of my friends said to me, 'If things keep on as they are, we'll all have to go begging.' I asked, 'Who from?'

"Many brokers did not lose money. They made fortunes on commissions while their customers went broke. The only brokers that got hurt badly were those that gambled on their own—or failed to sell out in time customers' accounts that were underwater. Of course, the brokerage business fell off badly, and practically all pulled in their belts, closed down offices and threw people out of work.

"Banks used to get eighteen percent for call money—money with which to buy stock that paid perhaps one or two percent dividends. They figured the price would continue to rise. Everybody was banking on it. I used to receive as much as twenty-two percent from brokers who borrowed from me. Twenty-two percent for money!

THE BIG MONEY

"Men who built empires in utilities would buy a small utility, add a big profit to it for themselves, and sell it back to their own public company. That's how some like Samuel Insull became immensely wealthy. The thing that caused the Insull crash is the same that caused all these frenzied financiers to go broke. No matter how much they had, they'd pyramid it for more.

"I had a great friend, John Hertz. At one time he owned ninety percent of the Yellow Cab stock. John also owned the Checker Cab. He also owned the Surface Line buses of Chicago. He was reputed to be worth $400 to $500 million. He asked me one day to join him on a yacht. There I met two men of such stature that I was in awe: Durant and Jesse Livermore.

"We talked of all their holdings. Livermore said: 'I own what I believe to be the controlling stock of IBM and Philip Morris.' So I asked, 'Why do you bother with anything else?' He answered, 'I only understand stock. I can't bother with businesses.' So I asked, 'Do men of your kind put away $10 million where nobody can ever touch it?' He looked at me and answered, 'Young man, what's the use of having ten million if you can't have big money?'

"In 1934—after he went through two bankruptcies in succession—my accountant asked if I'd back Livermore. He was broke and wanted to make a comeback in the market. He always made a comeback and paid everybody off with interest. I agreed to do it. I put up $400,000. By 1939, we made enough money so that each of us could have $1,300,000 profit after taxes. Jesse was by this time in the late sixties, having gone through two bankruptcies. 'Wouldn't it be wise to cash in?' I asked him. In those days, you could live like a king for $50,000 a year. He said he could just never get along on a pittance.

"So I sold out, took my profits, and left Jesse on his own. He kept telling me he was going to make the killing of the century. Ben Smith, known as 'Sell 'Em Short Ben,' was in Europe and told him there was not going to be a war. Believing in Smith, Livermore went short on grain.* For every dollar he owned, plus everything he could pyramid.

"When I arrived in Argentina, I learned that Germany invaded Poland. Poor Jesse was on the phone. 'Art, you have to save me.' I refused to do anything, being so far away. I knew it would be throwing good money after bad.

"A couple of months later, I was back in New York, with Jesse waiting for me in my office. The poor fellow had lost everything he could lay his hands on. He asked for a $5,000 loan, which, of course, I gave him. Three days later, Jesse had gone to eat breakfast in the Sherry-Netherlands, went to the lavatory and shot himself. They found a note made out to me for $5,000. This was the man who said, 'What's the use of having ten million if you can't have big money?' Jesse was one of the most brilliant minds in the trading world. He knew the crops of every area where grain grew. He was a great student, but always overoptimistic."

Did you sense the Crash coming in 1929?

"I recognized it in May and saved myself a lot of money. I sold a good deal of my stocks in May. It was a case of becoming fright-

---

* "Selling short is selling something you don't have and buying it back in order to cover it. You think a stock is not worth what it's selling for, say, it's listed as $100. You sell a hundred shares of it, though you haven't got the stock. If you are right, and it goes down to $85, you buy it at that price, and deliver it to the fellow to whom you sold it for $100. You sell what you don't have." Obviously, if the stock rises in value, selling short is ruinous. . . . Ben Smith sold short during the Crash and made "a fortune."

ened. But, of course, I did not sell out completely, and finished with a very substantial loss.

"In 1927 when I read Lindbergh was planning his memorable flight, I bought Wright Aeronautic stock. He was going to fly in a plane I heard was made by Wright. I lived in Milwaukee then. My office was about a mile from my home. When I left my house, I checked with my broker. By the time I reached my office, I had made sixty-five points. The idea of everything moving so fast was frightening. Everything you bought just seemed to have no ceiling.

"People say we're getting a repetition of 1929. I don't see how it is possible. Today with SEC* controls and bank insurance, people know their savings are safe. If everybody believes, it's like believing in counterfeit money. Until it's caught, it serves its purpose.

"In 1932 I came to New York to open an office in the Flatiron Building. Macfadden, the health faddist, created penny restaurants. There was a Negro chap I took a liking to that I had to deal with. He agreed to line up seventy-five people who needed to be fed. At six o'clock I would leave my office, I'd march seventy-five of 'em into the Macfadden restaurant and I'd feed 'em for seven cents apiece. I did this every day. It was just unbelievable, the bread lines. The only thing I could compare it with was Germany in 1922. It looked like there was no tomorrow.

"I remember the Bank Holiday. I was one of the lucky ones. I had a smart brother-in-law, an attorney. One day he said to me, 'I don't feel comfortable about the bank situation. I think we ought to have a lot of cash.' About eight weeks before the bank closings, we decided to take every dollar out of the banks. We must have taken out close to a million dollars. In Clyde, Ohio, where I had a porcelain enamel plant, they used my signature for money. I used to come in every Saturday and Sunday and deliver the cash. I would go around the department stores that I knew in Milwaukee and give them thirty-day IOUs of $1.05 for a dollar if they would give me cash.

"In 1933, the night Jake Factor, 'The Barber,' was kidnapped, an associate of mine, his wife, and a niece from Wyoming were dancing in a nightclub. Each of us had $25,000 cash in our socks. We were leaving the following morning for Clyde, and I was supposed

---

*Securities and Exchange Commission.

to bring in $100,000 to meet bills and the payroll. We were all dancing on $25,000 apiece. In the very place where Jake Factor was kidnaped for $100,000. The damn fools, they could have grabbed us and had the cash."

From Hard Times: An Oral History of the Great Depression.

GRADUATES V. OLIGARCHS

Paul Krugman

The notion that differences in education explain America's growing inequality simply does not stand up to scrutiny, as explained by a Nobel Prize–winning economist.

The economist Dean Baker made a really good point when he wrote about how the Occupy movement that began on Wall Street framed the inequality issue. Occupy focused on "the CEOs, the Goldman Sachs crew, the lobbyists and the other members of the one percent who have done incredibly well in the last three decades," Baker wrote and properly so.

Baker was chastising David Brooks, my fellow *New York Times* columnist, who wrote that these factors were not so important as "the gap between college-educated workers and those without a college degree."

Brooks called the inequality that Occupy brought into focus "blue inequality" because the elites whose income and wealth are growing tend to live along the coasts in urban centers that vote Democratic. The gap between those without college degrees and those who earned them is what Brooks called "red inequality," implying it is much more of a Heartland America concern.

The facts do not support the notion that education is at the heart of inequality. For starters, as Baker pointed out, "the ratio of the wages of those with just college degrees to those without college degrees has not risen much since the early 90s."

It's really awfully late in the game to be saying that the important inequality issue is college graduates versus nongraduates. It's not clear that this was ever true, and it certainly hasn't been true for a while.

I wrote about this in 2006, using Ben Bernanke's maiden testimony as chairman of the Federal Reserve, as an entry point. As I said then, Bernanke—like many others—fundamentally misread what's happening to American society.

What we're seeing isn't the rise of a fairly broad class of knowledge workers. Instead, we're seeing the rise of a narrow oligarchy: income and wealth are becoming increasingly concentrated in the hands of a small, privileged elite. The proof is right in the data we economists get paid to analyze and understand.

I think of Mr. Bernanke's position, which one hears all the time, as the 80-20 fallacy. It's the notion that the winners in our increasingly unequal society are a fairly large group—the 20 percent or so of American workers who have the skills to take advantage of new technology and globalization—and that they are pulling away from the 80 percent who don't have these skills.

Why would someone as smart and well informed as Bernanke get the nature of growing inequality wrong? Because the fallacy he fell into tends to dominate polite discussion about income trends, not because it's true, but because it's comforting. The notion that it's all about returns to education suggests that nobody is to blame for rising inequality, that it's just a case of supply and demand at work. And it also suggests that the way to mitigate inequality is to improve our educational system—and better education is a value to which just about every politician in America pays at least lip service.

The idea that we have a rising oligarchy is much more disturbing. It suggests that the growth of inequality may have as much to do with power relations as it does with market forces. Unfortunately, that's the real story.

Let me illustrate this point with some Congressional Budget Office data. First, a report issued in October 2011, titled *Trends*

in the Distribution of Household Income Between 1979 and 2007,
breaks out the income shares of the top 1 percent and the rest of the
top quintile (see the chart below). Notice that within the top 20 percent there has been no rise in the share of the 81st–99th group! It's
all about the top 1 percent. Second, even within the top 1 percent
the gains are going mainly to a small minority at the top of that
group.

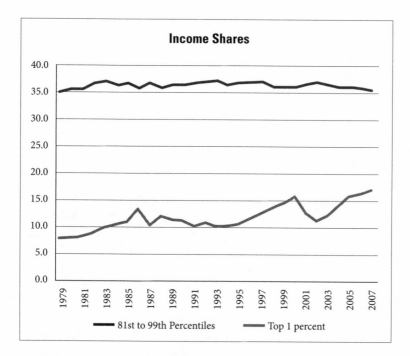

Another CBO report, *Historical Effective Tax Rates, 1979 to 2005,*
issued in 2008, looked inside the top 1 percent up through 2005 using slightly different methods. On the next page is another chart
with some of that data.

As you can see, the big gains have gone to the top 0.1 percent.
In 2000 and again in 2005, the top 0.1 percent's share of income
was the same as the nine times larger group from 99.0 percent to
99.9 percent.

So income inequality in America really is about oligarchs versus

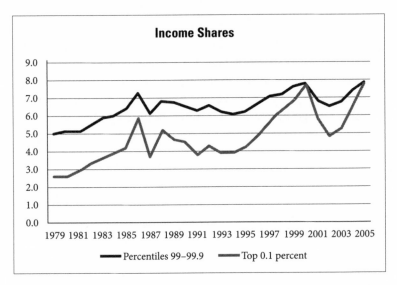

everyone else. When the Occupy Wall Street people talk about the 99 percent, they're actually aiming too low.

One last point: I see that David Brooks is arguing that the oligarchy issue, if it matters at all, is a coastal phenomenon, not the issue in the heartland. That is his "blue inequality" that "is experienced in New York City, Los Angeles, Boston, San Francisco, Seattle, Dallas, Houston and the District of Columbia. In these places, you see the top 1 percent of earners zooming upward, amassing more income and wealth."

Let me point out, then, that we have one country, with a tightly integrated economy. High finance is concentrated in New York, but it makes money from the United States as a whole. And even when oligarchs clearly get their income from heartland, red-state sources, where do they live? OK, one of the Koch brothers still lives in Wichita; but the other lives in New York City.

Put it this way: having much of the wealth your state creates go to people who are in effect absentee landlords, whose income therefore shows up in another state's statistics, doesn't mean that you have an equal distribution of income. Out of state shouldn't mean out of mind.

Look, I understand that some people find the notion that we've become an oligarchy—with all that implies about class relations—disturbing. But that's the way it is.

A version of this chapter originally appeared on November 1, 2011, in "The Conscience of a Liberal," the writer's New York Times *blog.*

EDUCATION

NO RICH CHILD LEFT BEHIND

sean f. reardon

The gap in test scores between poor and affluent children has widened, not because schools have changed, but because of preschool enrichment that only better-off parents can afford, a noted education scholar and sociologist explains.

Here's a fact that may not surprise you: the children of the rich perform better in school, on average, than children from middle-class or poor families. Students growing up in richer families have better grades and higher standardized test scores, on average, than poorer students; they also have higher rates of participation in extracurricular activities and school leadership positions, higher graduation rates and higher rates of college enrollment and completion.

Whether you think it deeply unjust, lamentable but inevitable, or obvious and unproblematic, this is hardly news. It is true in most societies and has been true in the United States for at least as long as we have thought to ask the question and had sufficient data to verify the answer.

What is news is that in the United States over the last few decades these differences in educational success between high- and lower-income students have grown substantially.

One way to see this is to look at the scores of rich and poor students on standardized math and reading tests over the last fifty years. When I did this, using information from a dozen large national studies conducted between 1960 and 2010, I found that the rich-poor gap in test scores is about 40 percent larger now than it was thirty years ago.

To make this trend concrete, consider two children, one from a family with income of $165,000 and one from a family with income of $15,000. These incomes are at the 90th and 10th percentiles of the income distribution nationally, meaning that 10 percent of children today grow up in families with incomes below $15,000 and 10 percent grow up in families with incomes above $165,000.

In the 1980s, on an 800-point SAT-type test scale, the average difference in test scores between two such children would have been about 90 points; today it is 125 points. This is almost twice as large as the 70-point test score gap between white and black children. Family income is now a better predictor of children's success in school than race.

The same pattern is evident in other, more tangible, measures of educational success, like college completion. In a study similar to mine, Martha J. Bailey and Susan M. Dynarski, economists at the University of Michigan, found that the proportion of students from upper-income families who earn a bachelor's degree has increased by 18 percentage points over a twenty-year period, while the completion rate of poor students has grown by only 4 points.

In a more recent study, my graduate students and I found that 15 percent of high-income students from the high school class of 2004 enrolled in a highly selective college or university, while fewer than 5 percent of middle-income and 2 percent of low-income students did.

These widening disparities are not confined to academic outcomes: new research by the Harvard political scientist Robert D. Putnam and his colleagues shows that the rich-poor gaps in student participation in sports, extracurricular activities, volunteer work, and church attendance have grown sharply as well.

More than 14,000 educators and education scholars gathered in 2013 for the annual meeting of the American Educational Research Association to discuss a familiar theme: can schools provide children a way out of poverty?

We are still talking about this despite decades of clucking about the crisis in American education and wave after wave of school reform. Whatever we've been doing in our schools, it hasn't reduced educational inequality between children from upper- and lower-income families.

Part of knowing what we should do about this is understanding how and why these educational disparities are growing. For the past few years, alongside other scholars, I have been digging into historical data to understand just that. The results of this research don't always match received wisdom or playground folklore.

The most potent development over the past three decades is that the test scores of children from high-income families have increased very rapidly. Before 1980, affluent students had little advantage over middle-class students in academic performance; most of the socioeconomic disparity in academics was between the middle class and the poor. But the rich now outperform the middle class by as much as the middle class outperform the poor. Just as the incomes of the affluent have grown much more rapidly than those of the middle class over the last few decades, so, too, have most of the gains in educational success accrued to the children of the rich.

Before we can figure out what's happening here, let's dispel a few myths.

The income gap in academic achievement is not growing because the test scores of poor students are dropping or because our schools are in decline. In fact, average test scores on the National Assessment of Educational Progress, the so-called Nation's Report Card, have been rising—substantially in math and very slowly in reading—since the 1970s. The average nine-year-old today has math skills equal to those her parents had at age eleven, a two-year improvement in a single generation. The gains are not as large in reading and they are not as large for older students, but there is no evidence that average test scores have declined over the last three decades for any age or economic group.

The widening income disparity in academic achievement is not a result of widening racial gaps in achievement, either. The achievement gaps between blacks and whites, and Hispanic and non-Hispanic whites have been narrowing slowly over the last two decades, trends that actually keep the yawning gap between higher- and lower-income students from getting even wider. If we look at the test scores of white students only, we find the same growing gap between high- and low-income children as we see in the population as a whole.

It may seem counterintuitive, but schools don't seem to produce much of the disparity in test scores between high- and low-income students. We know this because children from rich and poor families score very differently on school readiness tests when they enter kindergarten, and this gap grows by less than 10 percent between kindergarten and high school. There is some evidence that achievement gaps between high- and low-income students actually narrow during the nine-month school year, but they widen again in the summer months.

That isn't to say that there aren't important differences in quality between schools serving low- and high-income students—there certainly are—but they appear to do less to reinforce the trends than conventional wisdom would have us believe.

If not the usual suspects, what's going on? It boils down to this: the academic gap is widening because rich students are increasingly entering kindergarten much better prepared to succeed in school than middle-class students. This difference in preparation persists through elementary and high school.

My research suggests that one part of the explanation for this is rising income inequality. As you may have heard, the incomes of the rich have grown faster over the last thirty years than the incomes of the middle class and the poor. Money helps families provide cognitively stimulating experiences for their young children because it provides more stable home environments, more time for parents to read to their children, access to higher-quality child care and preschool and—in places like New York City, where four-year-old children take tests to determine entry into gifted and talented programs—access to preschool test-preparation tutors or the time to serve as tutors themselves.

But rising income inequality explains, at best, half of the increase in the rich-poor academic achievement gap. It's not just that the rich have more money than they used to; it's that they are using it differently. This is where things get really interesting.

High-income families are increasingly focusing their resources—

their money, time, and knowledge of what it takes to be successful in school—on their children's cognitive development and educational success. They are doing this because educational success is much more important than it used to be, even for the rich.

With a college degree insufficient to ensure a high-income job, or even a job as a barista, parents are now investing more time and money in their children's cognitive development from the earliest ages. It may seem self-evident that parents with more resources are able to invest more—more of both money and what Mr. Putnam calls "'Goodnight Moon' time"—in their children's development. But even though middle-class and poor families are also increasing the time and money they invest in their children, they are not doing so as quickly or as deeply as the rich.

The economists Richard J. Murnane and Greg J. Duncan report that from 1972 to 2006 high-income families increased the amount they spent on enrichment activities for their children by 150 percent, while the spending of low-income families grew by 57 percent over the same time period. Likewise, the amount of time parents spend with their children has grown twice as fast since 1975 among college-educated parents as it has among less-educated parents. The economists Gary Ramey and Valerie A. Ramey of the University of California, San Diego, call this escalation of early childhood investment "the rug rat race," a phrase that nicely captures the growing perception that early childhood experiences are central to winning a lifelong educational and economic competition.

It's not clear what we should do about all this. Partly that's because much of our public conversation about education is focused on the wrong culprits: we blame failing schools and the behavior of the poor for trends that are really the result of deepening income inequality and the behavior of the rich.

We're also slow to understand what's happening, I think, because the nature of the problem—a growing educational gap between the rich and the middle class—is unfamiliar. After all, for much of the last fifty years our national conversation about educational inequality has focused almost exclusively on strategies for reducing inequalities between the educational successes of the poor and the middle class, and it has relied on programs aimed at the poor, like Head Start and Title I.

We've barely given a thought to what the rich were doing. With the exception of our continuing discussion about whether the rising costs of higher education are pricing the middle class out of college, we don't have much practice talking about what economists call "upper-tail inequality" in education, much less success at reducing it.

Meanwhile, not only are the children of the rich doing better in school than even the children of the middle class, but the changing economy means that school success is increasingly necessary to future economic success, a worrisome mutual reinforcement of trends that is making our society more socially and economically immobile.

We need to start talking about this. Strangely, the rapid growth in the rich-poor educational gap provides a ray of hope: if the relationship between family income and educational success can change this rapidly, then it is not an immutable, inevitable pattern. What changed once can change again. Policy choices matter more than we have recently been taught to think.

So how can we move toward a society in which educational success is not so strongly linked to family background? Maybe we should take a lesson from the rich and invest much more heavily as a society in our children's educational opportunities from the day they are born. Investments in early-childhood education pay very high societal dividends. That means investing in developing high-quality child care and preschool that is available to poor and middle-class children. It also means recruiting and training a cadre of skilled preschool teachers and child-care providers. These are not new ideas, but we have to stop talking about how expensive and difficult they are to implement and just get on with it.

But we need to do much more than expand and improve preschool and child care. There is a lot of discussion these days about investing in teachers and "improving teacher quality," but improving the quality of our parenting and of our children's earliest environments may be even more important. Let's invest in parents so they can better invest in their children.

This means finding ways of helping parents become better teachers themselves. This might include strategies to support working families so that they can read to their children more often. It also means expanding programs like the Nurse-Family Partnership that have proved to be effective at helping single parents educate their children; but we also need to pay for research to develop new resources for single parents.

It might also mean greater business and government support for maternity and paternity leave and day care so that the middle class and the poor can get some of the educational benefits that the early academic intervention of the rich provides their children. Fundamentally, it means rethinking our still-persistent notion that educational problems should be solved by schools alone.

The more we do to ensure that all children have similar cognitively stimulating early childhood experiences, the less we will have to worry about failing schools. This in turn will enable us to let our schools focus on teaching the skills—how to solve complex problems, how to think critically, and how to collaborate—essential to a growing economy and a lively democracy.

This piece originally appeared on the New York Times *Opinionator blog on April 27, 2013.*

ACHIEVEMENT GAP

Editorial Projects of the Education Research Center

The disparity in how well students do in kindergarten through high school grows from unequal funding and other policies that give an advantage to children from better-off communities and put those from poorer communities at a distinct, and growing, disadvantage.

The "achievement gap" in education refers to the disparity in academic performance between groups of students. The achievement gap shows up in grades, standardized-test scores, course selection, dropout rates, and college-completion rates, among other success measures. It is most often used to describe the troubling performance gaps between African American and Hispanic students, at the lower end of the performance scale, and their non-Hispanic white peers, and the similar academic disparity between students from low-income families and those who are better off. In the past decade, though, scholars and policy makers have begun to focus increasing attention on other achievement gaps, such as those based on sex, English-language proficiency, and learning disabilities.

With the passage of the No Child Left Behind Act of 2001, closing achievement gaps among these various student groups became a focus of federal education accountability, and schools and districts were required to disaggregate student test scores and other performance data by student characteristics to enable better comparisons between groups. This created both greater awareness of racial disparities and rising concern about other kinds of achievement gaps. The attention led to more targeted interventions for different groups of students, but had not closed most achievement gaps to an appreciable degree a decade after the law passed.

While National Assessment of Educational Progress (NAEP) results show that, over time, black and Hispanic students have made great strides in improving performance in reading and mathematics, a breach still separated them from their white peers. For example, special analyses by the National Center for Education Statistics in 2009 and 2011 showed that black and Hispanic students trailed their white peers by an average of more than twenty test-score points on the NAEP math and reading assessments at fourth and eighth grades, a difference of about two grade levels. These gaps persisted even though the score differentials between black and white students narrowed between 1992 and 2007 in fourth-grade math and reading and eighth-grade math, National Center for Educational Statistics reports in 2009 and 2011 showed.

Students' high school course-taking patterns provide a slightly more positive progress picture. Data from the U.S. Department of Education show that students across the board greatly increased the average number of course credits they earned by graduation by 2009. Black students went from taking the least credit hours in 1990, 23.5, to the most of any student group in 2009, 27.4. Hispanic students increased their average credits from 24 to 26.5; white students from 23.7 to 27.3; and Asian American and Pacific Islander students from 24.2 to 27 credits during the same time period.

All student groups likewise improved the number of core academic courses they took during that time, with black students overtaking white students in their participation in core academic courses. But all other student groups continue to trail Asian American students in core coursework. However, both white and Asian American students were at least twice as likely to take classes considered academically rigorous in those subjects than black and Hispanic students. Fewer than 10 percent of black or Hispanic students participated in rigorous courses in 2009, National Center for Educational Statistics found.

Such disparities have also been evident in graduation-rate and college-success statistics. Changes in 2008 to federal regulations on educating students in poverty required school districts to be held accountable for the graduation rates of students in different racial, language, poverty, and disability groups. According to Editorial Projects in Education Research Center's annual Diplomas Count report, while each major racial and ethnic group had more students graduate as of the class of 2008, massive gaps remained between different groups of students. While 82.7 percent of Asian students and 78.4 percent of white students in the class of 2008 graduated on time, that was the case for only 57.6 percent of Hispanic, 57 percent of black, and 53.9 percent of American Indian students. Likewise, only 68 percent of male students graduated on time in 2008, compared with 75 percent of female students. Over the long term, only about one-half of male students from minority backgrounds graduate on time.

Under President Barack Obama's administration, the U.S. Department of Education also stepped up attention on gender and racial gaps in students' college-enrollment and college-success rates, toward a goal that the United States will lead the world in college graduates by 2020.

According to the American Council on Education's twenty-fourth annual status report on minorities in higher education, as of 2008, 38 percent of Americans ages 25–34 had earned at least an associate degree, while only 26 percent of African Americans ages 25–37 obtained a two-year degree and 18 percent of Hispanics in the same age group had obtained a two-year degree. Moreover, the U.S. Census Bureau reports that as of 2010, 36 percent of women ages 25 to 29 held a bachelor's degree or better versus only 28 percent of men in the same age group.

Achievement disparities are often attributed to socioeconomic factors. According to 2009 data from the Census Bureau, of all children younger than eighteen living in families, 15.5 million live in poverty, defined as a family of four with less than $21,947 per year. This includes 4.9 million, or about 10 percent, of non-Hispanic white children, and one in three black and Hispanic children, at 4 million and 5.6 million, respectively, a 2011 Annie E. Casey Foundation report showed.

According to a seminal study of language development in 1995, by age three, children in poverty have smaller vocabularies and lower language skills than children from middle-income families. Research has also shown that dropout rates tend to be higher for children who live in poverty. According to the U.S. Department of Education's 2011 Condition of Education report, about 68 percent of twelfth-graders in high-poverty schools graduated with a diploma in 2008, compared with 91 percent of twelfth-graders in low-poverty schools.

A recent study by the Annie E. Casey Foundation—*Double Jeopardy: How Third-Grade Reading Skills and Poverty Influence High School Graduation*—found that children who both live in poverty and read below grade level by third grade are three times as likely to not graduate from high school as students who have never been poor.

Researchers have tried to pinpoint why race and class are such strong predictors of students' educational attainment. In the 1990s, the controversial book *The Bell Curve* claimed that gaps in student achievement were the result of variation in students' genetic makeup and natural ability—an assertion that has since been widely discredited.

Many experts have since asserted that achievement gaps are the result of more subtle environmental factors and "opportunity gaps" in the resources available to poor versus wealthy children. Being raised in a low-income family, for example, often means having fewer educational resources at home, in addition to poor health care and nutrition. At the same time, studies have also found that children in poverty whose parents provide engaging learning environments at home do not start school with the same academic readiness gaps seen among poor children generally.

Education and school-funding policies can exacerbate these opportunity gaps. Analyses by the Education Trust, a Washington-based research and advocacy organization, and others have found that students in poverty and those who are members of racial minority groups are overwhelmingly concentrated in the lowest-achieving schools. For example, in California, black students are six times more likely than white students to attend one of the bottom third of schools in the state, and Latino and poor students are nearly four times as likely as white students to attend one of the worst-performing third of schools, the Education Trust reported in 2010.

Likewise, research has shown that good teaching matters and that poor and minority students tend to have less access to the most effective, experienced teachers with knowledge in their content field. One study of forty-six industrialized countries found the United States ranked forty-second in providing equitable distribution of teachers to different groups of students: for example, while 68 percent of upper-income eighth-graders in the U.S. study sample had math teachers deemed to be of high quality, that was true for only 53 percent of low-income students.

Some researchers are also exploring more subtle factors that can contribute to achievement gaps such as peer pressure, student tracking, negative stereotyping, and test bias. Research also has shown that students from a disadvantaged group can perform below their normal ability when confronted with negative stereotypes about their group. For example, in 2009 the Institute for Research on Education Policy and Practice at Stanford University found that specific student groups underperformed in stereotypical ways on state exit exams—girls performed worse on math, for example, or students from Asian American backgrounds scored lower on reading—suggesting that the high-stakes nature of the tests could contribute to students' performance anxiety.

In principle, the public has been behind closing the achievement gap, and schools have employed a variety of tactics to address it. Common reform recommendations have included reducing class sizes, creating smaller schools, expanding early-childhood programs, raising academic standards, improving the quality of teachers provided to poor and minority students, and encouraging more minority students to take high-level courses. Still, progress in reducing academic divides has been slow or nonexistent.

Achievement gaps seem likely to remain a focus in the next authorization of the Elementary and Secondary Education Act. The requirement that schools, districts, and states disaggregate students' test scores and graduation rates by race, gender, language, and socioeconomic status remains one of the few parts of No Child Left Behind with broad bipartisan support for reauthorization.

Moreover, the economic-stimulus law passed by Congress in 2009 required states to close achievement gaps and provide more equitable distribution of high-quality teachers for poor and minority students. Policy makers and educators hope to find new ways to close achievement gaps faster in the decade to come.

This article appeared in the July 7, 2011, issue of Education Week.

BACK TO SCHOOL

Mike Rose

Community colleges are crucial to improving the economic prospects of people from low- and moderate-income families, with many students long past their teen years, yet education budget cuts threaten their prospects at better jobs and incomes.

The majority of the more than ten million students in community colleges, and especially in adult-school academic and occupational programs, are from low- to modest-income backgrounds. And some live in poverty. For the most part, they have not benefited from high-performing schools or quality educational resources. They typically must work—some full-time or close to it—have family obligations, and have limited transportation. The schools and programs they attend provide the primary, if not only, avenue for them to further their education. This is particularly true in rural America. As a steady stream of reports on the American economy from federal, state, and private agencies have claimed, both workforce development as well as attainment of bachelor's and graduate degrees will stagnate without the achievement of this large and varied population.

It is in these institutions that we can get a measure of how we're doing as a society on a number of questions that are fundamental to our best sense of who we are. How well are we preparing students from a broad sweep of backgrounds for life after high school, and how adequate are the programs we have in place to remedy the failures of K–12 education? How robust is our belief in the ability of the common person, and what opportunities do we provide to realize that ability? Given the nature of Western capitalism, what mechanisms are there to compensate for boom-and-bust economic cycles, for "creative destruction," for globalization? Do we have an adequate social safety net, and how effective are we at providing people a second chance? How open and welcoming are our core institutions—such as postsecondary education—and how adaptable?

The problem is that these second-chance institutions are not living up to their promise, and the current political climate poses threats to their improvement and, in some cases, to their continued existence. Community college graduation rates offer one indicator of the limited effectiveness of our second-chance institutions. The majority of students entering community college say they want to graduate, but only about 30 percent complete a degree or credential or transfer within four years. There are a number of reasons offered for these disappointing results.

For all the diverse talents and strengths those entering the community college system bring to it, many students have a lot to overcome, ranging from poor educations and family disruptions to unstable employment, housing, and health care. They have not been on the educational fast track and don't come from families with much experience in higher education, so they aren't that familiar with institutional policies and norms. For older students, there's the additional burden of not having been in a classroom in decades. "I hated school," one woman told me, "and to be back in it is really strange." Some students, younger ones particularly, come because they know it will help them get a better job or because parents urge it or friends are going, but they don't have a particular goal in mind, which, combined with a lack of institutional savvy, leads to low levels of engagement, unfocused course selection, and sporadic attendance.

What is significant, though, is that some community colleges get better results than others with students who share similar background characteristics. Demography affects but does not determine achievement; what the college does matters. Let me here sketch the institutional barriers to student success. We find some of these barriers in the full range of postsecondary institutions, community college to Ivy League university, but they are especially vexing for the typical community college student who has fewer resources to overcome them.

At the policy and administrative level, many colleges—especially those in large higher ed systems—are hard to navigate: guidelines and requirements for matriculation, financial aid, or transfer are complicated by decades of independently made policy decisions that lack coherence. Counseling staff are overloaded (on some campuses a single counselor can be responsible for two thousand students). And different levels and kinds of advising (from an academic department, from the financial aid office, from the transfer center) can be fragmented, leading to contradictory advice. Even after spending a year or two at some colleges, I have a hard time wrapping my head around the many options and requirements involved in remedial courses in math, writing, and reading.

When it comes to curriculum and teaching, course sequences and requirements can be confusing. Here's a small but telling example: it's not uncommon that the three sequenced remedial writing courses leading to transfer-level English will have nonsequential, seemingly random numbers such as English 68, 25, and 30. The same holds true for reading and for math. Of more concern, little coordinated thought is typically given to how to address the limited skills and background knowledge of many of the students wanting to take academic or occupational courses. As for faculty, one finds—as in any profession—a wide range of competence and commitment, from people going through the motions to exceptionally gifted teachers deeply committed to their students. But community college teaching loads are daunting, and, increasingly, courses are taught by adjunct faculty holding down jobs on two or three campuses. So mounting a coordinated response to student need is difficult at best. As one instructor at a midwestern college put it, "It's hard to get the conversation going when we're all teaching five sections of writing."

Then there is the complex web of traditions, turf and status dynamics, and beliefs about institutional mission, the purpose of education, and the abilities of the student population. These symbolic and ideological issues emerge when you probe administrative structures or curriculum or staff and faculty behavior, and, to my mind, they represent the most formidable barriers to change. Some examples: the long-standing tension between the academic and the vocational mission of the community college; the deep-rooted erroneous beliefs about learning that shape most remedial programs; and the very different, frequently not articulated, philosophies of education held by staff and faculty.

On the campuses that are more successful, various combinations of enterprising faculty, department chairs and program directors, midlevel managers and top brass—though not always all these actors—are able to coordinate services and provide more structure and guidance for entering students, revise or create curricula that more directly address student needs, and develop ways to work through administrative and ideological tangles.

I want to return to those dreary statistics about student success. Though there is wide agreement that our second-chance institutions (and postsecondary institutions in general) have to do better, some of us are also concerned that these aggregated rates of completion of degrees and rates of transfer don't reflect the multiple reasons why people go to a community college—and why they leave. Even though the majority of students upon entry do say they want to complete a certificate or degree, many, in fact, shift to shorter-term goals, in some instances because of inadequacies in a college's services and curriculum, but also in response to personal needs, family demands, or opportunities in the job market.

One young man, a high school dropout with past addiction problems, entered an electrical construction program and over his first year got absorbed in school, developed some literacy and numeracy and trade skills, and began to see himself in a different light. He quit before completing the occupational certificate to join the navy where he could continue his education, clear his debts, and have a potential career before him. A woman with two kids already had a low-level job in the fashion industry, and she entered a fashion program to take four or five courses that built sufficient skills to get a better job in her company. Both of these people would be recorded as dropouts, a failure both for them and their college. It is also the case that approximately 60 percent of community college students attend more than one community college, so we won't get a complete picture of their postsecondary experience by focusing on their exit from the initial college.

There are efforts, therefore, to develop more discrete indicators of student progress and college effectiveness. How many students complete their remedial requirements within a certain time frame, or transfer-level English or math, or thirty units—a number associated with labor-market payoffs? These and other benchmarks correlate with student success, and they give a better indication of how well a college is doing its job. And, significantly, these more discrete measures can be used by an institution to create strategic counseling and instructional interventions, such as zeroing in on transfer-level math.

It is characteristic of our time to rely heavily on statistical measures in forming public policy; we count, and calculate averages and ratios, seeking clarity in numbers. I appreciate the value of statistical analysis and use it in my own work. But such analysis, especially the fairly broad kind used in policy making—tallies, percentages, trends—fills in only part of the picture of complex human reality. Some studies do combine interviews and other on-the-ground information with analysis of numerical data, but such studies are rare. The typical study would not capture the motives and decisions of that woman in the fashion program and the guy who joined the navy. Furthermore, no matter how refined the collection and analysis of statistical data, without knowledge of the history and culture and daily reality of the place from which the data were collected, policy makers can make huge blunders, as the history of failures in urban renewal and agricultural development illustrate. In general, the makers of education policy have not learned this lesson.

The heightened attention these studies of student success have brought to the community college (and likewise to adult school) has definitely put reform of two-year colleges on the map—a welcome development, for that segment of postsecondary education typically gets little attention. Federal and state governments and private foundations have sponsored initiatives aimed at increasing student success, and the many people within colleges who for some time have been pushing for improvements have received a welcome boost.

The issue I just mentioned about the need for intimate knowledge of institutions comes into play here. These initiatives naturally are geared toward results, more students hitting those aforementioned benchmarks and end goals. The ensuing pressure and accountability might jolt those campuses paralyzed by ossified traditions, infighting, and inertia. That would be a blessing. But we have to be careful about the mechanisms we put in place, for—as recent No Child Left Behind–driven K–12 reform has demonstrated—the fix can lead to unintended negative consequences. For example, there are proposals—and some attempts—to tie funding to these benchmarks: budgets will be affected by the percentage of students that exit remediation or gain those thirty units or complete a certificate or degree. This has a commonsense appeal, but one predictable result will be for formerly open-access colleges to put a floor on whom they admit, accepting only those who have a better chance of succeeding, limiting opportunity for the most vulnerable. Or small programs that are successful will be pressured to expand, to be brought to scale before they're ready or in a way that replicates the superficial features of the program but loses its heart, the qualities that make it work.

There is one other thing that worries me about the current reform environment. The continual broadcasting of high failure rates—statistics that, as I've been suggesting, might not tell the full story—can, over time, breed a sense of hopelessness in the public and lead policy makers to cut funds or redirect them. I've been watching, and have written about, this kind of thing happening in K–12 education. The headlines on the newspaper articles reporting on these studies of failure crystallize my concern: "Billions Spent in U.S. on Community College Students Who Drop Out" or "Failing Students Get Federal Aid." That sort of message can spark action, but it also leads to backlash and withdrawal of support.

The challenge as I see it is to be clear eyed and vigilant about the performance of our second-chance institutions but to use methods of investigation that capture a fuller story of the institutions and the people in them. As well, we need to find, study, and broadcast the many examples of successful work being done daily in these places and build our analysis and our solutions on illustrations of the possible.

America loves the underdog, the come-from-behind winner, the tale of personal redemption, the rags-to-riches story. In *Ragged Dick*, Horatio Alger's novel about an enterprising bootblack, one of the author's fictitious benefactors offers the following rosy observation about upward mobility in the United States: "In this free country poverty is no bar to a man's advancement." The belief that individual effort can override social circumstances runs deep in the national psyche. It's in Ben Franklin's writing, it's in Alger's immensely popular nineteenth-century novels, and it is a central tenet in conservative social policy today.

How noteworthy it is then that a recent issue of the influential conservative magazine *National Review* posed this question in bold print on its cover: "What's Wrong with Horatio Alger?" Above the question, the young Alger protagonist sits forlorn on a park bench, his shoeshine kit unused, an untied bundle of newspapers next to him, unsold. The standard political discourse from the Right contains no such question. The party line is that the market, if left alone, will produce the opportunity for people to advance, that the current sour economy—though worrisome and painful—will correct itself if commerce and innovation are allowed to thrive, and that the gap between rich and poor is, in itself, not a sign of any basic malfunction or injustice, for there are always income disparities in capitalism. For government to draw on the money some citizens have earned to assist those who are less fortunate is to interfere with market principles, dampen the raw energy of capitalism, and foster dependency. The opportunity to advance up the ladder of mobility is always there for those who work hard. This is a seamless story, made plausible by our deep belief in upward mobility.

But the author of the lead article in *National Review* cites statistics that pretty much all economists across the ideological spectrum confirm: upward mobility for people at the bottom rungs of the income ladder, limited during the best of times, is significantly diminished. Breaking the numbers out by race the author writes of "a national tragedy," that "Black and White children grow up in entirely different economic worlds." "Living up to our values," the writer suggests, "requires policymakers . . . to focus on increasing upward relative mobility from the bottom."

The *Economist*, not as fiscally conservative as *National Review* but in the same free-market ballpark, put it even more strongly in another recent cover story. The writers say that the real danger to the American economy is chronic, ingrained joblessness that is related to our social and economic structure: tens of millions of young, marginally educated people who drift in and out of low-paying, dead-end jobs and older low-skilled displaced workers, unable to find employment as industries transform and jobs disappear. This situation places a huge and, if left alone, intractable drag on the economy. Therefore, the editors recommend comprehensive occupational, educational, and social services, for America spends "much less as a share of GDP than almost any other rich country" on policies to get the hard-to-employ into the labor market.

This is the context in which we are considering our second-chance institutions. Many of the people we're discussing are facing hardships beyond what education alone can remedy, including inadequate housing, health care, child care, and, ultimately, employment—just a decent wage and a few benefits. But for some, improving English or math or gaining a GED certificate or an occupational skill or a postsecondary degree would contribute to their economic stability.

Yet, right at the point when they are most needed, our second-chance institutions are being threatened with severe budget cuts. Across the country, community colleges, adult schools, and literacy programs are reporting record enrollments at the same time they have to trim staff, classes, and services. A number of colleges can offer only a smattering of courses in the summer. Nationwide, hundreds of thousands of people are on waiting lists or simply denied admission. On the other side of this coin are rural and semirural institutions that have lost enrollment over the years because of changing demographic patterns. They are facing closure, even though for those still in the community, they are the only resource of their kind available. One more thing: the public library—an iconic American institution—is reducing hours and staff and closing local branches. And this is at a time when two-thirds of the nation's libraries provide the only free Internet access in their communities—and when government and employment information and forms are increasingly going online.

The immediate cause of these cuts is the terrible recession beginning in 2008. Policy makers face "unprecedented challenges" and "have no other choice" but to make cuts in education. Doing more with less has become, in the words of Secretary of Education Arne Duncan, "the new normal." The word *austerity* has entered our national conversation with a vengeance. As I write this, the Los Angeles Unified School District is considering eliminating its entire adult education program, twenty-four community schools, serving over 250,000 people.

I don't dispute the immense difficulty of budgeting in a recession nor the fact that education spending includes waste that should be eliminated. But when our situation is represented as inevitable and normal, the recession becomes a catastrophe without culpability. The civic and moral dimensions of both the causes of the recession and the way policy makers respond to it are neutralized.

What is especially worthy of scrutiny is the role right-wing economic ideology is playing in these policy deliberations—and as the economy improves, the Right's beliefs will still be a potent force in public policy. Antigovernment, anti–welfare state, antitax, this ideology forcefully undercuts broadscale public responses to hardship. Such responses are tarred as a "redistribution of wealth," moving money, as Rep. Paul Ryan puts it, from the "makers" to the "takers." Decisions are made on a ledger sheet profoundly bounded by simplistic assumptions about economics and opportunity and naive, often bigoted, beliefs about people who need help.

For the most part, conservatives support the idea of second-chance educational and training programs, but many would insist that the programs trim their costs and slash the financial aid that enables students to attend them. These policy makers also resist the kinds of services that many students need to continue their education: health and child care, rehabilitation programs, housing. So they support the idea of a second chance while undercutting most of what makes a second chance possible.

Equal opportunity is something every conservative affirms as a core American value. Yet in no realistic sense of the word does anything like equal opportunity exist toward the bottom of the income ladder. And some argue that opportunity is eroding toward the middle as well. Recent studies show that parental income has a greater effect on children's success in America than in other developed countries. A report from the Pell Institute, for example, shows an astonishing 47 percent gap in the attainment of bachelor's degrees between young people at the top half versus bottom half of our country's income distribution. As that writer in *National Review* noted, low-income children live in a different economic world.

Many of the students I've taught at UCLA who come from well-to-do families grew up in a world of museums, music lessons, tutoring, sports programs, travel, up-to-date educational technologies, after-school and summer programs geared toward the arts or sciences. All this is a supplement to attending good to exceptional public or private schools. Because their parents are educated, they can provide all kinds of assistance with homework, with navigating school, with advocacy. These parents are doing everything possible to create maximum opportunity for their kids, often with considerable anxiety and expense. There's no faulting them; poor parents would do the same if they could. But it would require quite a distortion to see young people from affluent and poor backgrounds as having an equal opportunity at academic and career success. To legitimize their view of the economy and society, then, conservatives have to justify advantage.

One way to account for unequal opportunity is to claim that intelligence is a factor and that the families and their children at the lower end of things are there because they're not that bright—so various compensatory programs, in fact, won't help that much. You'll certainly hear this kind of talk in private, and a few bold pundits like Charles Murray, of *The Bell Curve* fame, say it in public.

But scientifically it doesn't hold water, and it is so politically unpalatable that few politicians would risk uttering it.

Another way to explain away inequality—one that has a long history in the United States and is still very much with us—is the moral argument. People are at the lower end of the economy because of a failure of character; they engage in counterproductive behavior, lack a work ethic, don't complete things, and so on. They are a drain on the system, gaming it, on the dole. Since Ronald Reagan's infamous "welfare queen" invocation, conservative political discourse has been brimming with such imagery, as the 2012 GOP primaries demonstrated. There is both a theory of the social order and good, old-fashioned prejudice at play here—and both are enhanced by the social isolation of the rich from the poor.

I don't want to minimize the deep philosophical differences between the conservative and liberal perspectives on social issues, but I do think that some conservatives would be surprised to see firsthand the work ethic, the lack of excuses for previous bad behavior and blunders, the self-reliance, multiple responsibilities, and schedules of the people who populate poor communities.

I've been working with one group of students who begin classes at 7:00 A.M., then work, participate in student government, go to the library to study, and leave in the evening—usually by public transportation—to homes that are anything but stable (thus the refuge of the library). One young man is currently homeless, sleeping in his inoperable car parked at a friend's family's house. He's at school every day by 6:00 A.M. to clean up and get his day in order.

Of course there are people at their school who are drifting, drawing what resources they can, sometimes deluding themselves, sometimes consciously gaming the system. Allow me to note that the students I'm mentoring can point them out in a heartbeat—because they are not the norm. Furthermore, and it's a sign of the times that I even have to write this, such behaviors appear across the socioeconomic landscape. The deplorable thing is the degree to which moral and character flaws are disproportionately attributed to poor people. But if you are able to penetrate the ideological fog and actually enter other people's lives, you'll witness a quite different and much more complex human reality.

Finally, the Right justifies advantage by defining opportunity as an individual phenomenon and representing obstacles to mobility as clear and local and within one's personal power to overcome. This definition yields a particular version of the rags-to-riches story, which takes us back to the young Horatio Alger character sitting on that park bench. Conservatives use rise-from-hardship narratives to great effect, for the narratives confirm their claims about the ever presence of opportunity, regardless of background. But one of the most striking things about conservative celebrations of social mobility is that they are accounts of hardship with almost no feel of hardship to them. They reflect a kind of opportunity that exists only in fiction. Obstacles receive brief mention—if they're mentioned at all—and anger, doubt, or despair are virtually absent. You won't see the home health care worker whose back is a wreck or the guys at bitter loose ends when the factory closes. You won't see people, exhausted, shuttling between two or more jobs to make a living or the anxious scramble for minimal health care for their kids.

The Right's stories present a world stripped of the physical and moral insult of poverty. Characters move upward, driven by self-reliance, optimism, faith, responsibility. Though there might be an occasional reference to teachers or employers who were impressed with the candidate's qualities, the explanations for the candidate's achievements rest pretty much within his or her individual spirit. The one exception is parents: they are usually mentioned as the source of virtue. Family values as the core of economic mobility.

In the Alger originals, the lucky break, the fortuitous encounter is key to the enterprising hero's ascent. Alger's narrator states: "Not many boys can expect an uninterrupted course of prosperity when thrown upon their own exertions." It's worth dwelling on this sentence, for there's little play of chance and good fortune in the contemporary conservative version. Luck's got nothing to do with it. And you surely will not hear a whisper about legislation or social movements that may have enhanced opportunity, opened a door, or removed an obstacle. It would be hard to find a more radically individual portrait of achievement.

The stories of mobility that I know differ greatly from the

conservative script. To be sure, there is hard work and perseverance and faith—sometimes deeply religious faith. But many people with these same characteristics don't make it out of poverty. Discrimination is intractable, or the local economy is devastated to the core, or the consequences of poor education cannot be overcome, or one's health gives out, or family ties (and, often, tragedy) overwhelm.

The people who do succeed—and their gains are typically modest—often tell stories of success mixed with setbacks, of two steps forward and one back. Such stories reveal anger and nagging worry or compromise and ambivalence or a bruising confrontation with one's real or imagined inadequacies—"falling down within me," as one woman in an adult literacy program put it. This is the lived experience of social class. No wonder that these truer stories typically give great significance to help of some kind, both private and public. A relative, a friend, or a minister lends a hand. Family and community social networks open up an opportunity. A local occupational center provides training. The government's safety net—food stamps and welfare, Medicaid, and public housing—protects one from devastation.

It is, then, a tight bundle of reductive economic and social theory, a fanciful definition of opportunity, and negative beliefs about the poor that have become such a force in truly difficult budget negotiations, and there does not seem to be an equally powerful economic and moral countervoice in those deliberations to check it.

As the editors of the *Economist* pointed out, the United States does not currently have robust policies to help low-income people enter and thrive in the labor market. Among the few policy initiatives in place are ones aimed at increasing enrollments in postsecondary education, and several private foundations, notably Gates and Lumina, have been sponsoring such initiatives as well. These efforts are laudable; however, they reach a fairly small percentage of poor and low-income Americans and on average are targeted toward the more academically skilled among them—though many still require remedial English and mathematics.

The economic rationale for increased postsecondary education rests on some widely held—and continually broadcasted—assumptions. Work in the "new economy" requires more literacy, numeracy, and computer skills as well as so-called soft skills like collaboration and communication. A further assumption is that there is a "skills mismatch" between many Americans and the labor market; that is, there are jobs out there that go unfilled because the local labor pool doesn't possess the technological or behavioral skills to do the work. These beliefs have become gospel, repeated daily in policy speeches and documents and on opinion pages. And they do fuel enrollments in adult schools, colleges, and private occupational schools. There is some truth in them. A lot of the jobs that were available to someone with limited education in the mid-twentieth century have been automated and outsourced. And some specialized businesses across the country can't readily get the kind of employee they need. But the overall economic picture is more complicated.

First of all, in many sectors of the labor market, there are simply fewer jobs to be had because of changes in technology and the way work is organized. And Americans are working longer and harder, creating increases in production but not in jobs or salaries. Many jobs, both blue-collar and white, are also being broken down into components and outsourced. Your service representative is speaking to you from India or the Philippines. The traditional correlation between increased education and income still holds, but a whole lot of people with bachelor's degrees and beyond are out of work or working at a job that requires no college degree at all.

A particularly trenchant critique of the standard line on education and jobs is offered by political economist Gordon Lafer, who argues that the fundamental problem with the economy is the shortage of jobs and the absence of vigorous job-creation policies. It is a political "charade," as he puts it, to push job training as the solution to unemployment, for this approach shifts the blame for unemployment and income inequality onto workers themselves, onto their lack of "higher-order thinking skills," or "soft skills," or the "mismatch" between their skills and the skills that industry demands. In fact, the jobs aren't there, and short-term training in job-seeking strategies or basic skills does not make an appreciable difference in helping people get the limited number of jobs that do exist.

Lafer is targeting a particular set of policies and training programs primarily connected to the Workforce Investment Act, not necessarily the kinds of educational experiences I'm concerned with here, though there can be some overlap. But the larger point he makes is important here, for there is in the air the belief that education itself will lift people out of hard times. So let me be clear. I am not claiming that the education provided by second-chance institutions alone will guarantee mobility, be an economic magic bullet. I agree wholeheartedly with the call for better economic policy, for I see what happens when people work hard, build skills, gain a certificate or degree, and then go out into a world with no jobs or apprenticeships. It is indeed a cruel charade.

I am championing second-chance programs because I believe that when well executed they develop skills and build knowledge that can lead to employment but also provide a number of other personal, social, and civic benefits. There is an economic rationale for championing these programs—and these days the economic rationale is the only one that has a prayer of swaying policy makers—but school is about more than a paycheck.

To my mind, education and job creation are not an either-or proposition. There is a political battle over employment to be waged. And there is work to be done in the classroom. And at times the two come together. Students meet others in similar circumstances and broaden their understanding of their own hardships. They are exposed to economics, political science, history that, I'll be the first to admit, can simply be another bunch of stuff to memorize and get out of the way but also can provide perspectives on society and one's place in it. This is where good teaching is so important. Some students join clubs, trade organizations, or student government or get jobs on campus, all of which can provide the occasion to develop social networks and be exposed to new activities and bodies of knowledge. And as students become more literate and numerate, as they develop their interests or acquire new ones, as they learn trade skills, as they feel their minds working, this all affects the way they move through the world and act on it. One study suggests that nearly 20 percent of community college students decide to pursue further education after enrolling in their two-year institution. To the degree that educational programs and job creation are in conflict, it is solely because of political manipulation and not because the two are naturally antagonistic.

I believe deeply in what schooling can accomplish. And part of our problem—on the right and the left—has been that for decades we have reduced school, K–16, to an economic institution. But it is more than that, and throughout our history we have affirmed that education—for children and for adults, in the schoolhouse and in self-improvement associations—yields multiple benefits to self and society.

There are a number of means by which people can get a second chance in the United States: through education, through churches and faith-based institutions, through government programs and the military, through civic and community-based organizations, through labor unions, and through a wide range of private business and philanthropic initiatives. I'm focusing on education, and particularly on the community college and, to a lesser degree, the adult school. I refer to literacy programs, but did not have access to a substantial one during the writing of this essay, although I have in the past and will draw on that experience. In addition to libraries, community organizations, and churches, adult literacy instruction is also found in adult schools and some community colleges, so we will meet men and women along the way who are trying to learn to read and write.

Private occupational colleges—often called proprietary schools—have been in existence since the late nineteenth century (correspondence schools were one early example), and they have been undergoing a boom in the last few decades. They focus on specific job training, from fashion and culinary to engineering. As with any institution—particularly a rapidly growing one—there is a range of quality in proprietary schools, from ones that are well established and accredited to those that have been the subject of criminal investigation for fraud. Proprietary schools are not represented in this essay, for I want to focus on institutions that have a broader educational mission; even though community colleges and adult schools do offer occupational training (and we will witness a lot of it), that training, at least in theory, is embedded in a more educationally comprehensive institutional philosophy. I am also focusing on the

public domain, on institutions that the society sees as worth supporting as part of the public good, as integral to the development
of its citizens. This is an essay about the public, as well as personal,
meaning of a second chance.

From Back to School: Why Everyone Deserves a Second Chance at
Education.

EDUCATIONAL QUALITY AND EQUALITY

Linda Darling-Hammond

Six decades after a unanimous Supreme Court found "separate, but equal" to be both unconstitutional and inherently unequal, huge disparities remain that hamper opportunity for poor and minority children.

Of all the civil rights for which the world has struggled and fought for 5,000 years, the right to learn is undoubtedly the most fundamental. . . . The freedom to learn . . . has been bought by bitter sacrifice. And whatever we may think of the curtailment of other civil rights, we should fight to the last ditch to keep open the right to learn, the right to have examined in our schools not only what we believe but what we do not believe; not only what our leaders say, but what the leaders of other groups and nations, and the leaders of other centuries have said. We must insist upon this to give our children the fairness of a start which will equip them with such an array of facts and such an attitude toward truth that they can have a real chance to judge what the world is, and what its greater minds have thought it might be.

—*W.E.B. Du Bois,* The Freedom to Learn

Universal access to high-quality, intellectually empowering education for all citizens has long been a struggle.

Brown v. Board of Education was decided in 1954. Today the gaps in educational achievement between white and non-Asian minority students remain large, and the differences in access to educational opportunities are growing. Many students in the United States, especially low-income students and students of color, do not receive even the minimum education needed to become literate and join the labor market.

This is increasingly problematic, as the knowledge economy we now face demands higher levels of education from all citizens: about 70 percent of current U.S. jobs require specialized skill and training beyond high school, yet only about 75 to 80 percent of high school students graduate and only about 25 percent complete college.

Those who are undereducated can no longer access the labor market. While the United States must fill many of its high-tech jobs with individuals educated overseas, a growing share of its own citizens are unemployable and relegated to the welfare or prison systems. The nation can ill afford to maintain the structural inequalities in access to knowledge and resources that produce persistent and profound barriers to educational opportunity for large numbers of its students.

International studies continue to confirm that the U.S. educational system not only lags behind most other industrialized countries in mathematics and science achievement by high school but also allocates more unequal inputs and produces more unequal outcomes than its peer nations.

In contrast to European and Asian nations, which fund schools centrally and equally, the wealthiest U.S. school districts spend nearly ten times more than the poorest, and spending ratios of three to one are common within states.

These disparities reinforce the wide inequalities in income among families, with the most resources being spent on children from the wealthiest communities and the fewest on the children of the poor, especially in high-minority communities. This reality creates the disparities in educational outcomes that plague the United States and ultimately weaken the nation.

From the time southern states made it illegal to teach an enslaved person to read, throughout the nineteenth century and into the twentieth, African Americans, Native Americans, and, frequently, Mexican Americans faced de facto and de jure exclusion from public schools throughout the nation and experienced much lower quality education.

These disparities have continued. In 1991, Jonathan Kozol's *Savage Inequalities* described the stark differences between segregated urban schools and their suburban counterparts, which generally spent twice as much: places like Goudy Elementary School, which served an African American student population in Chicago, using "15-year-old textbooks in which Richard Nixon is still president" and "no science labs, no art or music teachers . . . [and] two working bathrooms for some 700 children," in contrast with schools in the neighboring town of New Trier (more than 98 percent white), where students had access to "superior labs . . . up-to-date technology . . . seven gyms [and] an Olympic pool."

More than a decade later, school spending in New Trier, at nearly $15,000 per student, still far exceeded the $8,500 per student available in Chicago for a population with many more special needs. Nationwide, many cities spend only half of what their wealthier suburbs can spend.

Recent analyses of data prepared for school finance cases in Alabama, California, Massachusetts, New Jersey, New York, Louisiana, South Carolina, and Texas have found that on every tangible measure—from qualified teachers and class sizes to textbooks, computers, facilities, and curriculum offerings—schools serving large numbers of students of color have significantly fewer resources than schools serving mostly white students. This description of one San Francisco school serving African American and Latino students was typical of others in the California complaint.

> At Luther Burbank, students cannot take textbooks home for homework in any core subject because their teachers have enough textbooks for use in class only. . . .
>
> For homework, students must take home photocopied pages, with no accompanying text for guidance or reference, when and if their teachers have enough paper to use to make homework copies. . . . Luther

Burbank is infested with vermin and roaches and students routinely see mice in their classrooms. One dead rodent has remained, decomposing, in a corner in the gymnasium since the beginning of the school year. The school library is rarely open, has no librarian, and has not recently been updated.

The latest version of the encyclopedia in the library was published in approximately 1988. Luther Burbank classrooms do not have computers. Computer instruction and research skills are not, therefore, part of Luther Burbank students' regular instruction. The school no longer offers any art classes for budgetary reasons. . . . Two of the three bathrooms at Luther Burbank are locked all day, every day. . . . Students have urinated or defecated on themselves at school because they could not get into an unlocked bathroom. . . . When the bathrooms are not locked, they often lack toilet paper, soap, and paper towels, and the toilets frequently are clogged and overflowing. . . . Ceiling tiles are missing and cracked in the school gym, and schoolchildren are afraid to play basketball and other games in the gym because they worry that more ceiling tiles will fall on them during their games.

Luther Burbank, like the schools described by Kozol, represents a growing number of "apartheid" schools that serve low-income racial and ethnic minority students exclusively in settings that are extraordinarily impoverished. In California, for example, many such schools are so severely overcrowded that they run a multitrack schedule offering a shortened school day and school year; lack basic textbooks and materials; do not offer the courses students would need to be eligible for college; and are staffed by a parade of untrained, inexperienced, and temporary teachers.

Such profound inequalities in resource allocations are supported by the increasing resegregation of schools over the decades of the 1980s and 1990s. In 2000, 72 percent of the nation's black students attended predominantly minority schools, up significantly from the low point of 63 percent in 1980. The proportion of students of color in intensely segregated schools also increased. More than a third of African American and Latino students (37 percent and 38 percent, respectively) attended schools with a minority enrollment of 90 to 100 percent. Furthermore, for all groups except whites, racially segregated schools are almost always schools with high concentrations of poverty. Nearly two-thirds of African American and Latino students attend schools where most students are eligible for free or reduced-price lunch.

Not only do funding systems and other policies create a situation in which urban districts receive fewer resources than their suburban neighbors, but schools with high concentrations of students of color receive fewer resources than other schools within these districts. And tracking systems exacerbate these inequalities by segregating many students of color within schools, allocating still fewer educational opportunities to them at the classroom level. As I describe below, these compounded inequalities explain much of the achievement gap that has often been attributed to genetic differences in intelligence or child-rearing practices or a "culture of poverty," rather than to the distribution of opportunity itself.

THE ACHIEVEMENT GAP

During the years following *Brown v. Board of Education*, when desegregation and early efforts at school finance reform were launched and the Great Society's War on Poverty increased investments in urban and poor rural schools, substantial gains were made in equalizing both educational inputs and outcomes. Gaps in school spending, access to qualified teachers, and access to higher education were smaller in the mid- to late 1970s than they had been before and, in many states, than they have been since. In the mid-1970s college-going rates were actually equivalent for a short period of time for white, black, and Hispanic students.

The gains from the Great Society programs were later pushed back. Most targeted federal programs supporting investments in college access and K–12 schools in urban and poor rural areas were reduced or eliminated in the 1980s. Meanwhile, childhood poverty rates, homelessness, and lack of access to health care also grew. Thus, it is no surprise that gaps in achievement began to widen again after the mid-1980s and have, in many areas, continued to grow in the decades since.

From All Things Being Equal: Instigating Opportunity in an Inequitable Time, *ed. Brian D. Smedley and Alan Jenkins.*

HEALTH CARE INEQUALITY

HEALTH AND INCOME INEQUALITIES ARE LINKED

Richard Wilkinson

People in countries with large inequality of income live shorter, more stressful lives, a British epidemiologist explains.

The United States, despite being richer and spending far more per person on medical care than any other country, comes in about twenty-fifth in the international rankings of life expectancy: it performs worse than most other developed countries. The most likely reason for its low health standards is that it is the most unequal of the developed countries. Britain's position in the international rankings of life expectancy also slipped when income differences widened during the last quarter of the twentieth century.

Differences among the rich developed countries are no longer related to the absolute standard of living and level of income.

The so-called diseases of affluence reversed their social distributions and became the diseases of the poor in affluent societies. Neither among the richest countries nor among the U.S. states is there much evidence of a relation between even twofold differences in real living standards and the life expectancy of the population. Yet within each of them there are large health inequalities related to relative income and social status. As the effects of absolute poverty have weakened, the social effects of relative deprivation have been unmasked and exposed to attention.

A tendency for health standards to be associated with absolute living standards has been replaced by an association with relative standards. Death rates in administrative areas of Taiwan were related to gross national product per capita in 1976. But in 1995, after life had been transformed by twenty years of extremely rapid economic growth, that relationship had weakened and been replaced by a different pattern. Instead of death rates being lowest in the areas with the highest incomes, the lowest death rates were in the areas with the smallest income differences.

We should probably think of income distribution in societies as a measure of the extent of social-class differentiation among the population. As a result, the number of excess deaths associated with health inequalities could be reduced, and average life expectancy for the society as a whole may be higher if we reduced inequality.

Some of the strongest associations between income distribution and health come from analyses of data for areas within the United States. Numerous studies have reported a close relationship between income distribution and age-adjusted death rates in the fifty states. The most egalitarian states, rather than the richest, are healthiest. The fact that average incomes in some states are twice as high as in others is unrelated to death rates.

Although the relationships between inequality and health have been shown at all ages, they seem to be strongest among men of working age. Interestingly, this is also the group in which health inequalities are usually largest, suggesting that income inequality and health inequalities are closely linked.

Death rates are lower in states in which income differences are smaller. The measure of income distribution used here is the proportion of societies' total income received by the poorest half of the population.

Inequalities in the distribution of market income (that is, income before the deduction of taxes or the addition of benefits) do seem to explain why some Canadian cities are healthier than others. The effect of inequality also shows up clearly among American cities. There is a slight tendency for the poorest cities to have higher death rates, but the really striking pattern is for the more unequal cities, which have higher death rates than the more equal ones.

Canadian public-health researchers Nancy Ross and Jim Dunn

put together data for 528 cities in five countries for which data were available on a comparable basis: Australia, Canada, Sweden, the United States, and the United Kingdom.

They found a striking tendency for death rates to be higher in cities where there is more inequality. The relationship appears consistent across all the cities, from the most unhealthy and unequal American ones to the healthiest and most egalitarian Swedish and Australian cities. The ordering is clear among the U.S. cities considered on their own, as it is among the British cities on their own. Two earlier analyses, using very different methods and data, also showed that income inequality and death rates are related among the 370 or so local government administrative areas of England.

Also, in the developed market democracies, obesity has been found to be related to inequality, and an analysis of data for the twenty regions of Italy has found a close relationship between the extent of income inequality and average life expectancy in each region.

DEVELOPING COUNTRIES

Analyses of international data from both richer and poorer countries have focused particularly on infant mortality. Robert Waldmann, using World Bank data on income inequality from seventy countries around 1970, found that after controlling for gross national product per capita, infant death rates were higher for more unequal countries. New Zealand public-health researcher Simon Hales and colleagues confirmed this using more recent data. For all levels of economic development, infant mortality rates tend to be lower in more egalitarian countries.

In the earliest of all the analyses of inequality and health, British epidemiologist G.B. Rodgers found relationships with death rates over a wide range of ages among a small number of richer and poorer countries.

A large number of studies have now reported empirical relationships between inequality and various health measures. Most of these relationships are statistically too strong to occur by chance alone more than one in a hundred times, or even one in a thousand times. We have seen that relationships have been reported among the fifty American states and 282 metropolitan areas of the United

States, among 528 cities in five developed countries, within cities in Britain and in Canada, regions of Russia, counties of Chile, and in areas of Brazil, Taiwan, and Italy.

This is powerful evidence that inequality of income and health are related.

Adapted from The Impact of Inequality: How to Make Sick Societies Healthier.

UNEQUAL QUALITY OF CARE

Mary E. O'Brien

Income plays a major role in determining the quality of health care people get, attests a doctor who volunteers annually in the Mississippi Delta.

Every summer I volunteer in the Tutwiler Clinic in the Mississippi Delta, one of the poorest areas in the country. For the Catholic nuns who operate the clinic, treatment never depends on payment; the nuns make ends meet through Medicare, Medicaid, the occasional insurance reimbursement, and charity. The quality of care is extraordinarily high by any standard, yet here the inequities of our health care system are dramatic. The starkest example of these inequities is the fact that many of my patients at the clinic simply have no expectation of being healthy as adults. They are poor and historically have not had access to qualified, caring doctors.

One Monday morning I arrived to find a muscular, middle-aged man waiting outside the clinic door, holding his ear and in obvious pain. He said he just wanted ear drops because he had to get to work or he'd lose a day's pay. When I examined his ear it was apparent he had a severe infection in his ear canal and outer ear. This condition is rarely seen in healthy people, but is a clear sign of uncontrolled diabetes. His blood sugar was five times normal, and it would have to be controlled before his ear infection would even respond to antibiotics. His blood pressure was sky high and he had a fever.

I explained all of this to him and urged him to go to the hospital in Clarksdale for immediate hospitalization. He looked at me as if I had two heads. "Sorry, Ma'am, but I just want drops for the ear and I'll go back to work. My boss is going to be angry because I'm late right now." Over the past few months he had lost about ten pounds and was constantly thirsty, two common signs of diabetes. He had attributed his weight loss and thirstiness to hard farm work in the hot Mississippi sun. He hadn't seen a doctor in years and had no idea that he had dangerously high blood pressure and diabetes. Although he had worked on the same plantation for twenty years and was now a foreman, he had neither health insurance nor an allowance for sick time. As to my suggestion of going to the hospital in Clarksdale, he flatly refused to consider it.

Over the next few hours at the clinic we gave him intravenous fluids and insulin to start bringing down his blood sugar for the ear infection. He agreed to come back twice a day, before and after work, to get insulin and IV antibiotics and to learn how to treat his diabetes and high blood pressure.

By the end of the week he looked much better. The clinic had provided all of his medicines and his treatment free. I'm sure that if his unbearably painful ear had not forced him to come to the clinic he would have collapsed working in the fields, another casualty of our inadequate health care system. It is estimated that at least 22,000 (and possibly more than 100,000) people die in the United States each year because they do not have health insurance and access to care.

This small clinic can serve only a tiny fraction of the residents of the Delta, most of whom are in desperate need of medical attention. But it offers a vision of the high-quality medical care that could be delivered to all residents of the United States if a single-payer health program were adopted, one that guarantees access to highly skilled clinicians without charge.

What are the essential elements that are necessary for high-quality health care, and how would a national health care system achieve this?

ACCESS

Quality of health care has little meaning if millions are unable to access care in the first place. We all need to be able to see a doctor when we are sick, so guaranteed and automatic health care coverage from birth to death is a must. This coverage must include not only care for illnesses and injuries but also preventive care, mental health care, medications, dental care, and long-term care.

This concept of access to health care is so important that in 2008 the American Cancer Society committed its entire $15 million advertising budget to promoting universal health care. Its chief executive, John R. Seffrin, said, "If we don't fix the health care system, that lack of access will be a bigger cancer killer than tobacco. The ultimate control of cancer is as much a public policy issue as it is a medical and scientific issue."

Those diagnosed with colon cancer who are uninsured have a 70 percent greater chance of dying within three years. Uninsured women diagnosed with breast cancer suffer an almost 50 percent higher risk of premature death. Halfway measures such as free screening for cancer offer little comfort to the uninsured or underinsured who realize that they will not be able to afford the high cost of treatment.

A SINGLE STANDARD OF EXCELLENT CARE

Whom would you point to who does not deserve equal high-quality care? The only way to create an equal opportunity to get high-quality health care is to have a single, comprehensive health care plan for all. This means no bare-bones plans whose high deductibles and co-pays effectively exclude us from health care. If the health care system treats all of us equally, then the most powerful among us will make sure that this is a top-notch system.

Our current system compromises the health care of all of us, insured and uninsured alike. Take the example of the severe overcrowding in hospital emergency rooms. Half of U.S. emergency rooms report daily overcrowding, with that number climbing to two-thirds of urban emergency rooms. This can result in vital delays in treatment, while overworked staff struggle to handle all of the patients. More than half a million ambulances are diverted to less crowded emergency rooms each year in the United States, delaying lifesaving care for the critically ill.

In many areas of the country, specially staffed and equipped trauma centers have closed because they are not profitable, forcing patients to lose those initial critical minutes of care that are so often vital in saving lives. Three-quarters of hospitals have difficulty finding specialists to take emergency or trauma calls. And despite all the rhetoric about preparedness, our overcrowded and underfunded emergency care system is ill prepared to respond to a major disaster—be it a natural one, a disease outbreak, or a terrorist attack.

CHOICE AND QUALITY OF CARE

We need to have free choice of doctors and hospitals, without being restricted by a managed-care plan or a constantly changing list of in-network providers—or being denied nonemergency care entirely for being uninsured. It is ironic that opponents of national health care cite their fears that Americans would lose freedom of choice under a national plan. Exactly the opposite would be true. With universal access and comprehensive coverage, free choice would be guaranteed. Closely related to this is the need for continuity of care, or what is sometimes referred to as a medical home, where a team of health care professionals including doctors, nurse-practitioners, and nurses knows us and our medical problems, takes care of us appropriately and efficiently, and advocates for the best medical care without any financial conflict of interest. Our care could also be coordinated when we see specialists or are hospitalized, and the number of medical errors caused by poor communication would be reduced.

The quality of health care and the outcome of different treatments must be measured and monitored so we can constantly fine tune and improve health care. But that is impossible in our current private system. The for-profit health insurance companies don't study the health or health outcomes of their clients in order to improve their services. Far from it. They monitor those who are sick and expensive to care for and try to exclude or drop them from their plans. In fact, it may surprise you to learn that almost all of the population data we have on the effectiveness of different medical treatments and outcomes come from our government-sponsored public health care programs—Medicare, Medicaid, and the Veterans Administration system.

Under a unified single-payer health care system there would be far greater accountability because we would have medical treatment and health outcomes data for everyone and we could better study and determine effective medical practice. We could monitor physician competency on a nationwide basis and identify the outliers providing poor care.

We rely on the competency of our doctors, but our current fragmented system renders it impossible to track a doctor's performance at an accepted medical standard. A good electronic medical record system could improve a doctor's practice through reminders for recommended screening (like Pap smears, mammograms, and cholesterol checks), guidelines for chronic-disease management, and alerts for drug interactions or improper doses of drugs. It could also detect practitioners who are far off the mark for appropriate medical care, something our current system has failed at miserably.

ELECTRONIC MEDICAL RECORDS

There is no doubt in anyone's mind—whether they be in big business, the medical establishment, or the highest levels of government—that a unified secure electronic medical records system must be created. Indeed, every major Democratic presidential candidate has made an electronic medical records system a cornerstone of his or her health care reform package. However, the overarching question is whether such a program can be realized without a single-payer health care delivery system. Already Microsoft, Google, and Texas Instruments have launched or are about to launch competing electronic medical records systems. It is obvious and predictable that a multiplicity of electronic medical records delivery systems will evolve and the important characteristics of the Veterans

Administration's medical records system—unified, affordable, and readily available—will disappear.

What we need is a system that scrupulously guards our medical privacy and confidentiality while affording health care professionals immediate access to a patient's medical history. Consider the case of a veteran who receives regular treatment at a veterans' hospital in New York. If the veteran were to suffer a heart attack or a life-threatening emergency while visiting relatives in Southern California, that vet could enter the nearest veterans' hospital, whose medical staff could have access to this vet's entire medical history within seconds, allowing them to proceed to the most informed course of treatment. The veterans' hospital system has in place a unified electronic medical records system that links all of its hospitals. This was invaluable after Hurricane Katrina, when thousands of veterans from New Orleans and surrounding areas sought health care at Veterans Administration facilities throughout the country. Nothing comparable would be possible in our present diffuse and fragmented health care system.

From a public-health standpoint, such a unified computerized database would permit early detection of epidemics like a severe flu season and allow prompt immunization to better control it. It would allow careful tracking of the incidence of cancer, heart disease, and depression so we could better study these chronic illnesses and allocate resources appropriately.

We need to combine the information from an electronic national database with strategic thinking to improve our systems for delivering health care more efficiently and cost effectively, while always having quality as our primary goal.

HEALTH PLANNING

Among the many benefits that would flow naturally from eliminating for-profit health-insurance companies and financial conflicts of interest would be a clear assessment and allocation of resources—to eliminate expensive redundancy of hospital and radiology facilities and to regionalize specialty surgery in accord with the knowledge that hospitals with a high volume of surgery have better proficiency and patient outcomes than hospitals with low volume. More focus could also be given to preventive health care.

PATIENT-PHYSICIAN RELATIONSHIP

At the heart of excellent health care is a patient's trusting and on-going relationship with a personal primary-care physician. A recent international study by the Commonwealth Fund showed that having a "medical home," where you have a regular doctor who knows your medical history, is easy to reach by phone during business hours, and will coordinate your care with other physicians or hospitals, is associated with more comprehensive and cost-effective care as well as greater patient satisfaction.

Clinicians need to have the time to listen carefully and respectfully to a patient's problems to determine appropriate, cost-effective treatment. The pressure on doctors to see patients in ten- to fifteen-minute appointments ultimately saves neither time nor money and leads to increasing frustration and medical errors.

A number of years ago I saw an elderly woman in a neighborhood clinic who had no regular doctor but had seen several different doctors over the past year, each of whom had added new and more potent medicines in order to control her blood pressure. She had lots of side effects from these medications, but her blood pressure remained dangerously high. She assured me that she took all of her medicines religiously and she denied adding any salt to her food. I asked her to describe in detail her actual meals: for breakfast, bacon and eggs; for lunch, canned soup; and for dinner, canned beans and rice. It turned out that she was getting a huge amount of salt in her diet that overwhelmed her medicines. She agreed to try to eliminate canned foods, and over several weeks her blood pressure was easily controlled with only two medications.

By my taking some extra time to explore her diet and then to educate her to the danger of ingesting large volumes of salt through prepared foods and to explain how her medicines operated in lowering her blood pressure, she was able to understand her high blood pressure and to take an active role in controlling it. If physicians are compelled to treat their patients at an assembly-line rate, too many subtle or complicated diseases will go unnoticed. Only a system dedicated to the optimal care of the patient—versus the optimum profits of insurance companies—will afford doctors the time that is needed to explore and diagnose thoroughly and competently. A single-payer system is the moral and economic answer to our current health care crisis.

Adapted from 10 Excellent Reasons for National Health Care.

REDUCING HEALTH CARE DISPARITIES

Olveen Carrasquillo and Jaime Torres

Racism pervades the provision of health care in America with severe consequences, as these authors show.

Disparities in health-insurance coverage must be addressed as an important first step toward eliminating the health care disparities that disproportionately affect the economically disadvantaged and people of color. Examples of such health care disparities include the black infant-mortality rate, which at 13.6 infant deaths per 1,000 live births is double that of non-Hispanic whites (NHWs) at 5.7. Another example is diabetes; 13 percent of Hispanics and 15 percent of black adults have diabetes versus 8 percent of NHWs.

The causes of these health disparities are complex and multifactorial and include issues related to the environment, poverty, housing, education, health behaviors, and even segregation and discrimination. Another important contributor to these health care disparities is the difference in quality of the health care received by racial or ethnic minorities versus that of NHWs. Examples of these health care disparities include blacks' receiving fewer bypass surgeries and kidney transplants than NHWs. Although blacks are one and a half times more likely to die from heart disease than whites, the rate of bypass surgery among whites was 9 per 1,000 versus 4 per 1,000 among blacks in 2001. Similarly, while over 50 percent of NHWs have received age-appropriate colorectal cancer screening, only 35 percent of Asians and Hispanics have had such tests.

In 1999, Congress commissioned the Institute of Medicine (IOM) to produce an in-depth report on health care disparities. The charge was to examine the existence of disparities that were not due to known factors such as health-insurance coverage and ability to pay. What the IOM found was that even after accounting for insurance, members of racial and ethnic minorities received lower-quality health care than NHWs. Yet, as this landmark report points out, disentangling the impact of known causes of disparities, such as access to affordable health insurance, from broader economic and social inequities is an "artificial and difficult distinction."

The IOM noted that while disparities in access to affordable quality health care are "likely the most significant barrier to equitable care," other factors such as bias, discrimination, and negative racial stereotypes are also important barriers to equitable care. Additional contributors to health care disparities included cultural and linguistic barriers, lack of a stable primary-care clinician, and fragmentation of the health care system.

The annual statistics published by the Census Bureau portray a dismal picture of health-insurance coverage among minorities. The data show that one-third of Latinos in the United States lack health-insurance coverage and 20 percent of both blacks and Asians in the United States are uninsured as well. In contrast, only 10 percent of NHWs are uninsured. Further, from 1987 to 2005, the proportion of the uninsured population in the United States that is minority has increased from 42 percent to 53 percent.

Among Latinos and Asians, the most vulnerable are immigrants. Over half of noncitizen Latinos and nearly a third of noncitizen Asians in the United States lack health coverage. It is also estimated that nearly 80 percent of undocumented immigrants lack insurance. However, even U.S.-born Latinos (over 60 percent of all Latinos are U.S. born) are twice as likely as NHWs to lack coverage.

Thus, immigration status by itself does not explain a large proportion of the disparities in health coverage between minorities and NHWs in the United States.

MEDICAL APARTHEID IN THE UNITED STATES

In the absence of a system of universal health care, a multi-tier health care system has developed in the United States, one that results in what can be described as health care segregation. In the highest tier are those who have private insurance coverage, usually through their employer or Medicare. These insurance programs are widely accepted by physicians and hospitals.

At the other end are the uninsured. In theory, they can pay for their health care services out of pocket. In reality, as most of the uninsured are either poor or middle class, they often forgo necessary care. Their alternative is to rely on a safety-net patchwork of providers, including community health centers, outpatient departments of public and some not-for-profit hospitals, and emergency rooms. While an important source of care for the uninsured, such patched-together systems are a far cry from the care received by privately insured and Medicare populations. In particular, access to subspecialty care and a stable source of outpatient medications are major barriers to care in these safety-net systems. While 85 percent of NHWs in this country belong to the highest tier of health care, only 63 percent of blacks and 50 percent of Hispanics belong to this top tier of access. Further, while racial and ethnic minorities make up less than a third of the U.S. population, over half of all persons in this lowest tier of health care are minorities.

In the middle tier are those covered through the various insurance programs serving the poor such as Medicaid and the State Children's Health Insurance Programs (SCHIP). These programs are critical components of the health care safety net and cover 40 million children and adults. Unfortunately, as is true for most other poverty programs, they suffer chronic underfunding and applicants face onerous eligibility and recertification requirements. In some states, over half of all persons who enroll are disenrolled in under a year. Further, when facing budgetary difficulties, limiting enrollment in these programs or rationing health care services through cutbacks of services covered is a favorite ploy of many legislators. Thus, for many enrollees, such programs are a far cry from the comprehensive, ongoing health care access that persons in the first tier enjoy.

The real reason that these underfunded programs are segregated is that in most states providers are paid at levels much lower than Medicare. As an example, in New York a private physician can be paid six times more to see a patient with Medicare versus Medicaid. As a result, fewer than half of all providers nationally choose to accept Medicaid patients. In many localities, this forces most Medicaid patients to receive care through the same network of safety-net clinics that exist for the uninsured. Further, access to subspecialty care in these settings is often as problematic as it is with the uninsured. In one large hospital in New York City, the wait for a Medicaid patient to see a gastroenterologist is eight months. In contrast, a patient with Medicare could be seen within two weeks in the private offices that are part of the same medical center but do not accept Medicaid patients. The government also reinforces this segregated system of care, because it provides additional subsidies or grants for designated safety-net providers and clinics to see Medicaid patients but does not make such funds available to providers in private practice. This segregationist system is quite effective at ensuring that those in the first tier receive a different level of care from those in the second and third tiers. A report by one advocacy coalition, Bronx Reach Coalition, extensively described this system of segregated care and unequal access faced by poor and predominantly minority patients as "Medical Apartheid."

Among the report's conclusions were that people who are uninsured or publicly insured (through Medicaid, Medicaid Managed Care, Family Health Plus, and Child Health Plus) are often cared for in separate institutions from those who are privately insured. The coalition also found that even within health care institutions, separate and unequal systems of care exist. The uninsured, people covered by Medicaid, and sometimes even those enrolled in Medicaid Managed Care, Family Health Plus, and Child Health

Plus receive poorer care in different locations, at different times, and by less trained physicians than those who are privately insured. Finally, the report shows that when patients are sorted according to their insurance status, this segregated care leads to different health outcomes.

Under a comprehensive national health-insurance plan, a wealthy NHW male would have the same level of coverage as a low-income black female. Detractors claim that this one-size-fits-all approach is not consistent with American values and that individuals should have the freedom to choose the level and quality of health care they wish to receive. However, such detractors have a hard time identifying persons who would want to receive low-quality health care. Clearly, under the mantra of choice, it would be minorities who would disproportionately be stuck in the lowest levels of health care. From a perspective of basic fairness, it is clear that having one system of care in which access to high-quality health care would be a right of all is far superior to one in which quality of coverage is determined by income.

DOES EVERYONE IN AND NO ONE OUT INCLUDE ALL IMMIGRANTS?

Immigrants contribute tens of billions of dollars to our economy, and the sustainability of programs such as Social Security and Medicare to a significant extent depends on taxes paid by such workers. Further, health costs for immigrants are about one-third those of NHWs. Ethical, religious, and humane issues could all be raised to support improving access to care for such immigrants. However, the main reason all immigrants would be included in national health insurance (NHI) is financial. Not only are immigrants relatively inexpensive to cover, but to exclude them would mean maintenance of very expensive administrative systems of billing and indirect and inefficient safety-net reimbursement mechanisms. Simply put, NHI would be much more costly if a system needs to be maintained to exclude 12 million undocumented persons. Thus, comprehensive coverage of all residents of the United States would be far more humane and less costly.

POLITICAL AND ORGANIZATIONAL SUPPORT FOR NHI AMONG MINORITIES

Since NHI is the only proposal for universal coverage that would ensure equitable high-quality health care for all, it has long been supported by the Congressional Black Caucus. Over half the members of the Congressional Hispanic Caucus also support HR 676. NHI also enjoys support among large minority medical groups such as the National Medical Association and the National Hispanic Medical Association. In response, the strategy favored by the insurance and pharmaceutical industries has been to partner with minority political leaders and organizations on other important disparities issues such as workforce diversity, cultural competency, and language barriers—but not on NHI. By lavishing groups with funding for other initiatives, these opponents of single payer hope not only to gain the goodwill of these political leaders and organizations but also to divert advocacy on behalf of NHI. Fortunately, so far this approach has had limited success, with the majority of minority leaders and organizations remaining strong advocates of NHI.

Will NHI end disparities? No. Health disparities are an extremely complex and multifaceted problem that has long plagued our society. As we've said earlier, disparities in health are due to a variety of factors—including environment, housing, poverty, education, and racism—that go far beyond just having insurance. Indeed, even in countries that have universal coverage, the wealthy and privileged enjoy better health status and find ways to receive better access to care than those in poverty. However, the magnitude of health care disparities in those countries is significantly less than in the United States. Many of us believe that once we have enacted a system of equitable, comprehensive coverage for all, we can then focus on addressing other important issues. These include ensuring a health care workforce whose diversity is reflective of our society, health care providers who are culturally and linguistically competent to provide care to persons from a wide variety of racial and ethnic backgrounds, and a health care delivery system that is free of the many racial and ethnic biases and stereotypes that plague our society. But since disparities in access to quality health care are a major contributor to disparities in health, health insurance is the key driver of many health care disparities, and efforts to address disparities must start with the most glaring and obvious factor.

Adapted from 10 Excellent Reasons for National Health Care.

UNIVERSAL HEALTH CARE

Leo W. Gerard

Profits would grow if health care were universal, the president of the most progressive industrial workers' union shows.

Today the nation is faced with a private/public health care financing system that has left one-third of the American people with either inadequate health insurance or no coverage at all. Forty-nine percent of people with insurance tell pollsters they are somewhat or completely unprepared to cope with a costly medical emergency over the coming year.

Twenty-nine percent of people with underinsurance often postpone medical care because of costs, problems compounded by the fact that incomes have been relatively stagnant for active workers and are in decline for those on fixed incomes. Health-insurance premiums are going up while benefits are going down.

Four percent of middle-income families—those earning between $40,000 and $80,000 annually—lost employer-based health insurance between 2000 and 2005. Four percent may sound small, but it represents two million families. Half of those families lost their insurance because their employers abandoned health-insurance programs, another 15 percent because their premiums became unaffordable.

Union negotiators and health care program administrators have spent years pulling rabbits out of hats to compensate for the increasing costs of health care. Introducing generic drugs, preferred-provider organizations, as well as raising deductibles and co-pays have all been strategies developed to patch a collapsing system. Despite these "innovations," employers' costs of group health insurance rose from $331 billion in 2000 to $514 billion in 2005, or about 9 percent of total wage and salary costs.

Many of today's collective bargaining disputes are driven by health care costs.

Rather than joining labor to lobby for universal, affordable health care, private employers are abandoning financial responsibility for health care costs at the rate of about 5 percent per year, reducing the number of group-plan participants, driving down employee living standards, and further undermining private-sector health care financing. As employer definancing of health care continues unabated, the move to a national system will no longer be a choice; it will be a necessity in order to maintain any health care system whatsoever.

Employers increasingly point to the disadvantage they suffer when competing globally, especially companies operating in the many nations that have developed uniform, government-supported health care. In those nations, even where financing is derived from both private and public sources, administration of the system and guidelines for care have become publicly supported social services.

In the United States, where financial accounting standards require employers to carry their long-term liabilities for retiree health care on their balance sheets, unions are put in the unenviable but inevitable position of having to press demands for health care benefit coverage in bargaining not only for their existing dues-paying members but also for a considerable number of retirees. Especially in the industrial sectors of the economy, the number of retirees whose interests must be represented often far exceeds the number of active members, as was the case with United Steelworkers (USW) negotiations with the Goodyear Tire and Rubber Company and the United Automobile Workers negotiations with the auto industry.

It is little wonder, then, that in negotiations with these companies, unions have felt compelled by the twin goals of preserving and

securing retiree benefits and keeping employers competitive to negotiate Voluntary Employee Benefits Associations (VEBAs), trusts
funded by the companies and administered by boards of trustees
independent of the employer. Because their assets will be immune
from any potential bankruptcy of the employer, these VEBAs provide continuing and secured health care benefits for current and future retirees while lifting a significant body of health care liabilities
that employers are obliged to carry on their books. And their assets
can be increased through contributions negotiated in future contract
bargaining.

No competitor of General Motors or Goodyear elsewhere in the
industrialized world carries such liabilities or obligations, as all are
beneficiaries of health care subsidized by their governments in one
fashion or another. Only in the United States must these obligations
be secured through collective bargaining if workers and retirees are
to have any hope of receiving health care benefits. The value of securing such benefits is of course not lost on those workers who have
enjoyed health care coverage only to see it wiped out by their employers' bankruptcies.

CRUEL IRONY

That retired union members should be among those most victim-
ized by the nation's health care crisis is cruelly ironic, for the ori-
gins of America's current health care financing system are rooted
in labor-management collective-bargaining agreements forged
during World War II. Negotiators introduced enhanced health care
benefits as a reward for workers during a period when wage increases were restricted by war-policy measures. These benefits soon
became a standard part of employment compensation.

The result was a stable financial base for the growth and improvement of health care systems across the nation. Communities
had money for hospitals and infrastructure. The medical profession
was able to upgrade its capabilities, do more research, and profes-
sionalize care. Financing was handled by a growing private insurance industry that was dominated by nonprofit-style carriers.

There was another, less noticed outcome of America's health care
evolution. Health care professionals began to enjoy a new upper-
middle-class status, and health-insurance executives became in-

creasingly acquisitive as they gained control of significant pools of health-insurance reserves. Eventually a system that had been non-profit in character morphed into a for-profit enterprise, with costs spiraling out of control as the health-insurance industry became concerned with the bottom line rather than providing a real health care benefit to working Americans.

Rife with inefficiency and shaped by the drive for profit and ex-orbitant executive compensation, the private financing system is inherently ill equipped to provide equitable health care for all of America's population, let alone to continue to provide it afford-ably to workers with a union contract. As the costs of care have increased, often much more rapidly than the rate of inflation, the deficiencies of a system that relies disproportionately on employer-based financing have become more apparent.

The inefficiency and rising costs of the American health care system have ripple effects throughout the economy, affecting not only unions but all Americans. Health care costs impede efforts to reverse the United States' massive trade deficits, which are further eroding competitiveness and well-paying jobs. Our product and service costs are driven up by the refusal to implement an efficient health care system. Some estimates cite the waste in our health care system as representing as much as 7 percent of the nation's produc-tive capacity (gross domestic product). Since we are a debtor nation, these costs flow directly into the national debt and further weaken our national financial strength.

The best face that can be put on the unwillingness of corpo-rate executives to abandon our broken system in favor of universal health care is their misbegotten belief that the current system can be stabilized enough to make the costs amenable to effective busi-ness planning. Yet, in reality, as things stand today, businesses have no leverage whatsoever over either quality or price. Their only "con-trol" is over the amount of coverage they will pay for—an approach they all too frequently default to in contract negotiations.

A national single-payer system would relieve corporations of the burden of health-insurance administration, stabilize costs, and give corporations the global level playing field they want. Businesses can play a major role in solving the health care dilemma, therefore, by overcoming their blind resistance to a national system and insisting instead that a national plan be designed that provides their employees with proper coverage without runaway costs. Universal coverage through a single-payer system offers the best hope of achieving these goals.

Adapted from 10 Excellent Reasons for National Health Care.

U.S. HEALTH CARE COSTS THE MOST—
BY FAR

David Cay Johnston

America spends far more than any other modern country on health care yet alone lacks universal coverage. If America had in place the French system, which the World Health Organization says is the world's best, the savings in 2010 would have been enough to eliminate the federal income tax that year.

Here is how much America's health care system costs: in 2010 Americans spent $2.64 per person for health care for each dollar spent by the thirty-three other countries with modern economies. The United States spent $8,233 per capita compared with an average of $3,118 in the other thirty-three countries, according to data compiled by the Organization for Economic Cooperation and Development. And those are not simple currency transactions used to compare dollars: the OECD used PPEs (purchasing power equivalents) to get the best possible measure of relative costs.

A growing share of federal tax dollars, in direct spending and in tax breaks, is going to U.S. health care as the population ages. Yet while the thirty-three other modern countries provide universal care, about one in six Americans lacks health insurance and another one in ten is covered for only part of the year. America's health care system, more accurately described as a sick-care non-system, totaled 17.6 percent of the economy in 2010, compared to an average of 9.2 percent in the other thirty-three countries, the OECD data show.

Here is another way to think about the cost of health care. The World Health Organization says France has the best health care system in the world, while the United States ranks thirty-seventh. The French system cost 11.6 percent of its economy in 2010, six percentage points less than the 17.6 percent of the American economy devoted to health care.

How much is six percentage points of the American economy, the extra burden Americans bore compared to the French? In 2010 it was equal to almost the entire federal income tax, which came to 6.3 percent of American gross domestic product. In other words, all else being equal, if Americans had put the French system in place in 2010 they could have eliminated the federal income tax that year. In 2013 they could have eliminated about half of income taxes. That is just measuring the American costs that are above the French cost when measured as a share of the economy.

Now consider the total cost, public and private, of U.S. health care. It is significantly greater than the total of corporate and indi-

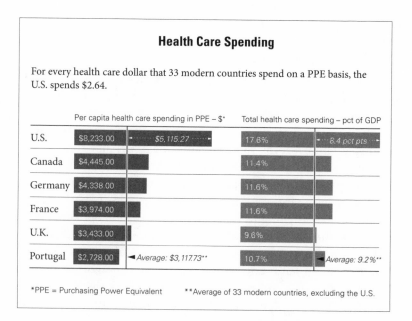

Health Care Spending

For every health care dollar that 33 modern countries spend on a PPE basis, the U.S. spends $2.64.

	Per capita health care spending in PPE – $*		Total health care spending – pct of GDP	
U.S.	$8,233.00	$5,115.27	17.6%	8.4 pct pts
Canada	$4,445.00		11.4%	
Germany	$4,338.00		11.6%	
France	$3,974.00		11.6%	
U.K.	$3,433.00		9.6%	
Portugal	$2,728.00	Average: $3,117.73**	10.7%	Average: 9.2%**

*PPE = Purchasing Power Equivalent   **Average of 33 modern countries, excluding the U.S.

vidual income taxes, as well as payroll taxes. For each dollar paid in all three of those taxes in 2010, health care came to $1.29.

Take a look at your pay stub to get an idea of the kind of money being spent on a system that fosters personal bankruptcy, bedevils small business, and leaves the United States ranked thirty-first among the thirty-four OECD countries in preventing premature death.

Capitol Hill Republicans say the federal government is "structurally and financially broken" and that "three programs—Medicare, Medicaid, and Social Security—account for over 40 percent of total spending." These costs, the GOP says, are "harming job creation and growth," while "projections of future spending growth are nothing short of catastrophic, both economically and socially." The Republicans offer what they say is a solution—a promise to "empower millions of seniors to control their personal health care decisions," a vow immediately followed by a promise to cut federal spending.

The clearest explanation of what that would mean comes from Representative Paul Ryan of Wisconsin, the 2012 Republican vice presidential nominee. Before he started obfuscating during the campaign, Ryan laid out his plans in detail. He boasted that by changing Medicare from a plan that provides treatment for every older American into one that gives seniors a fixed sum to buy their own health insurance, taxpayers would save through 2084 the present equivalent of $4.9 trillion. What Ryan proposes is to change Medicare from a defined-benefit plan into a defined-contribution plan, which is to say from whatever health care an older American needs to whatever he or she can afford on a fixed budget.

His plan would, for sure, save the net present equivalent of almost $5 trillion. What Ryan did not mention is that for each tax dollar his plan saves, older Americans would have to spend $8 out of pocket.

We know how Ryan's plan would raise total costs because of work by David Rosnick and Dean Baker, economists at the Center for Economic Policy and Research, which promotes government policies that it says would benefit workers and the poor. Rosnick and Baker applied the same formula that Ryan (or his staff) applied to the same Congressional Budget Office data not just for Medicare spending, but for private spending as well. For a long time, private health care costs have been rising faster than Medicare's.

It makes no sense to spend $8 out of pocket to save $1 in taxes. Beyond that, older people do not have the money to cover those higher costs. A tenth of Americans age seventy-five and older live below the official poverty line. Another 24 percent have only a tad more.

Every indicator shows that Americans do not have enough for their old age and that a shrinking number have pensions. Ryan and many other, but not all, Capitol Hill Republicans also say they want to cut future Social Security benefits, if not kill the program. So if older Americans have less income how would they cope with higher private medical costs? Ryan will not answer questions about that, but the answer is obvious: they will die sooner for lack of medical care.

Why would any Americans under age fifty-five, whose health care benefits Ryan wants to cut when they reach sixty-five, think they can afford to spend $8 to save $1 of tax? After withering criticism, Ryan softened his plan, saying those who wish to may stay in traditional Medicare. Anyone not rich who can count would stick with Medicare. That means Ryan's promised $4.9 trillion of taxpayer savings would never materialize. Alan Grayson, the combative one-term Democratic representative from Florida, got it right when he said on the House floor in 2009: "The Republican plan— don't get sick and if you do get sick, die quickly."

In the 2012 elections, the Democratic platform called for universal health care. "We will end the outrage of unaffordable, unavailable health care," it said, though that party promise remained unfulfilled for six decades. Indeed, President Nixon had agreed to universal health care back in the early 1970s, but union leaders put him off for a year, hoping for an even better deal, and ended up with nothing when the Watergate scandal consumed the White House.

President Barack Obama's Patient Protection and Affordable Care Act will enable those with preexisting conditions and twentysomethings without work to get health insurance starting in 2014. But the Obama plan does nothing to address the larger economic problem: American health care costs too much and needs replacement, not a nip and tuck.

Portugal, with half the income per person as America, provides universal health care for its citizens. Cuba, the CIA tells us, ranks fortieth in infant mortality, while the United States is nine steps lower at forty-ninth, an astonishing fact given U.S. spending compared to the poverty induced by Castro's collectivist economic policies.

Doing worse than Portugal and Cuba is not just costly, it is immoral. Americans should be ashamed that they rank behind Cuba in any measure of health care and quality. And they should be angry that they pay so much but get less than the rest of the modern world in quality and reach of care.

INEQUALITY KILLS

Stephen Bezruchka

For nearly two hundred years America was one of the healthiest coun-tries, but no more. A public health expert explains what changed and how we can make Americans healthier.

Around the time of the founding of the United States, it was one of the healthiest places in the world. Even though what we think of as quality health care or public health services were not around yet, the common cause of developing a nation pro-vided a strong sense of community and that solidarity proba-bly supported a relatively healthy population. Around 1900, the movement to get the fecal matter out of the water produced vast health improvements by reducing the risk of infectious disease. Rising living standards and public health improvements contin-ued so that by 1950, shared economic growth had produced "the good life" in America. At that time we were one of the world's longest-lived countries.

But something happened around 1970: the United States began focusing on the business of medical care, rather than on produc-ing health. This happened at the same time that income inequality started rising, a rise that has continued. The ranking of U.S. health in relation to other countries began to fall, until today, over thirty nations have better health by many measures than the United States. We've lost touch with the conditions that promote health and need to refocus on finding them.

What is health? For individuals the actual definition of health is difficult, although there are healthy ranges for measurements such as blood pressure, cholesterol, and body weight. However, for populations there are a number of well-accepted measures of health. Average length of life, or measures that include the quality of those years, as well as rates of death in infancy or childhood are commonly used and can be compared for different populations and countries. Mortality rates in general, describing the ages at which people are likely to die, are accepted designations of population health and correlate very highly with people's own descriptions of how healthy they are.

For a country like the United States, normal health status should be comparable to what the healthiest nations achieve. What is the relative health status of Americans? A good place to begin the discussion is a book issued in 2013, *U.S. Health in International Perspective: Shorter Lives, Poorer Health* by the U.S. Institute of Medicine (IOM). The institute was authorized in 1970 as a branch of the National Academy of Sciences to provide unbiased, science-based advice to decision makers and the public on matters of the nation's health. Today it has an annual budget of fifty million dollars and is headed by Harvey Fineberg, former provost of Harvard University and prior to that the dean of the Harvard School of Public Health. These facts suggest that the IOM is headed by a scholar who is recognized by academics of the highest order.

Fineberg summarized the basic message of the book in the foreword. "Americans die sooner and experience more illness than residents in many other countries," he wrote. "Americans with healthy behaviors or those who are white, insured, college-educated, or in upper-income groups appear to be in worse health than similar groups in comparison countries."

The comparison countries Finberg referred to were the other rich nations with comparable data. The IOM report and other data show that the United States has higher rates of deaths from heart attacks, motor-vehicle crashes, violence (especially firearm induced), and AIDS than the thirty other most developed countries. We are at the bottom of most lists that rank mortality levels among the wealthy countries, and worse off than some middle-income nations as well. This well-documented fact is quite unknown to the great bulk of Americans, who will suffer the consequences nonetheless.

Infant death rates, those occurring in the first year of life, are a particularly sensitive measure of health in a population. According to a U.S. Centers for Disease Control and Prevention report released in 2013, our infant mortality rate is about 6.1 deaths for every thousand live births. Sweden has an infant mortality rate less than half of ours, 2.1 deaths per thousand births. If we had Sweden's rate of infant deaths, the United States would have around forty-seven fewer infants dying every day in the United States. That is what is achievable: every day forty-seven babies wouldn't die if we had Sweden's rate of infant deaths.

Why do we rank so badly in health? The IOM report spends about 150 pages explaining the U.S. health disadvantage. The U.S. health care system was not, in a surprise to many, a focus of this explanation. Many of the usual measures of the success of a health care system are favorable in the United States, such as the observation that we have lower levels of cholesterol and blood pressure than people in many longer-lived countries. The United States also has higher rates of cancer screening and lower stroke mortality than other healthier rich nations.

Yet those successes of the health care system do not make us healthy. The most generous estimate of the impact of health care on the health of societies is on the order of 10 percent, and may well be less than that. As the IOM report suggests, we need look elsewhere to understand why we die so young in this country.

The report points out ways that the political system is linked to our relatively high infant mortality, those forty-seven babies wasted every day. They relate those deaths to our corporatist political system and actually point the finger at our media and advertising as being at least partly responsible.

The report concludes that while the American health care system is far from perfect, and is the subject of about 42 percent of all world health spending, its failings explain only a small part of the

U.S. health disadvantage. The same is true for our public health system of clinics and services to prevent or address specific problems. Fixing the health care system won't do it.

The distinction between health and health care is a critical one, but something that seems not to be well understood by the lay public, health care professionals, or policy makers. Every time we hear the word *health*, we should ask ourselves whether that term refers to health itself, or to the much more limited concept of health care. Making that distinction will help us find the road to health.

If the culprit is not health care, are individual health-related behaviors, often blamed for the high death rates in some groups, causing our low ranking in health? Apparently not. Americans smoke less than both men and women in the healthier countries, so tobacco, though important, is not a significant cause for our higher mortality. Diet and other similar individual behaviors prevalent in the United States also don't account for our health disadvantage compared to other rich nations.

When asked to identify solutions to our poor health status as a nation, many respond that we need more education. Many see education as the solution to a wide range of problems. But on average the U.S. population has more years of schooling than in any other country in the world. And while we spend a great deal of money on education, we don't get much bang for those bucks. The IOM report points out that reading, science, and mathematics outcomes for U.S. fifteen-year-olds are poor compared to other countries. Just as with health care, we spend a great deal on education and have little to show for it.

The IOM report presents appalling information about violence and firearm deaths in the United States. But although we have very high rates of violent deaths for young people compared to other rich nations, that risk is a sideshow, too. The violent deaths of children are terrible events, but if we count up, for example, all the school shootings, they average out to about ten deaths a year. However tragic for the individual families, youth violence is an insignificant cause of our relatively limited life spans.

The report also includes a long section on the factors for our high death rates. Among the main causes cited are poverty, income inequality, low social status, stress, epigenetics (factors on the genome telling your genes to switch on or off, speak loudly or whisper, that are influenced by a host of environmental factors broadly considered and are transmitted across generations), and early-life disadvantage. Although recent attention has been paid to the rising economic inequality in the United States, the links of that trend to our health have not been presented to the public. Those associations remain buried in academic research.

The life-course perspective in particular is out of the public eye. Looking more deeply into research on the effects of early life, it is possible to estimate that roughly half of our health as adults is programmed from the time of conception to around two years of age. The importance of these "first thousand days" is the subject of increased interest and study, and explains a lot about the difficulties of focusing on short-term interventions to improve health. Countries with healthier populations structure this formative period by making it easier for parents to parent. In practical terms, this means that in modern societies where most people work outside the home, providing paid parental leave is the single most effective social intervention that can be undertaken for improving health. It is can be thought of in the same light as public sanitation systems that make water safe to drink. We all benefit, rich and poor alike, from clean water, from sewage treatment, from immunizations and other public health measures.

Everyone in a society gains when children grow up to be healthy adults. The rest of the world seems to understand this simple fact, and only three countries in the world don't have a policy, at least on the books, for paid maternal leave—Liberia, Papua New Guinea, and the United States. What does that say about our understanding, or concern, about the health of our youth?

Differences in mortality rates are not just a statistical concern— they reflect suffering and pain for very real individuals and families. The higher mortality in the United States is an example of what Paul Farmer, the noted physician and anthropologist, calls structural violence. The forty-seven infant deaths occur every day because of the way society in the United States is structured, resulting in our health status being that of a middle-income country, not a rich country.

There is growing evidence that the factor most responsible for the relatively poor health in the United States is the vast and rising inequality in wealth and income that we not only tolerate, but resist changing. Inequality is the central element, the upstream cause of the social disadvantage described in the IOM report. A political system that fosters inequality limits the attainment of health.

The claim that economic inequality is a major reason for our poor health requires that several standard criteria for claiming causality are satisfied: the results are confirmed by many different studies by different investigators over different time periods; there is a dose-response relationship, meaning more inequality leads to worse health; no other contending explanation is posited; and the relationship is biologically plausible, with likely mechanisms through which inequality works. The field of study called stress biology of social comparisons is one such way inequality acts. Those studies confirm that all the criteria for linking inequality to poorer health are met, concluding that the extent of inequality in society reflects the range of caring and sharing, with more unequal populations sharing less. Those who are poorer struggle to be accepted in society and the rich also suffer its effects.

A recent Harvard study estimated that about one death in three in this country results from our very high income inequality. Inequality kills through structural violence. There is no smoking gun with this form of violence, which simply produces a lethally large social and economic gap between rich and poor.

If we face the grim reality of our failure to support the health of the public in the United States, it's critical to identify approaches to change the system that isn't working. The last part of the IOM report lays out ideas for what to do, saying that we know enough to act without requiring more research. Their call to action is the need to alert the public to our alarmingly low relative health status and stimulate a national discussion about it.

But who should lead that discussion? The report suggests that it should come from independent, nonpartisan, objective organizations. Who are those groups in the United States? Scientists clearly are not the best source of information, since a large proportion of the American public distrusts science, scientific bodies, and their knowledge. For example, despite clear scientific evidence, Americans are less likely than people in other rich countries to believe climate change is taking place. In one study, America had the smallest proportion of people believing in evolution among more than sixty countries reviewed.

Agnotologists—those who introduce ignorance into our scientific debates—have been hard at work creating a misinformed American public.

The corporate-dominated media seem oblivious to the impact of inequality and almost never point out our poor health status relative to other nations. A vast array of philanthropic and non-governmental organizations in the United States deals mostly with the symptoms of our sick society and not with the basic conditions causing the disease.

Creating awareness and understanding of the basic problems constraining our achievement of better health will be a major challenge. Americans as a people simply have not been good at evaluating information in a critical manner. A very successful ploy of advertisers is the endless repetition of simple statements that stick in people's minds. That process of "manufacturing consent" has been used widely in political spheres as well; a few years ago the widely repeated slogan "Iraq Has Weapons of Mass Destruction" had the public enraged, supporting the invasion of Iraq despite any evidence to support the accusation.

To save those forty-seven infant lives every day, we could take a similar action, and create a broken record to run throughout the entire range of public spheres, from local and county governments to the national administration, Congress, and the courts, with the message: "Americans Die Younger Than People in All the Other Rich Nations." If that statement were included in every speech made by governmental leaders and other public figures, repeated over and over, it might stimulate us to invade our own nation to improve its health status. Only widespread understanding of the problem we face will lead us to develop effective solutions.

The IOM report also discussed looking at healthier countries to see if some of their policies impacting health could be applicable here. The U.S. public is generally ignorant of some very good examples of "what can be done" among European countries. For those who recoil at the idea that we could learn anything from other countries, a look at our own not so distant history points out what Americans thought, and did, before we became so lethally unequal. In 1969 a Republican president proposed a Family Assistance Plan that would have guaranteed a basic income for all American families. Editorial opinion then was 95 percent in favor of such support to families. Our values at that time were to decry the poverty in our midst to try to make it vanish from the country. President Nixon's bill passed the House of Representatives, then languished in the Senate. When Nixon became embroiled in the Watergate scandal it died—along with a credible, feasible plan to strengthen the health of families in this country and prevent what was soon to become a relentless decline in our relative health.

We can return to those values and pledge to support healthy families. Let's leave that club we are in with Liberia and Papua New Guinea, and join those nations that recognize the importance of early life. We could start by granting every family paid leave, beginning with pregnancy and continuing for the first two years after a child's birth. The first thousand days are when parental well-being and care matter the most. Studies demonstrate that paid leave policies have important health benefits for infants, although we may have to wait a generation or two for the process to bring about major improvements in the population at large.

Tackling inequality directly would have a greater impact on health than any more direct "health" intervention, and the time may be ripe for those actions. We could follow the lead of other countries and consider having a maximum pay ratio within companies; Switzerland, for example, has proposed that the salary ratio of CEO to the lowest-paid worker should not be greater than 12:1. We could return the maximum tax rates to the levels they were when we were much healthier relative to other nations; many today are shocked to hear that in 1966 the highest marginal tax rate was 70 percent. Similarly, we could tax corporations at rates that more realistically reflect their profit levels as we did in the past. These efforts will be resisted by the elite, although even the top 1 percent will be healthier when there is less inequality.

Another beneficial measure would foster more employee-owned enterprises. Already 130 million Americans participate in ownership of co-op businesses and credit unions. Public banks, as an alternative to corporate, profit-oriented ones, could stabilize the public economy. North Dakota has had a state bank for over ninety years, and that state suffered far less during the 2008–9 economic meltdown than the rest of the country.

The basic changes needed will only occur if we address current government policies that mostly serve the rich. While the United States is not alone in this regard, the excesses in our system, which some call a kleptocracy, limit what ordinary people can demand from their government. The rich do not face the same constraints, as was so clearly evident in the bailouts during the recent economic crisis. Changing this power imbalance is the real challenge we face.

Finally, let's monitor our efforts in getting back our health. We need to look at progress in reducing inequality and make sure that information is widely known. We need to track the U.S. standing in the Olympics of health—the ranking of countries by health outcomes. While the United States wins gold medals in the Billionaire, Incarceration, and Health Care Spending Olympics, we are not even in the start-up for the final day's race in the Health Olympics.

What gets measured gets done. Let's measure health outcomes and have every American know how much shorter their lives are than they need to be. That will have us watching for progress. The president should report on our health and inequality goals in the annual State of the Union speech.

Countries can set health goals, just as the United States set a goal to land a human on the moon in the 1960s. We monitored progress toward that goal and were eventually successful. The United Kingdom, for example, set a child poverty reduction goal a few years ago and monitors success toward that aim. Australia has set a goal of being the healthiest nation in the world by 2020.

It will not be easy, but they have outlined a plan and are monitoring progress.

The United States also regularly sets goals. The effort began with the Healthy People 2000 outcomes; but when we failed to reach those targets, we set more lofty ones for 2010—which again we didn't achieve. For 2020 we need to set realistic goals, benchmarks, and strategies for getting there, and we need to achieve them. Those strategies need to include meaningful social and economic changes that will give everyone in the country a chance of growing up, and living a long and healthy life.

Every single day that we delay, another forty-seven American babies will die needlessly.

DEBT AND POVERTY

JAILED FOR BEING IN DEBT

Chris Serres and Glenn Howatt

Minnesota's leading newspaper, following up on a tip that the number of arrest warrants was rising, discovered in 2011 that collection agencies used sheriff's deputies to arrest people with unpaid debts, many of whom were released after posting bail equal to the debt. Since the three-part series by Minneapolis Star Tribune *reporters Serres and Howatt ran, newspapers in Arkansas, Georgia, and other states have shown how widespread this practice is.*

As a sheriff's deputy dumped the contents of Joy Uhlmeyer's purse into a sealed bag, she begged to know why she had just been arrested while driving home to Richfield after an Easter visit with her elderly mother.

No one had an answer. Uhlmeyer spent a sleepless night in a frigid Anoka County holding cell, her hands tucked under her armpits for warmth. Then, handcuffed in a squad car, she was taken to downtown Minneapolis for booking. Finally, after sixteen hours in limbo, jail officials fingerprinted Uhlmeyer and explained her offense— missing a court hearing over an unpaid debt. "They have no right to do this to me," said the fifty-seven-year-old patient-care advocate, her voice as soft as a whisper. "Not for a stupid credit card."

It's not a crime to owe money, and debtors' prisons were abolished in the United States in the nineteenth century. But people are routinely being thrown in jail for failing to pay debts. In Minnesota, which has some of the most creditor-friendly laws in the country, the use of arrest warrants against debtors has jumped 60 percent over the past four years, with 845 cases in 2009, a *Star Tribune* analysis of state court data has found.

Not every warrant results in an arrest, but in Minnesota many debtors spend up to forty-eight hours in cells with criminals. Consumer attorneys say such arrests are increasing in many states, including Arkansas, Arizona, and Washington, driven by a bad economy, high consumer debt, and a growing industry that buys bad debts and employs every means available to collect.

Whether a debtor is locked up depends largely on where the person lives, because enforcement is inconsistent from state to state, and even county to county.

In Illinois and southwest Indiana, some judges jail debtors for missing court-ordered debt payments. In extreme cases, people stay in jail until they raise a minimum payment. In January, a judge sentenced a Kenney, Illinois, man "to indefinite incarceration" until he came up with $300 toward a lumber yard debt.

"The law enforcement system has unwittingly become a tool of the debt collectors," said Michael Kinkley, an attorney in Spokane, Washington, who has represented arrested debtors. "The debt collectors are abusing the system and intimidating people, and law enforcement is going along with it."

How often are debtors arrested across the country? No one can say. No national statistics are kept, and the practice is largely unnoticed outside legal circles. "My suspicion is the debt collection industry does not want the world to know these arrests are happening, because the practice would be widely condemned," said Robert Hobbs, deputy director of the National Consumer Law Center in Boston.

Debt collectors defend the practice, saying phone calls, letters, and legal actions aren't always enough to get people to pay.

"Admittedly, it's a harsh sanction," said Steven Rosso, a partner in the Como Law Firm of St. Paul, which does collections work. "But sometimes, it's the only sanction we have."

Taxpayers foot the bill for arresting and jailing debtors. In many cases, Minnesota judges set bail at the amount owed.

In Minnesota, judges have issued arrest warrants for people who owe as little as $85—less than half the cost of housing an inmate overnight. Debtors targeted for arrest owed a median of $3,512 in 2009, up from $2,201 five years ago.

Those jailed for debts may be the least able to pay.

"It's just one more blow for people who are already struggling," said Beverly Yang, a Land of Lincoln Legal Assistance Foundation staff attorney who has represented three Illinois debtors arrested in the past two months. "They don't like being in court. They don't have cars. And if they had money to pay these collectors, they would."

THE COLLECTION MACHINE

The laws allowing for the arrest of someone for an unpaid debt are not new.

What is new is the rise of well-funded, aggressive, and central-ized collection firms, in many cases run by attorneys, that buy up unpaid debt and use the courts to collect.

Three debt buyers—Unifund CCR Partners, Portfolio Recovery Associates Inc., and Debt Equities LLC—accounted for 15 percent of all debt-related arrest warrants issued in Minnesota since 2005, court data show. The debt buyers also file tens of thousands of other col-lection actions in the state, seeking court orders to make people pay.

The debts—often five or six years old—are purchased from com-panies like cell-phone providers and credit-card issuers, and cost a few cents on the dollar. Using automated dialing equipment and teams of lawyers, the debt-buyer firms try to collect the debt, plus interest and fees. A firm aims to collect at least twice what it paid for the debt to cover costs. Anything beyond that is profit.

Portfolio Recovery Associates of Norfolk, Virginia, a publicly traded debt buyer with the biggest profits and market capitaliza-tion, earned $44 million last year on $281 million in revenue—a 16 percent net margin. Encore Capital Group, another large debt buyer based in San Diego, had a margin last year of 10 percent. By comparison, Walmart's profit margin was 3.5 percent.

Todd Lansky, chief operating officer at Resurgence Financial LLC, a Northbrook, Illinois–based debt buyer, said firms like his operate within the law, which says people who ignore court orders can be arrested for contempt. By the time a warrant is issued, a debtor may have been contacted up to twelve times, he said.

"This is a last-ditch effort to say, 'Look, just show up in court,'" he said.

GO TO COURT—OR JAIL

At 9:30 A.M. on a recent weekday morning, about a dozen people stood in line at the Hennepin County Government Center in Minneapolis.

Nearly all of them had received court judgments for not paying a delinquent debt. One by one, they stepped forward to fill out a two-page financial disclosure form that gives creditors the information they need to garnish money from their paychecks or bank accounts.

This process happens several times a week in Hennepin County. Those who fail to appear can be held in contempt and an arrest warrant is issued if a collector seeks one. Arrested debtors aren't officially charged with a crime, but their cases are heard in the same courtroom as drug users.

Greg Williams, who is unemployed and living on state benefits, said he made the trip downtown on the advice of his girlfriend who knew someone who had been arrested for missing such a hearing.

"I was surprised that the police would waste time on my petty debts," said Williams, forty-five, of Minneapolis, who had a $5,773 judgment from a credit-card debt. "Don't they have real criminals to catch?"

Few debtors realize they can land in jail simply for ignoring debt-collection legal matters. Debtors also may not recognize the names of companies seeking to collect old debts. Some people are contacted by three or four firms as delinquent debts are bought and sold multiple times after the original creditor writes off the account.

"They may think it's a mistake. They may think it's a scam. They may not realize how important it is to respond," said Mary Spector, a law professor at Southern Methodist University's Dedman School of Law in Dallas.

A year ago, Legal Aid attorneys proposed a change in state law that would have required law-enforcement officials to let debtors fill out financial-disclosure forms when they are apprehended rather than book them into jail. No legislator introduced the measure.

Joy Uhlmeyer, who was arrested on her way home from spending Easter with her mother, said she defaulted on a $6,200 Chase credit card after a costly divorce in 2006. The firm seeking payment was Resurgence Financial, the Illinois debt buyer. Uhlmeyer said she didn't recognize the name and ignored the notices.

Uhlmeyer walked free after her nephew posted $2,500 bail. It took another $187 to retrieve her car from the city impound lot. Her eighty-six-year-old mother later asked why she didn't call home after leaving Duluth. Not wanting to tell the truth, Uhlmeyer said her car broke down and her cell phone died.

"The really maddening part of the whole experience was the complete lack of information," she said. "I kept thinking, 'If there was a warrant out for my arrest, then why in the world wasn't I told about it?'"

JAILED FOR $250

One afternoon last spring, Deborah Poplawski, thirty-eight, of Minneapolis was digging in her purse for coins to feed a downtown parking meter when she saw the flashing lights of a Minneapolis police squad car behind her. Poplawski, a restaurant cook, assumed she had parked illegally. Instead, she was headed to jail over a $250 credit-card debt.

Less than a month earlier, she learned by chance from an employment counselor that she had an outstanding warrant. Debt Equities, a Golden Valley debt buyer, had sued her, but she says nobody served her with court documents. Thanks to interest and fees, Poplawski was now on the hook for $1,138.

Though she knew of the warrant and unpaid debt, "I wasn't equating the warrant with going to jail, because there wasn't criminal activity associated with it," she said. "I just thought it was a civil thing."

She spent nearly twenty-five hours at the Hennepin County jail.

A year later, she still gets angry recounting the experience. A male inmate groped her behind in a crowded elevator, she said. Poplawski also was ordered to change into the standard jail uniform—gray-white underwear and orange pants, shirt and socks—in a cubicle the size of a telephone booth. She slept in a room with twelve to sixteen women and a toilet with no privacy. One woman offered her drugs, she said.

The next day, Poplawski appeared before a Hennepin County district judge. He told her to fill out the form listing her assets and bank account, and released her. Several weeks later, Debt Equities used this information to seize funds from her bank account. The firm didn't return repeated calls seeking a comment.

"We hear every day about how there's no money for public services," Poplawski said. "But it seems like the collectors have found a way to get the police to do their work."

THREAT DEPENDS ON LOCATION

A lot depends on where a debtor lives or is arrested, as Jamie Rodriguez, forty-one, a bartender from Brooklyn Park, discovered two years ago.

Deputies showed up at his house one evening while he was playing with his five-year-old daughter, Nicole. They live in Hennepin County, where the Sheriff's Office has enough staff to seek out people with warrants for civil violations.

If Rodriguez lived in neighboring Wright County, he could have simply handed the officers a check or cash for the amount owed. If he lived in Dakota County, it's likely no deputy would have shown up because the Sheriff's Office there says it lacks the staff to pursue civil debt cases.

Knowing that his daughter and wife were watching from the window, Rodriguez politely asked the deputies to drive him around the block, out of sight of his family, before they handcuffed him. The deputies agreed.

"No little girl should have to see her daddy arrested," said Rodriguez, who spent a night in jail.

"If you talk to fifteen different counties, you'll find fifteen different approaches to handling civil warrants," said Sgt. Robert Shingledecker of the Dakota County Sheriff's Office. "Everything is based on manpower."

Local police also can enforce debt-related warrants, but small towns and some suburbs often don't have enough officers.

The *Star Tribune*'s comparison of warrant and booking data suggests that at least one in six Minnesota debtors at risk for arrest actually lands in jail, typically for eight hours. The exact number of such arrests isn't known because the government doesn't consistently track what happens to debtor warrants.

"There are no standards here," said Gail Hillebrand, a senior attorney with the Consumers Union in San Francisco. "A borrower who lives on one side of the river can be arrested while another one goes free. It breeds disrespect for the law."

Haekyung Nielsen, twenty-seven, of Bloomington, said police showed up at her house on a civil warrant two weeks after she gave birth through Caesarean section. A debt buyer had sent her court papers for an old credit-card debt while she was in the hospital; Nielsen said she did not have time to respond.

Her baby boy, Tyler, lay in the crib as she begged the officer not to take her away.

"Thank God, the police had mercy and left me and my baby alone," said Nielsen, who later paid the debt. "But to send someone to arrest me two weeks after a massive surgery that takes most women eight weeks to recover from was just unbelievable."

THE SECOND SURPRISE

Many debtors, like Robert Vee, thirty-six, of Brooklyn Park, get a second surprise after being arrested—their bail is exactly the amount of money owed.

Hennepin County automatically sets bail at the judgment amount or $2,500, whichever is less. This policy was adopted four years ago in response to the high volume of debtor-default cases, say court officials.

Some judges say the practice distorts the purpose of bail, which is to make sure people show up in court.

"It's certainly an efficient way to collect debts, but it's also highly distasteful," said Hennepin County District Judge Jack Nordby. "The amount of bail should have nothing to do with the amount of the debt."

Judge Robert Blaeser, chief of the county court's civil division, said linking bail to debt streamlines the process because judges needn't spend time setting bail.

"It's arbitrary," he conceded. "The bigger question is: Should you be allowed to get an order from a court for someone to be arrested because they owe money? You've got to remember there are people who have the money but just won't pay a single penny."

If friends or family post a debtor's bail, they can expect to kiss the money goodbye, because it often ends up with creditors, who routinely ask judges for the bail payment.

Vee, a highway construction worker, was arrested one afternoon in February while driving his teenage daughter from school to their home in Brooklyn Park. As he was being cuffed, Vee said his daughter, who has severe asthma, started hyperventilating from the stress.

"All I kept thinking about was whether she was all right and if she was using her [asthma] inhaler," he said.

From the Hennepin County jail, he made a collect call to his landlord, who promised to bring the bail. It was $1,875.06, the exact amount of a credit-card debt.

Later, Vee was reunited with his distraught daughter at home. "We hugged for a long time, and she was bawling her eyes out," he said.

He still has unpaid medical and credit-card bills and owes about $40,000 on an old second mortgage. The sight of a squad car in his rearview mirror is all it takes to set off a fresh wave of anxiety.

"The question always crosses my mind: 'Are the cops going to arrest me again?'" he said. "So long as I've got unpaid bills, the threat is there."

This article first appeared in the Minneapolis Star Tribune *on June 6, 2010.*

AMERICA'S POVERTY "TAX"

Gary Rivlin

Charging high fees has become a big business in America, with Wall Street financing the firms that make short-term, very high interest loans.

It's expensive being poor, the writer James Baldwin famously said. Baldwin uttered those words fifty years ago, long before the working poor became a big business—long before the invention of the payday loan, rent-to-own, and a long list of diabolically clever ideas that entrepreneurs have devised to get hundreds-of-millions-of-dollars rich off those with thin wallets.

Call it a poverty tax. It's the hundreds of dollars, if not thousands, in extra fees people making $20,000 or $25,000 or $30,000 a year pay because they have lousy credit or because they have no savings.

Add up all the profits pocketed by all those payday lenders, check cashers, subprime auto lenders, and other Poverty, Inc. enterprises and divide it by the forty million households the Federal Reserve says survive on $30,000 a year or less. That works out to around $2,500 per household, or a poverty tax of around 10 percent.

The corner check casher takes the biggest bite, at least from those fifteen million or so Americans who have no bank account—the so-called unbanked. In the main, these are people who've bounced too many checks or otherwise messed up their relationship with a bank.

How much does the average check-cashing customer fork over? According to Matt Fellowes, who investigated the high price of being poor as a researcher with the Brookings Institution, the typical unbanked worker bringing home $22,000 a year spends roughly $800 to $900 a year in check-cashing fees. That figure tops $1,000 annually when you include the fees the unbanked pay for money orders and the additional fees check cashers charge (around $2 a check) when you need to pay your bills.

The payday lender—those in the business of making horrifically expensive loans against a person's next paycheck, her social security check, or, increasingly, an unemployment check—takes another big cut of the meager earnings of the working poor. The single mom struggling to get by on $20,000 a year is forever falling a few bucks short before payday, but that's the brilliance of the payday industry, which dates back to the early 1990s. In less than ten minutes, she'll have a few hundred dollars cash in her hands, no questions asked— and then be charged a fee that works out to an annual interest rate of 400 percent.

The average payday customer pays between $600 and $700 a year in fees. More than ten million people avail themselves of a payday lender each year.

The rent-to-own industry draws less than half that many customers but generates around the same revenues as the payday business. The genius of rent-to-own is that its proprietors have figured out how to collect $1,400 in weekly installments on the same child's bedroom set you could pick up for $600 with a credit card. Can't afford a computer for the kids? No problem. The corner rent-to-own store also carries laptops and PCs, along with flat screens, washers and dryers, and living room sets.

The rent-to-own customer, of course, could choose to set aside some money each week until she has saved enough to buy the item in a retail store. She could frequent a secondhand shop. But for essentials there's the risk of being dubbed a negligent parent by the authorities or family, and can you blame the security guard making $25,000 a year or home health aide bringing in $15,000 annually for wanting to come home to a comfortable easy chair and a large flat-screen TV? The point is that the rent-to-own customer is typically paying two and a half times as much as those who have the means to buy retail.

The average rent-to-own customer spends around $1,200 a year. That means the typical rent-to-own customer pays an extra $700 annually because he or she doesn't have the cash or credit to buy it at a store.

Those living on the bottom of the economic pyramid pay more in a wide array of other ways. The subprime insurance market is its own racket, and even mainstream insurers charge more for auto insurance if you live in an unsafe neighborhood where robberies are more common. Select credit-card companies still cater to those with a subprime credit score of less than 620—but you'll pay dearly for the privilege of carrying that plastic in your pocket. For instance, there's First Premier, which charges a $95 application fee and both a $45 annual fee and a $6.25 "monthly servicing fee" for a card carrying an APR of 36 percent, which at least is better than the 49.9 percent card it was peddling last year.

And then there's the steep cost of financing your car if you're one of the fifty million or so Americans suffering from a subprime credit score. Rather than a car loan carrying an annual interest rate of around 5 percent, the subprime customer pays interest rates of 18 or 20 or 25 percent a year, if not more.

The person paying 20 percent interest on a $10,000 car loan will pay $900 more each year on a five-year loan compared to the person paying an interest rate of 5 percent on that same loan amount.

Thankfully, a good portion of the working poor never resort to a payday loan. They avoid paying the steep rates charged by the local Rent-A-Center. Plenty of people earning less than $30,000 a year have a checking account and good credit. There's also help on the horizon as the new Consumer Financial Protection Board has singled out payday loans and subprime auto finance as two of its top priorities.

Yet don't underestimate the ingenuity or hunger for profits driving those who the author Mike Hudson dubbed "merchants of misery." A few years back, I attended the annual Check Cashers Convention, where I sat in on a ninety-minute presentation dubbed, "Effective Marketing Strategies to Dominate Your

Market." Speaking to a standing-room-only crowd, a consultant named Jim Higgins shared his tips for turning the $1,000-a-year check cashing or payday customer into one worth "$2,000 to $4,000 a year." Pens scribbled furiously as he tossed out ideas: raffle off an iPod. Consider scratch 'n win contests. Institute the kind of customer reward programs that has worked so well for the airlines. And for those who are only semiregulars, offer a "cash 3, get 1 free" deal. After all, Higgins told the crowd, "These are people not used to getting anything free. These are people not used to getting anything, really."

Adapted from Broke, USA: From Pawnshops to Poverty, Inc.—How the Working Poor Became Big Business.

HUNGER IN AMERICA

Donald S. Shepard, Elizabeth Setren, and Donna Cooper

The number of hungry Americans rose sharply with the Great Recession, exacting a costly toll in damaged lives and economic losses—about which it was easy to remain ignorant, as documented by three researchers in a study published by the Center for American Progress.

The Great Recession and the tepid economic recovery swelled the ranks of American households confronting hunger and food insecurity by 30 percent. In 2010, about 48.8 million Americans lived in food-insecure households, meaning they were hungry or faced food insecurity at some point during the year. That's 12 million more people than faced hunger in 2007, before the recession, and represents 16.1 percent of the U.S. population.

Yet hunger is not readily seen in America. We see neither newscasts showing small American children with distended bellies nor legions of thin, frail people lined up at soup kitchens. That's primarily because the expansion of the critical federal Supplemental Nutrition Assistance Program helped many families meet some of their household food needs.

But in spite of the increase in Supplemental Nutrition Assistance Program funding, many families still have to make tough choices between a meal and paying for other basic necessities. In 2010 nearly half of the households seeking emergency food assistance reported having to choose between paying for utilities or heating fuel and food. Nearly 40 percent said they had to choose between paying for rent or a mortgage and food. More than a third reported having to choose between their medical bills and food.

What's more, the research in this paper shows that hunger costs our nation at least $167.5 billion due to the combination of lost economic productivity per year, more expensive public education because of the rising costs of poor education outcomes, avoidable health care costs, and the cost of charity to keep families fed. This $167.5 billion does not include the cost of the Supplemental Nutrition Assistance Program and the other key federal nutrition programs, which run at about $94 billion a year.

We call this $167.5 billion "America's hunger bill." In 2010 it cost every citizen $542 due to the far-reaching consequences of hunger in our nation. At the household level, the hunger bill came to at least $1,410 in 2010. And because our $167.5 billion estimate is based on a cautious methodology, the actual cost of hunger and food insecurity to our nation is probably higher.

This report also estimates the state-by-state impact of the rising hunger bill from 2007 through 2010. The rise in America's hunger bill since the onset of the Great Recession affected every state. Fifteen states experienced a nearly 40 percent increase in their hunger bill compared to the national increase of 33.4 percent. The sharpest increases in the cost of hunger are estimated to have occurred in Florida (61.9 percent), California (47.2 percent), and Maryland (44.2 percent).

Our research in this report builds upon and updates a 2007 report, *The Economic Costs of Domestic Hunger*, the first to calculate the direct and indirect cost of adverse health, education, and economic-productivity outcomes associated with hunger. This study extends the 2007 research, examining the recession's impact on hunger and the societal costs to our nation and to each of the fifty states in 2007 and 2010. It also provides the first estimate of how much hunger contributes to the cost of special education, which we found to be at least $6.4 billion in 2010.

The 2007 report estimated America's hunger bill to be $90 billion in 2005, sharply lower than the $167.5 billion bill in 2010. We argue that any policy solutions to address the consequences of hunger in America should consider these economic calculations. The reason:

we believe our procedures for expressing the consequences of this social problem in economic terms help policy makers gauge the magnitude of the problem and the economic benefits of potential solutions.

In this paper we do not make specific policy proposals beyond adopting our methodology for calculating hunger in America, but we do point out that expanding the Supplemental Nutrition Assistance Program to all food-insecure households could cost about $83 billion a year. While we do not recommend this approach, we note that nonetheless it would cost the nation much less than the most recent hunger bill in 2010 of $167.5 billion.

There are other policy approaches that also could achieve sustained reduction in hunger and food insecurity—approaches that rely on a mix of federal policies to boost the wages of the lowest-wage earners, increase access to full-time employment,

AMERICA'S HUNGER BILL IN 2007 AND 2010 IN BILLIONS OF 2010 DOLLARS

Elements of the hunger bill	2007	2010	Increase
Health conditions			
Poor health	$28.7	$38.9	$10.2
Depression	$22.2	$29.2	$7.1
Suicide	$15.8	$19.7	$3.9
Anxiety	$12.9	$17.4	$4.5
Hospitalizations	$12.1	$16.1	$4.0
Upper gastrointestinal disorders	$4.2	$5.7	$1.4
Migraines, colds, and iron deficiency	$2.5	$3.5	$1.0
Total illness costs	$98.4	$113.1	$14.6
Lower educational productivity and lifetime earnings			
Drop out due to grade retention	$5.1	$6.9	$1.9
Drop out due to absenteeism	$4.2	$5.8	$1.6
Special education	$4.6	$6.4	$1.8
Total productivity and education costs	$13.9	$19.1	$5.3
Charity costs	$13.2	$17.8	$4.6
Total	$125.5	$167.5	$42.0

and modestly expand federal nutrition programs. These policies are consistent with the variables used to allocate federal nutrition funding to states under the Emergency Food Assistance Program. In using the state's poverty and unemployment rates, this program recognizes that improved economic conditions reduce hunger and the need for emergency support.

Our calculations based on our research enable us to break out the consequences of hunger and food insecurity in America fairly rigorously (see previous page).

If the number of hungry Americans remains constant, on a lifetime basis, each individual's bill for hunger in our nation will amount to about $42,400 (based on the average life expectancy of 78.3 years per the U.S. Census Bureau).

Of course, the average American doesn't receive a real bill for these costs. Instead, the costs are reflected in taxes, our contributions to charities that address hunger, and the costs paid directly and indirectly for the poor health condition of those who are hungry and their lower productivity.

Federal programs can and do address hunger and food insecurity directly. To a large measure they help mitigate enormous economic and societal costs of hunger. For instance, without federal funds supporting the more than 42 million Americans with Supplemental Nutrition Assistance Program benefits, America's hunger bill would have skyrocketed. If high levels of unemployment continue and wage stagnation remains, the number of hungry and food-insecure families will either stay the same or rise. So, too, will America's hunger bill.

What remains unchanged from our original research in 2007 is the most salient point: "The nation pays far more by letting hunger exist than it would if our leaders took steps to eliminate it."

Adapted from Hunger in America: Suffering We All Pay For, *a 2011 report by the Center for American Progress.*

GEORGIA'S HUNGER GAMES

Neil deMause

In 1996, Congress and President Clinton agreed to "end welfare as we know it." Families are now limited to sixty months of lifetime assistance, but even that promise is illusory in some states, as this journalist, who specializes in subsidies, found in Georgia.

When the economy crashed in 2008, millions of Americans lost their jobs. Applications for food stamps soared. So did attendance at emergency food providers—soup kitchens and food pantries—that help the estimated fifty million people, working and nonworking, who can't afford enough groceries to get through the month.

Unlike past economic downturns, though, the welfare rolls barely budged. Where fifteen years ago 68 percent of poor Americans received cash via Temporary Assistance to Needy Families (as welfare was officially renamed in 1996), today only 27 percent of Americans with incomes low enough to qualify for cash benefits receive them. The resulting welfare gap has left at least four million families with neither jobs nor cash aid.

The size of the welfare gap, however, varies widely from state to state. In states like California and Maine, which have focused on getting their poor citizens into jobs programs, about two-thirds of the eligible still receive welfare.

On the opposite end of the spectrum is Georgia, which over the past decade has set itself up as the poster child for the ongoing war on welfare. Even as unemployment has soared to 9 percent and 300,000 Georgia families now live below the poverty line—50 percent more than in 2000—the number receiving cash benefits has all but evaporated: barely 19,000 families receiving TANF remain, all but 3,400 of which were cases involving children only. That's less than 7 percent, making Georgia one of the toughest places in the nation to get welfare assistance.

NO POINT IN APPLYING

What's Georgia's secret? According to government documents, interviews with poor Georgians, and those who work with them, it's simple: combine an all-Republican state government out to make a name for itself as tough on freeloaders; a state welfare commissioner so zealous about slashing the rolls that workers say she handed out Zero candy bars to emphasize her goal of zero welfare; and federal rules that, regardless of who's in the White House, give states the leeway to use the 1996 law's requirement for "work activities" to slam the door in the face of their neediest. This has created a land that welfare forgot, where a collection of private charities struggle to fill the resulting holes.

For the Atlanta Community Food Bank, that means sending out more than three million pounds of canned goods, bread, and other groceries each month to churches in and around Atlanta to help feed the state's growing number of poor and near poor. The food bank's staff also helps arrange for free income tax preparation services, and helps the city's poor apply for food stamps and Medicaid.

One thing the food bank staff and volunteers don't discuss, though, is welfare. Says food bank advocacy and education director Laura Lester: "We don't even send anybody in to apply, because there's just no point."

It's a state of affairs that's left an increasing number of Georgians with nowhere to turn. Teresa, a single mom of a two-year-old living in a domestic-violence shelter, tells of how she broke down and applied for cash benefits after fleeing an abusive relationship—only to be chastised by state welfare officers who asked, "Wouldn't you rather work?" Eventually, Teresa says, "I was sitting there crying—I just didn't know what else to do. I said, you've gone from letting people sit on their butt and collect money to the very opposite of that."

Ultimately, it didn't matter. In the end, she was rejected. The reason? Failing to fill out her paperwork correctly.

One of the common misconceptions about welfare reform is that under the grand bargain that Newt Gingrich and Bill Clinton agreed to in 1996, a new regime was put in place: if you won't work (or at least look for work), you'll no longer get a government check. In fact, though, welfare reform is less a single law than fifty separate experiments, as Washington provided states with a broad framework under which they are free to set their own rules on time limits, grant levels, and work requirements for those seeking help.

Immediately after the new law was put in place, the welfare rolls plunged by two-thirds—though no one could say for certain whether this was because people were leaving the rolls for jobs or merely sinking deeper into poverty.

In Georgia, the number of Georgians receiving welfare in 2004 leveled off at about 54,000 families—roughly 30 percent of poor Georgia. That year Governor Sonny Perdue, the state's first Republican governor since Reconstruction, hired a new commissioner to head Georgia's Department of Human Services. Beverly "B.J." Walker, a fifty-four-year-old black woman from Chicago, had been an obscure school curriculum consultant best known as the wife of Chicago's airport commissioner when Republicans chose her to run a pilot project in 1995 to streamline state government services. Soon she rose to run Chicago's welfare programs as well.

Walker quickly gained a reputation for a get-tough attitude toward welfare recipients that rivaled other states. "What B.J. emphasized was that everybody who can work, should work," says Joseph Antolin, who was an Illinois state welfare official when Walker arrived on the scene.

What that meant was that those who wouldn't work—or preferred, say, to go back to school to increase their chances of landing a good job—would be quickly pushed off the rolls. One of her first steps, Antolin recalls, was to shoot down plans to expand GED classes and vocational college courses for the poor. Her philosophy, he says, was "you essentially have to throw them in the pool and let them learn how to swim."

In Georgia, Walker seemed focused on a single goal: keeping people from getting benefits by any means necessary. New applicants soon found themselves being handed flyers emblazoned with slogans like "TANF is not good enough for any family," "TANF = work now," and "We believe welfare is not the best option for your family." Allison Smith of the Georgia Coalition Against Domestic Violence says the reality was that local welfare offices "were really taking a lot of steps to dissuade people from applying—or once they had applied, they were doing things to make the process really cumbersome and difficult."

Smith's colleagues began documenting reports of welfare applicants being discouraged from applying for benefits. Among the entries in their reports: making them go through sixty job searches a week or come to eight orientations. Ordering a woman in her seventh month of pregnancy to take a waitress job that would require her to be on her feet all day. Telling a mother living in a shelter that if she applied for Temporary Assistance to Needy Families her children would be taken away.

"They were trying to make me feel bad that I was trying to get money," says Teresa of her experience seeking benefits. "They told me that taxpayers are paying for it—I used to pay my taxes, you know?"

Kelda O'Neal, a young grandmother currently caring for an extended family of fifteen in her DeKalb County home, had a similar experience. "They treat you like you're in a jail facility," she said. O'Neal received benefits until her husband, a truck driver, applied for disability after suffering a mental breakdown following the murder of his daughter. He was told he would have to first attend sixty to ninety days of a state work program. When he missed one appointment, the state not only rejected him, but ended her $133 in monthly benefits as well.

Missed appointments are a common reason for rejected TANF

applications in Georgia. Failure to meet state job search rules—which require thirty days of job search before a first check will be cut—is another. Teresa says she was told that to have her welfare application processed she'd have to file twenty-four job applications per week. "That was really hard, because I couldn't find any places that were hiring," she says. She was approved for benefits, but only so long as she then performed twenty-four hours a week of community service, plus twelve hours of job search, which she struggled to do during the limited computer time available at the domestic-violence shelter.

Eventually, she had her benefits cut off. The reason? Failing to properly record the phone numbers of her job contacts.

The Georgia Department of Human Services has long insisted that it does not actively strive to deny benefits. (Walker departed in 2011, but her policies endure.) Indeed, there's nothing in written state guidelines telling workers to focus on turning applicants away. But bureaucracies do not operate based only on written instructions. There are subtle ways to tell welfare workers what they must do to keep their jobs.

CANDY BARS SEND A MESSAGE

One of these unwritten measures involved Zero candy bars, according to Smith. Senior officials handed out the candy bars to staff as a not-so-subtle reminder that the goal was to have no one receiving welfare, she says. "That was the goal, workers were telling us. The message was 'zero TANF.'" A DHS spokesperson replies that the state "has no information" on the distribution of candy bars by the department.

In any case, the share of approved welfare applications fell by half, from 40 percent to 20 percent, during Walker's tenure, according to Liz Schott, a senior fellow at the Center on Budget and Policy Priorities, a Washington nonprofit research organization that advocates for the poor. Two-thirds of denials were due to either withdrawal of the applications or failure to complete application procedures. That suggests not-so-subtle threats, like telling homeless mothers their children would be taken away, encouraged people to give up.

As for getting Georgia's poor back to work—the ostensible goal of welfare reform—the numbers are unpromising. Georgia has bragged about its rising "work participation" rate—a key metric set down by Congress to ensure that states followed federal work rules by insisting that at least half of welfare recipients were engaged in "work activities," which can include anything from actual employment to searching for a job. However, the Center on Budget and Policy Priorities found that far fewer poor Georgians were engaged in "work activities" under Walker. The only reason the percentages had increased was that the number of people getting cash aid had plummeted even faster.

Asked whether having barely one in a hundred of the state's poor receiving cash is an acceptable result, Ann Carter, the Georgia policy director for Temporary Assistance to Needy Families, replies, "I don't know that that's a yes-or-no question." If a dwindling number of people are successfully receiving benefits, she implies, that's their decision, not the state's: "Our withdrawal rate dictates whether they want to comply with the program, or they don't."

She adds that the state offers job seekers help getting to job interviews, such as a new car battery or transit passes, and now lets them conduct job searches at home—provided that they have a computer with Internet access.

And what of the hundreds of thousands who got welfare and then left? About 70 percent were employed during their first year after leaving the program, but more than 80 percent remained below the federal poverty level.

A 2006 state study found that one thing that did help get people off Temporary Assistance for Needy Families and into work was increased child-care assistance. That program is now threatened with funding cuts.

It shouldn't be this way, says O'Neal, the young grandmother, as she prepares to file TANF paperwork yet again for her daughter, hopefully this time with a better result. "All of these people coming down here are not people just looking for handouts," she says. "You got a lot of people who have worked hard pretty much all their lives and have paid taxes. And now they're in need, and they can't get what they need. And it's so sad."

A version of this chapter appeared in December 2012 on Slate.com *and was reported in partnership with the Investigative Fund at the Nation Institute.*

LIVING DOWN TO EXPECTATIONS

Stephen Pimpare

Poor people often blame themselves and accept the stereotype that they have moral flaws. But poverty reflects broad societal failings more than individual shortcomings, a social-welfare expert shows. Often these people divert their eyes and try to make themselves invisible, a tendency you can observe if you address each person who serves you or performs what society regards as menial labor by name and look them in the eye.

> I have no mercy or compassion in me for a society that will crush people, and then penalize them for not being able to stand up under the weight.
>
> —*Malcolm X*

Throughout our history, poverty has usually been understood to be rooted in personal, moral failure: weakness of character, the absence of a work ethic, and disdain for the norms of society at large spread like a disease from person to person, from family to family, and produce entire communities beset with vice and despair.

Some even suggest that poor Americans inhabit an entirely separate culture, a "culture of poverty," one that manifests itself, according to anthropologist Oscar Lewis (1914–1970), in seventy-five distinct traits. Among them, we find a hatred and fear of the police; the absence of participation in mainstream institutions (and a distrust of them); low marriage rates; a "present-time" and fatalistic orientation; territoriality; early sexual activity; female-centered families; a lack of impulse control; a "tolerance for pathology"; and feelings of marginality, helplessness, dependence, and inferiority.

It is the urban poor, others have argued, who are especially distinct, and their inability or unwillingness to alter these "pathologies" is the chief cause of their poverty. As Jacob Riis (1849–1914) professed long before Lewis: "The thief is infinitely easier to deal with than the pauper, because the very fact of his being a thief presupposes some bottom to the man."

It is the supposed passivity among the very poor that often draws the attention of politicians, reformers, and critics of welfare. But it has been prominent even among more liberal voices. American socialist Michael Harrington wrote this in *The Other America*, his 1962 book credited with bringing the Kennedy administration's attention to poverty:

> The other America does not contain the adventurous seeking a new life and land. It is populated by the failures, by those driven from the land and bewildered by the city, by old people suddenly confronted with the torments of loneliness and poverty, and by minorities facing a wall of prejudice . . . the other America is becoming increasingly populated by those who do not belong to anybody or anything. They are no longer participants in an ethnic culture from the old country; they are less and less religious; they do not belong to unions or clubs. They are not seen, and because of that they themselves cannot see. Their horizon has become more and more restricted, they see one another, and that means that they see little reason to hope.

Harrington is not quite blaming poor people for their state, but he seems to suggest that there is little that can be done in the face of such deeply ingrained norms. Others have concluded that trying to relieve poverty is therefore futile, or even counterproductive. If people are poor, it is their own fault. In a land of such opportunity, after all, how else could we explain it?

NO CITY ON A HILL

It is in many ways our oldest and most enduring national myth, one that has taken many forms: the streets are paved with gold. With hard work, any American can achieve anything. Any boy (or girl, we now add) can grow up to be president. We're a beacon to the world, a land of freedom and opportunity. Even before leaving the *Mayflower* and stepping on our shore, William Bradford (1590–1657) proclaimed in 1630, "We must consider that we shall be as a City upon a Hill, the eyes of all people are upon us."

In 1699, Governor Bellomont of New York boasted, "I believe there is not a richer populace anywhere in the King's dominions," and, when the creation of a workhouse was first suggested, he reported that the Assembly "smiled at [the proposal] because there is no such thing as a beggar in this town or county." Years later, novelist Herman Melville continued the myth.

> Such a being as a beggar is almost unknown; and to be a born American citizen seems a guarantee against pauperism.

America's most famous French visitor, Alexis de Tocqueville (1805–1859), famously remarked upon it in his 1835 book *Democracy in America*:

> No novelty in the United States struck me more vividly during my stay there than the equality of conditions. It was easy to see the influence of this basic fact on the whole course of society.... Men there are nearer equality in wealth and mental endowments, or, in other words, more nearly equally powerful, than in any other country of the world or in any other age of recorded history.

Benjamin Franklin (1706–1790), thanks to his rags-to-riches *Autobiography*, must also take part of the blame for this enduring

trope, but even Gordon Wood, an eminent historian of our founding era, finds this Shining City evident from our earliest stirrings
of resistance to Britain: "The social conditions that generically are
supposed to lie behind all revolutions—poverty and economic
deprivation—were not present in colonial America . . . the white
American colonists were not an oppressed people; they had no
crushing imperial chains to throw off." We should give Wood
credit, and note his caveat (white American colonists), but even so,
his assertion is unfounded.

Recent research by historians of the colonial era shows that
claims of a relatively free and equal society, one without dire need,
are without much merit, and that it was "a poor man's country for
many of its citizens." The number of those needing and receiving
aid rose throughout the eighteenth century. Mobility even then was
limited, especially in the cities, and poverty was a constant presence throughout people's life spans. Many had to rely upon assistance from churches, private aid societies, friends, neighbors, and
family, and by the time of the American Revolution, local officials
spent perhaps as much effort in "warning out" (or expelling) the
nonresident poor as they did in caring for residents in need.

By the end of the eighteenth century, all large American cities
had discovered the need for almshouses and workhouses. Women,
then as now, were disproportionately poor and reliant upon public
aid, a condition that grew worse, not better, over the course of the
eighteenth century. And during that period, while the number of
landholders rose, so too did the number who were born and died
without property. Infant mortality rates in the colonies were no
lower than in England, and as historian Gary Nash (1933–) writes,
"among the mass of those who sought opportunity in the British
American colonies, it is the story of relentless labor and ultimate
failure that stands out."

Historian John K. Alexander noted in 1980 that in the late 1700s
Philadelphia "had far more social distance between classes and far
more class conflict than is often supposed . . . thus questioning the
claim that the late colonial and revolutionary periods were marked
by a high degree of social unity, harmony, and simple humanitari-
anism." Wood himself admitted "wealth was more unequally distributed after the Revolution than before."

Simple narratives of abundance and opportunity, of progress and prosperity, will no longer do. Poverty and inequality have been a constant presence in this country, and the causes have been constant, too: disruption and dislocation brought by war and large-scale economic change; sickness, death, fire, and natural disaster; seasonal fluctuations in the demand for labor; discrimination based on race, ethnicity, and gender; the power conferred by inherited wealth and status; and a political system that inhibits the ability of majorities to exert their will over elite minorities. Yet we have been unwilling to acknowledge this, and instead of relieving poverty we blame poor Americans for their condition, rationalizing our neglect with disdain for their supposed lack of aspiration, their poor work ethic, their despair.

A RATIONAL SURRENDER

Oscar Lewis wrote of the culture of poverty that "there is nothing in the concept that puts the onus of poverty on the character of the poor," for it is the effects of poverty that he has documented, not the causes.

The diminished expectations, the refusal to participate in mainstream institutions, the cynicism, and other characteristics we might indeed find among very poor people—these are not marks of moral failure, he insists, but complicated (if unconscious) strategies used by those with little discernible power and little cause for hope to protect themselves from disappointment. It first developed centuries ago, Lewis argued, as a reaction to the tumultuous transition from feudalism to capitalism.

We've now seen enough into the lives of poor Americans to understand how diminished expectations, or even utter hopelessness, might, alas, be prudent, given the formidable obstacles to their survival, let alone success. If one expects nothing, after all, it is more difficult to be disappointed. The anthropologist Elliot Liebow observed it in the men he chronicled in *Tally's Corner*, his insightful 1967 book on the lives and attitudes of poor black men who hung out on a sidewalk in the nation's capital: "Convinced of their inadequacies, not only do they not seek out those few better-paying jobs which test their resources, but they actively avoid them, gravitating in a mass to the menial, routine jobs which offer no challenge—and therefore pose no threat—to the already diminished images they have of themselves."

Adapted from A People's History of Poverty in America, *part of the People's History book series edited by the historian Howard Zinn.*

POLICY

HOW ECONOMICS IS BIASED TOWARD THE RICH

Moshe Adler

Modern economics operates from certain assumptions, two of which stack the deck in favor of the rich, an economist shows.

Economic laws are not made by nature. They are made by human beings.

—*Franklin D. Roosevelt*

The search for a definition of economic efficiency began with the emergence of democracy.

With democracy came, for the first time in history, the need to ask explicitly whom government should serve. Kings were never bothered by this question. "L'état, c'est moi," Louis XIV of France declared in the early eighteenth century—"the state is me." But who should a government "of the people" and "for the people" serve, when some of the people are rich and some are poor?

In 1793 the French "people" executed Louis XVI and proceeded to ratify in a referendum a constitution that guaranteed income redistribution in the form of public relief and public schooling. ("People" is in quotation marks because not all the French wanted the king executed, nor did all of them vote for the constitution.)

But how much should be redistributed? The constitution of 1793 did not say, and the political process that could have determined it was thwarted by the government before it started. A group of citizens, "The Conspiracy of Equals," demanded that the constitution be implemented, but the group was disbanded when its leader, François Noël Babeuf, was sent to the guillotine. Luckily, a contemporary of Babeuf, the wealthy British philosopher Jeremy Bentham (1748–1832), addressed the question.

Bentham based his theory of the efficient degree of redistribution on three building blocks:

the happiness of a society consists of the sum of the happiness of each of its members,

an efficient allocation of resources is one that maximizes the happiness of society, and

the happiness that a person gets from an additional dollar (or English pound) decreases as the number of dollars that person has increases.

In the language of economics, "happiness" has long since been replaced by "utility," and Bentham's theory is known, therefore, as Utilitarianism. Utility, which in the algebra of economists is shown as U, is made of tiny units called "utils." Utils are derived from money. Each additional dollar buys additional utils, and the number of utils that each additional dollar buys is called "the marginal utility of money."

More income yields more utility, but while an extra dollar always brings additional utility, this additional utility gets smaller as a person's income increases. Because each added dollar is less significant to one's well-being, the marginal utility of money decreases with the amount of money a person has. Think about how much an extra dollar might mean to someone scraping by with not enough to afford food on the last day of the year compared to a billionaire having one more dollar. That extra dollar is worth a great deal to the poor person who can quell his hunger, but is immaterial to the billionaire.

Because a rich person has more money than a poor person, if a dollar is transferred from the rich to the poor, the loss of utility to the rich will be less than the gain in utility to the poor. The transfer of a dollar from the rich person to the poor person will therefore increase the sum of utilities of these two individuals.

Where should the process of redistribution stop?

Bentham believed that redistribution should stop when each person has the same amount of money, because this will maximize the sum of their utilities. To Bentham, the pie of happiness is biggest—and therefore Utilitarian efficiency is achieved—when it is divided exactly equally.

Bentham was an effective agitator for equality. But Utilitarianism as a yardstick for economic efficiency did not survive the century in which it was developed. It was supplanted wholly and with complete success by another definition of efficiency, one invented by an Italian economist, Vilfredo Pareto (1848–1923). If Utilitarianism is still mentioned in economics textbooks at all, it is summarily dismissed as a historical curiosity on the way to the truth: Pareto efficiency.

How and why did Pareto dismiss Utilitarianism? Let's begin with the why.

At the end of the nineteenth century, inequality in Europe was so extreme that a socialist revolution had become a real possibility. Pope Leo XIII was moved enough by the prevailing economic disparity that in 1891 he issued an encyclical letter, *Rerum Novarum* [Of New Things], which was devoted to "The Condition of the Working Classes," and in which he wrote: "The whole process of production as well as trade in every kind of goods has been brought almost entirely under the power of a few, so that a very few rich and exceedingly rich men have laid a yoke almost of slavery on the unnumbered masses of non-owning workers."

This would seem to lay the groundwork for a call to redistribute "the whole process of production." In fact, though, the pope objected strongly to redistribution through the power of the state. The rich should have no legal obligation to assist the poor, the pope asserted: "These [assisting the poor] are duties not of justice, except in cases of extreme need, but of Christian charity, which obviously cannot be enforced by legal action."

Pareto also opposed redistribution, arguing that Bentham

was not necessarily right in his analysis. Bentham assumed that the only difference between a rich person and poor person was in how much money they had: given the same amounts of money they would have similar amounts of utility. It is this similarity between the rich and the poor that led Bentham to conclude that transferring a dollar from the rich to the poor would hurt the rich less than it would help the poor.

But according to Pareto rich people and poor people may be fundamentally different. In this scenario transferring money from the rich to the poor could actually hurt the rich more than it would help the poor. Pareto used an extreme hypothetical example to illustrate this possibility: *What if the rich actually enjoy the poverty of the poor?*

If that is so, reducing poverty by redistribution may hurt the rich more than it would help the poor, Pareto argued. "Assume a collectivity made up of a wolf and a sheep," Pareto explained. "The happiness of the wolf consists in eating the sheep, that of the sheep in not being eaten. How is this collectivity to be made happy?"

Economists do not usually cite this passage in explaining Pareto's objection to Utilitarianism. Instead they ask what if the rich and the poor do not have the same utility function but instead, by chance, the rich happen to derive greater utility from a given quantity of money than the poor do.

This theory argues that just like a poor person, a rich person also derives greater utility from her first dollar than from her last one. But a rich person's utility from her *last* dollar may exceed the poor person's utility from her *first* dollar.

Economists do not claim that this situation actually exists, only that it may exist. Because utility is not measurable, this possibility simply cannot be ruled out. And if this is indeed the situation, then Bentham's argument does not hold, and redistribution is therefore not justified.

Bentham acknowledged this possibility. "Difference of character is inscrutable," he said. But, he argued, a large difference in character between the rich and the poor was so unlikely that the government would make fewer mistakes if it operated under the assumption that the rich and the poor are similar, than if it operated under the assumption that they are fantastically different.

The economist Abba Lerner (1903–82) noted that Bentham was just applying the first principle of statistics: when it is not known that things that appear the same are really different, the best we can do is to assume that they are the same. This is why, with gambling dice, we assign the probability of 1/6 to each face of a die.

Unlike Bentham or Lerner, Pareto did not concern himself with the question of how likely it was that redistribution would hurt the rich more than it would help the poor. For him this theoretical possibility, no matter how remote, was reason enough to reject the level of equality as a yardstick of economic efficiency. And based solely on this theoretical possibility, the entire economics profession removed the distribution of resources from its definition of economic efficiency and replaced it with Pareto's own definition.

Like Bentham, Pareto also equated efficiency with maximizing the well-being produced by society's resources. But while Bentham allowed for the possibility that this would require the redistribution of these resources from the rich to the poor, Pareto ruled this possibility out from the start. According to him, an allocation of resources is efficient if it cannot be changed in a way that will make at least one person better off without making anybody else worse off. This definition is indifferent to the distribution of society's resources. Today we call this Pareto efficiency, but economists usually omit the name Pareto. They equate efficiency with Pareto efficiency, ignoring the existence of competing definitions, including that of Utilitarian efficiency .

The concept of *Pareto efficiency* is a critical building block of all modern-day economics. A related and equally important concept is known as a *Pareto improvement*. A reallocation of resources is a Pareto improvement if it makes at least one person better off without making anybody worse off. When a Pareto improvement is possible, the allocation of resources is NOT Pareto efficient.

To use an extreme example that illustrates the concept, if the total income of a society were concentrated in the hands of just one person while everybody else went hungry, this would be Pareto efficient. Why? Because it would be impossible to feed the hungry without taking some money away from the rich.

We can see how economists use Pareto efficiency in actual policy making by looking at what happened during a food crisis and how a president of the American Economic Association wanted to reform the health care system.

In 1997 several Asian countries experienced a financial crisis that started when foreign investors slowed the pace of their investments in these countries. Indonesia was particularly sensitive to the decline in the inflow of dollars because all of its wheat, one-third of its sugar, and one-tenth of its rice are imported, and all of a sudden the country did not have enough dollars to pay for basic food. The government of Indonesia asked the IMF for a loan, but the IMF saw this request as an opportunity to enforce Pareto efficiency. The government of Indonesia subsidized food prices at the time, but these subsidies violate Pareto efficiency; the IMF made the loan contingent upon the abolition of the subsidies.

Why are food subsidies Pareto inefficient? Because in many cases it would be possible to give poor people cash directly instead of paying for subsidies, and the result would be both a lower cost to the taxpayer and higher utility to the poor. To see why, suppose that the world price of a loaf of bread is two dollars but that the subsidized local price to the consumer is only fifty cents (the taxpayer pays the extra four and a half dollars). Suppose also that with this low price a poor person buys three loaves of bread and pays for them a dollar and a half, but that she would have preferred to have not three, but only two loaves of bread, provided she could also have an extra dollar in her pocket. Under these conditions, the food subsidy would be Pareto inefficient. To see why, let's examine a possible Pareto improvement.

Let the government abolish the subsidy and give the poor person three and a half dollars in cash instead. The poor would then buy two loaves of bread for two dollars each and because she would be spending only fifty cents of her own money instead of a dollar and a half, would have an extra dollar in her pocket. The taxpayer would also be better off because she would spend only three and a half dollars for the transfer payment instead of spending four and a half dollars on the subsidy. Since both the poor and the taxpayer would be better off, this would be a Pareto improvement. And since a Pareto improvement is possible, food subsidies are not Pareto efficient.

Of course, people are the best judges of what they need and therefore giving poor people money directly is no doubt better than subsidizing a particular good that they buy. No policy is better for dealing with the consequences of inequality than reducing inequality itself. The only problem is that we live in a world in which it is much easier for governments to give things than to give money. In the United States, for instance, there is much less resistance to the food-stamps program than there is to welfare payments. Therefore, when subsidies are abolished, people are rarely adequately compensated for their loss, and Indonesia was no exception to this rule. When the IMF economists demanded that the government end its food subsidies in order to establish "market-based pricing," Larry Summers, the deputy U.S. secretary of commerce, backed them, and President Clinton even called President Suharto of Indonesia from Air Force One to demand that he comply. And comply Suharto did.

In the riots that ensued, five hundred people died in the capital, Jakarta, alone.

The Nobel Prize–winning economist Joseph Stiglitz, who was the chief economist of the World Bank at the time, called the food riots in Indonesia "the IMF Riots." "When a nation is down and out," Stiglitz told the London newspaper the *Observer*, "the IMF takes advantage and squeezes the last pound of blood out of them. They turn up the heat until finally the whole cauldron blows up." The *Observer* obtained secret International Monetary Fund documents in which the IMF's managers revealed that they expected "social unrest" in response to the policies they would impose, and that they decided to respond to these riots with "political resolve."

How does utilitarianism apply to food subsidies? If poor people will experience hunger without subsidies, it is clear that the gain in utility from the subsidies to the poor would exceed the loss in utility to the rich who would pay for them. Of course, utils are not measurable. Weighting the relative gains and losses requires judgment, and mistakes are possible. But food subsidies may be Utilitarian efficient even if they are not Pareto efficient.

Now let's look at the two definitions of efficiency as they apply to health care, which in the United States, until Obamacare, not only the poor but most middle class people could not afford. In 2004 Martin Feldstein, who had served as President Reagan's chair of the Council of Economic Advisers, received the highest recognition that economists give to one of their own: presidency of the American Economic Association. Feldstein devoted a large part of his presidential address to health insurance.

Health insurance was, of course, a very fitting topic for the president of the American Economic Association to address, since some fifty million Americans were without health insurance at the time, despite the fact that many of them worked full-time and despite the fact that even families with insurance were often crushed financially when they were faced with a catastrophic illness. Given the crisis in health care, one might have expected Feldstein to talk about how to provide health insurance to more Americans or, perhaps, how to remove unhealthy limitations on health care put in place by health maintenance organizations or HMOs.

Instead, Feldstein told the audience that health insurance in United States faced a problem because deductibles and co-payments were too low, and as a result people went to the doctor too many times: "They [low co-payments] also lead to an increased demand for care that is worth less than its cost of production."

To a noneconomist, the prime example of inefficient medical care would probably be cosmetic surgery, because it diverts doctors, nurses, and operating rooms away from real medical problems. But to an economist, cosmetic surgery is actually the prime example of efficient medical care. Why? Because cosmetic surgery is not medically necessary.

Because cosmetic surgery is not necessary, it is not covered by insurance. Without insurance a patient will never have cosmetic surgery, unless he is able to pay for it. This guarantees that the surgery is not "worth less than its cost of production." Real medical care is covered by insurance, and this is why, according to Martin Feldstein, it may be "worth less than its cost of production."

The following example illustrates Feldstein's argument that low co-payments lead to medical care that is "worth less than its cost of production." Suppose that the cost of a doctor's visit is $100 and that Poor, who is uninsured, cannot pay more than $20 for the visit. This means that the doctor's visit will not take place.

Now, let's change the example by assuming that Poor is insured and there is no co-payment, so insurance covers the $100. Under these circumstances the visit would take place, even though it is "worth less than its cost of production," which is the $100 that Poor cannot pay.

Is the visit Pareto inefficient? In other words, had the insurance company offered Poor a sum that is less than the cost of the visit—say, $95—to not visit the doctor, would Poor have accepted it? After all, Poor would have $95 in her pocket for a visit for which she was willing to pay $20.

It would be wrong to simply assume that she would, because Poor may nevertheless prefer to see the doctor than to take the money. In that case the visit to the doctor would be Pareto efficient even if without health insurance it would have been skipped. Economists are so accustomed to equating the worth of a good to a person with how much that person can afford to pay for it that Martin Feldstein could make this equation the pivotal element of his American Economic Association presidential address. The two are not the same, and this is precisely why insurance exists: to let people see the doctor when they cannot afford to.

Keep in mind that not seeing the doctor may mean that a treatable condition can worsen, causing a more severe illness and even death. But in his speech Feldstein did not consider such matters. Economists often do this, looking at hypothetical examples without context.

Currently, an employer who provides health insurance to her employees may deduct the premium payments from the company's income for tax purposes. Feldstein wanted to disallow this deduction in order to make health insurance more expensive because this would make it Pareto efficient. When insurance becomes more expensive to employers, Feldstein explained, poor employees will be forced to settle for higher deductibles and higher co-pays, which means that they will use less medical care. If Feldstein's advice were followed, the poor would have paid with their lives, because increases in co-pays lead patients to forgo immunization, cancer screening, and lifesaving drugs.

Needless to say, according to Feldstein's logic, while medical care for the poor may be worth less than its cost, this does not hold for the rich. To continue our example, let's suppose that Rich is willing to pay $101 for a doctor's visit. To dissuade Rich from going to the doctor, the insurance company would have to offer her this sum or more; but the doctor's fee is less than that, so an offer will not be made. In other words, a low co-payment rate for the rich would be Pareto efficient because the rich don't really need it.

Feldstein's recommendations were ignored, and under Obamacare co-pays for preventive medical procedures were abolished altogether. Does tax-subsidized health insurance increase the sum of utilities in society? Nothing gives greater utility to people than their health. The gain in utility to a patient who visits the doctor probably exceeds the loss in utility to those who pay for it. As for people who would make excessive visits to the doctor, there are other ways to channel behavior than a price mechanism that denies care.

Economists object to the redistribution of goods because giving poor people cash would achieve an even greater good. To reiterate, when dealing with the consequences of inequality, no policy is more effective than reducing the inequality itself. But to oppose policies that would alleviate shortages of food, housing, health care, or many other goods ostensibly because they are not as effective as income redistribution is duplicitous.

People are poor because under the banner of economics, the deck is stacked. What we need is economics for the rest of us.

Adapted from Economics for the Rest of Us: Debunking the Science That Makes Life Miserable.

DON'T DRINK THE KOOL-AID

Robert Kuttner

Inequality is as much a political problem as an economic one, one of America's top economic journalists writes. Ignoring trillions in wasted individual investments while riling up anger over even minor waste in government is part of the problem—and so is the change in who reports the news.

A number of chapters in this volume document the shocking increase in inequality in America. My message is simple: it does not have to be that way. It does not have to be that way economically or politically.

The Right has a story to tell about inequality. It's a simple story, which has been swallowed whole by elite opinion and a lot of ordinary Americans. If you want an economy that works efficiently, it says, you have to tolerate a great deal of inequality.

I've devoted much of my career as an economics writer and a polemicist to disproving that argument. The simplest refutation is to refer back to periods of American history when we had significantly greater equality, both of opportunity and of result, and stronger economic growth; we can also point to other countries that have much less inequality than the United States does and work better economically.

It's not hard to see why they do. A prosperous economy demands investment in children, in health, in education, in job training, in public systems, in the commons generally. If you have tens of millions of people not living up to their potential as economic beings, by definition your society is going to be less productive than it could be. If you spend almost 18 percent of the gross domestic product on health care because private, profit-motivated insurance companies are taking thirty cents out of every premium dollar, you are not going to have a society that is as healthy as it ought to be.

Equality works. Extreme inequality does not. Out of the grotesque opportunism that we've seen among owners of great wealth in the past ten years has come a colossal waste of financial capital and human energy.

The stock-market bubble of the late 1990s induced investors to put vast resources into enterprises that never paid back a nickel of return; they only lined the pockets of insiders. If the government squandered money on this scale, conservatives and conservative investment bankers would be up in arms. But they're not, of course. When the government wastes hundreds of dollars, they tell us it's an outrage; when the market wastes trillions of dollars, it's a lamentable glitch. This is not economics. This is ideology, pure and simple.

Why has our society become so much more unequal in the past twenty-five years? It's a trick question. The technical or policy answer involves a systematic weakening of what might be called equalizing institutions, which defend the commonwealth against the forces of wealth and concentrated power. To maintain a social contract of the kind that existed in this country during the postwar decades, you need a government to administer it; to help people climb out of poverty, you have to tax the wealthy and put some of the proceeds into opportunity-making programs.

But in a global economy with no global government, there is no entity capable of enforcing rules or effectively collecting taxes and directing public investment. I am a citizen of the United States of America. I am not a citizen of the Republic of NAFTA. There is no Republic of NAFTA, and that is exactly the way big business wants it.

And so, in addition to the alleged economic efficiency of freer trade, business gets another benefit: it wipes away all of the social institutions that have been built through great struggle by ordinary people and their governments over the past hundred years.

That is really the insidious influence of globalization. It is not just that jobs move to countries where people are desperate enough to work for starvation wages, or where publics are too powerless to demand environmental standards. No, it is the fact that we are left with no democratically accountable institution capable of setting ground rules. We could have had a brand of globalization in which the ability to sell products to the United States depended on meeting certain social minimums, involving wages, organizing rights, environmental standards, treatment of children, and so on. But because that was not the globalization that corporate America sought, it is not what has evolved.

So the real answer to the question, "Why have we become so much more unequal?" has to be a political answer. The forces that yearn for a restoration of the kind of polity we had in the robber baron era of the late 1800s have become far stronger over the past quarter century; that, in essence, is why organized labor has shrunk since 1970 from 35 percent to 9.3 percent of the American workforce in 2012 and under 7 percent of private-sector workers.

That's what encourages giant corporations to demand huge tax "incentives" before they move in anywhere, and then to move out with impunity as soon as another jurisdiction offers a better deal. That's why, in so many areas, property rights now take precedence over human rights, social rights, and labor rights. The instruments and institutions that allow us to choose to become a more egalitarian society have simply been removed from the realm of democratic citizenship.

We cannot fully blame this change on one political faction or party. Too often, over the past twenty-five years, both parties have been drinking the same Kool-Aid. Too much of the time, Democrats have presented themselves as the "me too" party. "We do not really like government either," they say. "We love big business, too. Let the free market decide." We heard far too much of that from our last two Democratic presidents, Jimmy Carter and Bill Clinton.

There are several explanations for this self-defeating rhetoric. First of all, it is the result of money becoming paramount in politics—becoming the medium of politics. If you spend most of your waking hours courting the wealthy, you start talking their language; you instinctively seek to reassure your donors, and you cease paying attention to building, validating, and energizing your base. As the Democrats have become more artful fund-raisers, their message to the base has become muddy, and populism has become a dirty word.

The news media have abetted the process. When I started out in journalism, a reporter was a kind of average person who wore cheap suits and identified with the downtrodden. Today, the most influential journalists, who make six- and seven-figure incomes, with a few in the eight-figure class that starts at $10 million per year, give well-paid lectures to trade associations and hobnob with elites. Hardly any of them identify with ordinary people. One of the daunting tasks that faces us, in addition to taking back American politics, is taking back the American press so it does not contribute more to justifying our worsening inequality.

From Inequality Matters: The Growing Economic Divide in America and its Poisonous Consequences, *ed. James Lardner and David A. Smith.*

SOCIAL SECURITY REDUCES INEQUALITY—EFFICIENTLY, EFFECTIVELY, AND FAIRLY

Nancy Altman and Eric Kingson

Two scholars who served on the staff of President Reagan's 1982 National Commission on Social Security Reform explain that Social Security does more to reduce income inequality and prevent poverty among the old in the United States than any other program, public or private, while providing crucial protection for orphans and the disabled. And, contrary to widely circulated claims, they show it does not add one dollar to the federal government's budget deficits and can remain financially sound as long as our government exists.

Generations of Americans built our Social Security system to provide basic and widespread protection against loss of earnings arising from the death, disability, or retirement of working Americans—for themselves, their families, and those who follow. Like the Constitution or other major institutions, it requires modest adjustments from time to time, but its basic structure is sound. It has worked well for seventy-seven years, never failing to meet its obligations, even during the deep recession that followed the near collapse of the economy in 2008. There is no reason it can't continue to do so as long as the United States is around.

Social Security gives concrete expression to widely held and time-honored American commitments. Grounded in values of shared responsibility and concern for all members of society, it reflects an understanding that, as citizens and human beings, we all share certain risks and vulnerabilities; and we all have a stake in advancing practical mechanisms of self- and mutual support. It is based on the belief that government—which is simply all of us acting collectively—can and should uphold these values by providing practical, dignified, secure, and efficient means to protect Americans and their families against risks they all face.

Social Security runs seamlessly and efficiently—less than 1 percent of its expenditures are for administration.

Social Security provided monthly benefits in 2013 to 57 million Americans:

37 million retired workers

2.3 million spouses of retired workers

3.9 million aged widow(er)s

8.9 million disabled workers

256,000 disabled widow(ers) ages 50 to 66

3.5 million children under age 19

1 million severely disabled dependent adult children

160,000 spouses of disabled workers, and

146,000 spouses of deceased workers caring for dependent children.*

Although Social Security's benefits are modest, they are extremely important for the vast majority of beneficiaries, especially those with low and moderate incomes. The average benefit is about $15,000 a year for retired workers; about $12,700 a year for survivors of workers; and about $11,700 for disabled workers and their families.

Sixty percent of households with at least one person aged sixty-five or over reported income of less than $32,602 in 2010 income About three-quarters of all the income going to those households comes from Social Security. Occupational pensions

---

*You can look up the latest data, posted each month, by the Social Security Administration, Office of the Actuary.

make significant contributions to the aggregate incomes going to households in the three highest quintiles, but fall short of Social Security, which is not surprising when considering that roughly six out of ten private-sector employees do not have private pension protections.

Without Social Security, the official U.S. poverty rate among the

IMPORTANCE OF SELECTED SOURCES OF INCOME TO ELDERLY (65+) HOUSEHOLDS BY QUINTILES, 2010

Percent of Total Income from:	All Aged Units	Quintiles				
		Q1	Q2	Q3	Q4	Q5
		Under $12,554	$12,554–$20,144	$20,145–$32,601	$32,602–$57,956	$57,957 and over
Social Security	36.7%	84.3%	83.3%	65.7%	43.5%	17.3%
Occupational Pensions	18.6%	2.9%	6.9%	15.9%	25.8%	19.1%
Earnings	30.2%	2.4%	4.1%	9.6%	19.4%	44.9%
Income from Assets	11.4%	1.8%	2.6%	5.4%	7.8%	16.1%
Public Cash Asistance	.5%	.7%	1.6%	.5%	.2%	.1%
Other	2.6%	1.6%	1.4%	2.8%	3.3%	2.4%

Social Security Administration, Table 10.5, income of the Population 55 or Older, 2021, February 2012.

aged would jump from 9 percent to nearly 50 percent—about the same rate as in the 1920s and early 1930s, prior to the enactment of Social Security. Poverty rates for older Americans living alone and for minorities are even higher than the rate of poverty among all aged, and those subgroups are, on average, more dependent on Social Security.

From the beginning, Social Security has been structured to address two goals—social adequacy along with individual equity. Social adequacy means that even the lowest benefits will provide at least a minimal level of support. The ideal, though not fully achieved, is that those who work their entire lives should not have to retire into poverty. Those who work and contribute should benefit from that work, and receive higher benefits than they would simply from means-tested welfare. Individual equity means that all workers receive a fair benefit in relation to their work effort and level of contributions. Social Security has been well designed to balance these twin goals.

One way these twin goals are achieved is through the use of a progressive benefit formula. The way Social Security calculates benefits is one of the most ingenious and important features of the program. Its benefit formula ensures that long-term, low-wage workers receive a proportionately larger benefit relative to their contributions, though a lower absolute dollar amount, than high-wage workers. At the same time, the Social Security contributions of high-wage workers are recognized by a larger monthly benefit in absolute dollar terms, but a proportionately smaller benefit relative to their contributions. For workers retiring at the full retirement age of sixty-six years in January 2012, Social Security benefits replaced about 26 percent of earnings for those with earnings consistently at the maximum taxable earnings ceiling, about 41 percent for average earners, and about 55 percent for those with earnings at 45 percent of median wage, which the year before was $26,965 or less than $519 a week.

Social Security's protections are by far the most important life and disability safeguard available to virtually all the nation's seventy-five million children under age eighteen. Through Social

Security, working Americans who are married with two young children, for example, earn life-insurance protections with a present value around $550,000 dollars. They earn similar protections for themselves and their families in the event of a severe and permanent disability.

In 2013, 4.5 million dependent children—about 3.5 million under age nineteen and 1 million adults disabled before age twenty-two—received Social Security checks totaling about $2.7 billion per month. Another 3.4 million children who do not receive benefits live in households with one or more relatives who do. Social Security benefits lift 1.3 million children out of poverty.

As much as children need Social Security protections when young, those hoping to work, especially if they plan to have children or retire one day, also need it. The Social Security Administration estimates that 25 to 30 percent of twenty-year-olds will become disabled prior to age sixty-seven and one in eight will die. Disability insurance, a benefit rarely offered by employers, provides vital protection over the course of one's life. Further, nothing approaches Social Security in terms of providing secure retirement-income protection. Neither stock-market fluctuations nor inflation undermines its value. As billions of dollars of pension and home-equity "wealth" disappeared in the Great Recession, there was no risk of Social Security failing to meet its obligations.

By providing an orderly way for individuals to pay for benefits during working years in exchange for protections against premature death, disability, and retirement, Social Security takes some of the tension out of family life and reinforces the dignity of many. Knowing that one's parents have Social Security often frees up the generation in the middle to direct more family resources toward their own children.

Given what a central role Social Security plays in the lives of the overwhelming number of America's families, it is no surprise that virtually every poll shows large majorities consider Social Security crucial to their and the nation's well-being and do not want to see benefits cut. This is true across all demographic groups—women, people of color, old, young—as well as across the political spectrum—Democrats, independents, and Republicans, union and even Tea Party supporters.

While there is much skepticism, especially among young adults, about its future, Social Security remains one of the few public services that citizens are willing to pay for. A 2013 Matthew Greenwald & Associates online survey of two thousand people ages twenty and above, commissioned by the nonpartisan National Academy of Social Insurance, showed that "Americans value Social Security, want to improve benefits, and are willing to pay more to maintain and expand its benefit protections." Specifically, the poll found that:

Roughly four out of five say they value Social Security for themselves, their families, and for the sound protection it provides to tens of millions of beneficiaries;

More than four-fifths say that benefits are too low for retirees and three-quarters favor improving retirement protections for working Americans;

and more than four out of five believe it should be preserved for future generations even if it requires increasing payroll-tax contributions.

Of course, like the nation's highways, Social Security needs to be maintained. The system, a public trust, is carefully monitored. Political squabbling aside, the Congress has always managed to adjust the system when necessary.

The Social Security system as currently structured is fully affordable. Indeed, higher benefits are affordable. At its most expensive, around 2035, when most if not all of today's baby-boom generation is fully retired, Social Security will cost, as a percentage of the nation's gross domestic product, less than other industrialized countries such as Germany, France, and Japan spend on their old age Social Security programs in 2013.

The American program is conservatively managed. Every year, its board of trustees issues a report projecting Social Security's future income and outgo for the next three-quarters of a century. This is a longer valuation than private pensions use and longer, indeed, than most other countries use for their Social Security programs. The most recent report indicates that over the next seventy-five years, Social Security will have a projected shortfall of less than 1 percent of GDP.

That shortfall could be eliminated by increasing the rate at which Social Security contributions are assessed by just 1.31 percentage points to 7.51 percent of covered wages, but there are much more progressive ways to eliminate the shortfall. Several modest changes could ensure that the program is fully funded for everyone alive today. One change we believe should be made is increasing the maximum amount of wages on which Social Security's contributions are assessed. Contributions are assessed only on the wages that are insured against loss.

Congress has expressed its intent that 90 percent of all wages be insured against loss, but because wages at the top have grown so much faster than average wages over the last few decades, the percentage of wages covered has declined. Restoring the maximum so it once again covers 90 percent of all wages would eliminate about a third of the projected shortfall. Gradually phasing out the maximum so that high-income employers eventually pay the same rate as the vast majority of their employees on all their earnings would, depending on how this change is structured, eliminate roughly 80 to 90 percent of the projected shortfall. It would also mean somewhat increased benefits for higher-income workers.

Other streams of revenue that could eliminate Social Security's projected shortfall while addressing income inequality would be a modest tax on annual incomes above $1 million, or a modest tax on financial speculation. Numerous other approaches exist. All would impose modest increased costs on those at the top without cutting Social Security's modest, but vital, benefits.

Since it was first proposed in 1935, many conservatives have vehemently opposed Social Security. They assert that Social Security's universal wage insurance is an inappropriate role of government. They believe Social Security somehow restricts freedom and turns the nation into a collection of people dependent on government. Yet Americans continue to work hard while continually demonstrating overwhelmingly support for Social Security.

This popularity is the reason it is hard to find any politician who says he or she does not support Social Security; they all say they want to "strengthen" it. Generally, one can only discern their true motives by studying what they are proposing. Despite the time-tested ability of Social Security to meet all its obligations, in good times and bad, there are those who falsely claim it is unsustainable. Others, in the name of fiscal austerity or claims about insolvency, want to compromise Social Security's basic protections by reducing its modest benefits through subtle but damaging changes. One would be cutting the cost of living adjustment, which prevents benefits from eroding over time. Another proposal is to raise the retirement age, which amounts to an across-the-board benefit cut for retirees, a cut which would fall hardest on those in physically demanding jobs or in poor health. There are, and will be, other proposals to portray benefit cuts as strengthening the system.

The worst proposals are to radically transform Social Security by privatizing, which would put people at the mercy of the stock and bonds markets as well as cost much more to administer or to add means-testing which would deny benefits to higher-income workers. Either of these ideas would destroy the fundamental features that have made Social Security so successful, and wildly popular, which is what opponents of Social Security want to destroy so they can end the program.

Occasionally the veil slips, and politicians let their true views out. At a private fund-raiser on May 17, 2012, presidential candidate Mitt Romney said, in an apparent reference to, among others, Social Security beneficiaries, "There are 47 percent of the people . . . who are dependent on government, who believe that they are victims, who believe that government has a responsibility to care for them." Similarly, his vice presidential running mate, Congressman Paul Ryan, has divided Americans into so-called takers and makers. The reality is that Social Security is not a government handout. It is a benefit that is earned and paid for through hard work.

Because of all the organized attacks based on falsehoods told about Social Security, the public lacks confidence in its future, concerned that it may not be there when they, their children, and grandchildren need it. Ask most young people whether they think Social Security will be there when they need it, and a large majority says "no."

Ask those same young people whether they think Social Security benefits, averaging just around $15,000 a year for today's retired workers, should be increased, and most answer "yes." These young people seem to understand that behind all the numbers, all the technical talk about Social Security, are real people—their grandparents, parents, a classmate whose father died, and another whose mother is severely disabled. And, as the economy changes, it becomes increasingly apparent that they, like their parents, will need this system as they travel through life.

Americans today face a serious retirement-income crisis. Data published by the Retirement Research Center at Boston College suggest that nearly two-thirds of today's workers will be unable to maintain their standards of living in retirement, even if they work until age sixty-five. Nevertheless, political and media elites seem to think that still larger cuts are sensible—both for today's and tomorrow's beneficiaries—and only a courageous few have voiced the need to expand, not cut, Social Security.

Today's debate is less about today's seniors than tomorrow's. Our nation's children have a huge stake in the preservation of Social Security. Even more than their parents and grandparents, they stand to gain the most from the organized efforts of older Americans to strengthen the program, not cut it. The United States can unquestionably afford Social Security. The issue about its future is not one of mathematics or even demographics, but politics.

The case for expanding Social Security is strong. It is more efficient, secure, universal, and fair in its distribution than any private-sector counterpart is or could ever be, no matter how structured. The reason? Wage insurance works best when all workers are covered under the same plan and the coverage starts at the beginning of their working lives. The only entity that can mandate this kind of universal program is the federal government and it has.

In reality, Social Security is the nation's most successful, popular, and just social program, the "poster child" for government working well on behalf of the American people and playing a major role in reducing inequality.

ARGUMENTS FOR AND AGAINST
INCOME INEQUALITY
Thomas L. Hungerford

Some researchers argue that inequality is a social good. In this chapter a former Congressional Research Service economist examines the issues, including three key factors that contribute to rising inequality.

For more than two centuries social scientists and philosophers have been concerned with issues surrounding the distribution of income or income inequality. For example, the economist and philosopher Adam Smith discussed these issues as early as 1776 in his classic book *An Inquiry into the Nature and Causes of the Wealth of Nations*. Modern academics have been writing on income-inequality-measurement issues for at least a century. Policy makers have also long been interested in income-inequality issues. The Congressional Budget Office, a research arm of Congress, has documented that income inequality has been increasing in the United States over the past thirty-five years.

The Obama administration has stated that one of its tax-reform principles was to observe the "Buffett rule." It is named for Warren Buffett, the investor who disclosed that he pays 17 percent of the income reported on his tax return in federal income and payroll taxes, half the rate paid by his secretary. The Obama administration describes the rule this way: "no household making over $1 million annually should pay a smaller share of its income in taxes than middle-class families pay."

There are reasoned arguments about whether rising income inequality is harmful or beneficial to society. The classic argument against rising income inequality is that the rich get richer and the poor get poorer. This can increase poverty, reduce well-being, and reduce social cohesion. Consequently, some argue that reducing income inequality may reduce various social ills. Additionally, research across national boundaries has demonstrated that large income and class disparities adversely affect health and economic well-being.

In contrast, others argue that rising inequality is nothing to worry about and point out that over the long run average real income has been rising, so while the rich are indeed getting richer, the poor are not necessarily getting poorer. In addition, some researchers and policy analysts argue that some income inequality is necessary to encourage innovation and entrepreneurship—the possibility of large rewards and high income are incentives to bear the risks. Without large rewards there would be less investment and innovation, these researchers argue, and total incomes would be smaller.

Furthermore, some have argued that income or social mobility—movement up and down within the income distribution—reduces income inequality and increases well-being. However, research in recent years has shown that income mobility is not very great in the United States. Mobility either remained unchanged or decreased since the 1970s, my research and that of others have shown.

Among the potential causes of the increase in after-tax income inequality between 1991 and 2006 are changes in labor income (wages and salaries), changes in capital income (interest income, capital gains, dividends, and business income), and changes in taxes. These reasons are not mutually exclusive—a change in labor or capital income could also affect the amount of taxes paid, which affects observed inequality of after-tax incomes.

Earnings inequality has been increasing since at least the late 1960s. Increased salaries, bonuses, and stock options partially explain this. Higher pay for CEOs, managers, financial professionals, and athletes accounts for 70 percent of the increase in the share of income going to the richest Americans.

This growth at the top, various scholars argue, is the result of government policies that favor elites, changes in education levels and skills, declining unionization or the falling value of the minimum wage, which in real terms fell from $6.57 per hour in 1996 to $5.57 per hour in 2006. There is disagreement on whether more women entering the workforce starting in the 1970s has increased or decreased inequality of earnings.

An increasing share of income for high-income tax filers is from capital income—capital gains, dividends, interest, rents, and business income from partnerships and S-corporations. The concentration and growth of capital income was thrust into the debate over increasing income inequality with the Occupy Wall Street movement in 2011. Across the country Occupy raised questions about growing wealth and income from financial investments and corporate executive pay and stock options, while millions of people were out of work.

Proposed legislation to increase the tax rate on carried interests received by managers of hedge funds and private-equity funds has also drawn attention to how we measure income and how we tax income. These managers of other people's money pay taxes at the lower rates for capital gains, rather than the higher rates paid by other workers, including managers of stock mutual funds and executives at corporations. This lower rate is allowed even though the managers may not have any of their own capital at risk, but rather get paid for their success at investing other people's money.

Capital income is concentrated among higher-income tax filers because they tend to own more wealth, both investments like stocks and bonds but also businesses. The number of partnerships and S-corporations (whose profits and tax liabilities flow through to the owners) steadily increased from 1991 to 2006. The number of partnerships increased by 1.4 million over this period and the number of S-corporations increased by 2.2 million. Most of the income from these entities flows to high-income Americans.

Tax policy has also been identified as a possible cause for rising income inequality. While the individual income-tax system is progressive, at least to the level of 99.9 percent of reported income, and has been since it was introduced in 1913, the trend has been toward lower marginal tax rates. This means the trend is toward a less progressive tax system. This, in turn, implies more inequality over the long run as those with higher incomes can save more because their tax burden is smaller and their investments will grow faster on an after-tax basis. The long-term effect is like that of a snowball gathering more as it rolls along.

But by far the largest contributor to increasing income inequality, regardless of how inequality is measured, is changes in income from capital gains and dividends. Policies that further concentrate capital ownership at or near the top of the income distribution will thus increase income inequality.

INEQUALITY OF HAZARD

Frank Ackerman and Lisa Heinzerling

*The poor live with much more pollution than the affluent under
government policies that concentrate toxic discharges where people with little income and even less political power live. The assumptions of cost-benefit analysis encourage this sort of inequality
of hazard, as an economist and an environmental law professor
explain.*

The environmental justice movement emerged in the 1980s
with disputes about the siting of undesirable facilities in communities of color. A protest in North Carolina, at the proposed
site of a landfill for polychlorinated biphenyls (PCBs)—highly
toxic and persistent chemicals that have been banned in this country and many others—is often cited as the launching point of
the movement. This protest inspired several national studies on
the siting problem; the studies eventually provided clear statistical evidence that racial minorities were more likely to live near
hazardous-waste dumps.

In the early years of the movement, there was a lengthy discussion of whether this uneven burden was primarily based on the
legacy of racial discrimination or the stark facts of economics. But
underlying that debate is the more profound question of why a

market economy produces, and condones, such a marked inequality of hazard.

Siting decisions are only one of the many ways that injustice manifests itself in health and environmental policy. For example, government decisions about which polluters to target for enforcement actions and possible financial penalties, and about where and how thoroughly to clean up contaminated sites, have also been shown to be correlated with race and ethnicity—and not in a way that works to the advantage of minorities.

Even the building blocks of health and environmental regulation—scientific assessments of risk—are often infused with assumptions that ignore or intensify racial and ethnic inequality. Assessments of the risk from eating fish contaminated with hazardous chemicals, for example, have often failed to account for the higher fish consumption of certain groups, such as Native Americans. Likewise, studies on pesticide risk often have assumed that the people exposed to pesticides have the body weight and other physiological characteristics of adults, yet many farmworkers bring their children to the fields with them when they work. Assumptions like these have the effect of understating risks to minority racial and ethnic groups, and thus threaten to reduce the health protections afforded these groups.

Likewise, there is increasing concern that the current enthusiasm for market-mimicking regulatory approaches—like pollution trading—has overlooked the potential for injustice in these approaches. A pollution-trading program in Southern California, for example, allowed marine terminals to avoid installing expensive new pollution-control equipment by buying old, highly polluting cars. That got the clunkers off the road. And it meant that increased pollution at the marine terminals was "traded" for lower pollution from cars.

Such systems are supposed to promote efficiency by lowering the total cost of pollution control; in this case, removing old cars from the road is a cheaper way to reduce emissions than controlling air pollution at marine terminals.

Unfortunately, the program did not always reduce pollution from cars; many of the scrapyards where the cars ended up just put the old, dirty engines into other cars that went right back on the roads. More significantly, the pollution levels in the mostly Latino, low-income neighborhoods surrounding the marine terminals went sky-high, thanks to emissions from the terminals (because increased pollution at these facilities, in just a few neighborhoods, was supposedly being traded for decreases on the roads throughout a four-county area).

Eventually the car-scrapping program was itself scrapped due to these problems. A seemingly sophisticated market mechanism only succeeded in creating inequality and environmental injustice because the more intense pollution continued in the poorer areas near the port.

There are multiple lessons to be learned from this experience. One is the power of the Enron effect: when a complex new market is introduced, the most profitable short-run strategy, if you understand the market, may be simply to cheat. It will take some time for everyone else to figure out what is going on, and until they do you can make out, literally, like a bandit. Those who like to invent market mechanisms should note the importance of transparency in new institutions, and the essential role of law enforcement.

A deeper lesson is the potential connection between pollution trading and inequality. Even if the California trading system had worked as intended—that is, even if the scrapyards had actually scrapped the dirty old engines—its effect would have been to trade reduced pollution in neighborhoods where the old cars were previously being driven for increased pollution around the marine terminals. Thus the efficiency achieved by the trading system, consisting of lower total costs for pollution reduction, would have come at the expense of shifting pollution into poorer neighborhoods.The economists who originally came up with the idea of pollution trading, more than thirty years ago, would not have been surprised to learn that the California trading program created heavily polluted "hot spots." In fact, they thought something like this might happen, and embraced the idea. In their naive optimism, they thought that local variation in pollution levels would be associated with freedom of choice, not with inequality of power and income.

J.H. Dales, a Canadian economist who is often credited with first introducing the idea of pollution trading, concluded that it would be a good idea to allow lots of pollution in some places while allowing very little in others. Polluting an already polluted area was better, Dales thought, than spreading the pollution around so that every place was dirty. "We all benefit from variety," Dales wrote in his 1968 book *Pollution, Property and Prices.*

If, for example, urban rivers are polluted but rivers in the countryside are kept pristine, the avid angler could enjoy city life yet still drive to a beautiful countryside to fish. Dales referred to his idea, following the lead of British economist E.J. Mishan, as the "separate facilities" approach.

But Dales forgot one important fact: people might live near each of his separate facilities, and living with pollution around them might harm more than their enjoyment of fishing. When the people who live around the "facilities" we've chosen to keep polluting are disproportionately African American, Hispanic, poor, or otherwise socially disadvantaged, even the term "separate facilities" has a sinister echo. It was, after all, racially separate facilities on passenger trains that the U.S. Supreme Court endorsed in its infamous nineteenth-century decision in *Plessy v. Ferguson*, with the impossible proviso that the facilities be "separate but equal." The preference for "separate facilities" built into the original case for pollution trading makes it no surprise to learn that trading programs can worsen existing environmental inequalities.

It is widely agreed, at least in principle, that values like freedom and fairness are important considerations in health, safety, and environmental policy. Yet we have seen that market mechanisms such as pollution trading can work against fairness.

The problem is equally severe when it comes to monetization and cost-benefit analysis. Like life and health, the values discussed in this chapter do not come with price tags attached. There is no meaningful way to assign dollar values to risks when the upper limit of potential harm is unknown, when the risk is involuntary, or when the risk is unfairly distributed.

When the upper limit of potential harm is unknown, it is simply not possible to assign a number to the health and environmental benefits obtained by avoiding the harm. The number must either remain blank—in which case it will often be arbitrarily treated as if it were zero—or be based on a hopelessly speculative, perhaps misleadingly reassuring, guess.

In its unpredictability, terrorism closely resembles some of the major, uncertain, potentially unbounded environmental risks, such as climate change, in that reasonable, precautionary policies must be developed based on our current, imperfect understanding of the threats. Waiting for an impossibly precise measurement of the risks—or relying on wildly speculative, low-end predictions about the probability of harm—is a dangerous and shortsighted strategy for climate change, for terrorism, and for other fundamental threats to our future.

Likewise, the very nature of involuntary risks also defies monetization and creates troubles for cost-benefit analysis. The risks that led the Environmental Protection Agency to assume a value of $6.1 million for a human life are not the same kinds of risks that government often regulates. In the workplace setting involved in deriving that figure, the risks of death on the job are sometimes said to be voluntary; workers choose their jobs, the theory goes, based on their acceptance of a certain risk in return for a certain wage. Yet the choice of jobs is a somewhat more ambiguous process in reality, perhaps best described as partly, or occasionally, voluntary. However, in the environmental setting, risks are not allocated, even in theory, according to market transactions. No one has asked the citizens of Los Angeles whether they will accept money in return for dirty air; they just get the dirty air without being asked.

Some analysts have tried to incorporate the involuntary nature of environmental risks into cost-benefit analysis by proposing a higher dollar value for human life in the environmental setting, based on the claim that people will be willing to pay more to avoid involuntary risks than to avoid voluntary ones. This view misses the fundamental problem with translating involuntary risks to human life and health into dollars.

The philosophical premise of cost-benefit analysis is that a person is the best judge of his or her own welfare. When someone consents to accept an increased risk in exchange for money, the theory says that this choice should be respected for the sake of both freedom and rationality. But the same cost-benefit analysts don't seem to think that people are very good judges of their own welfare when it comes to perceiving and assessing risks.

Aside from any other problems with this theory, the premise of rational, free choice obviously collapses when it comes to involuntary exchanges, which, by definition, take place without a person's consent. An involuntary exchange is one forced on you, such as having to breathe dirtier air, if you live near the Port of Los Angeles, after that clunker car program.

Involuntary exchanges tell us nothing about a person's true willingness to pay for benefits. No one, we suppose, would advocate using the money forked over to robbers or the ransom paid to kidnappers as evidence of the value of life or health.

It is possible, of course, that some voluntary market exchanges could exist with respect to involuntary risks. For example, a person might buy bottled water in order to avoid the risk associated with her contaminated tap water. Or she might buy an air filter to mitigate the risk from air pollution in her neighborhood. Thus, it could be argued, involuntary risks pose no special challenge for economic analysis based on "willingness to pay." Such alternatives may not be practical in every case: to avoid climate change, will each person buy an unspoiled individual ecosystem, her own private Idaho?

But even when private expenditures, as for bottled water, could provide technical solutions, there is still a central issue to confront: who should have the right to go about her daily business without seeking permission from the people she affects—the polluter or the polluted?

If the consumer had a right to clean water, then whoever wanted to engage in activities that would contaminate her drinking water would have to seek her permission—and probably pay her—to go ahead with those activities. It may well be that a person would demand a much higher amount for her consent to have her drinking water contaminated than she would pay to filter or replace her water, once it was contaminated. She might even, for example, believe that her entitlement to clean water is not something to be bargained away, or she might have a moral aversion to the idea of befouling drinking water for economic profit.

In any case, market interactions between polluter and polluted likely would be very different from interactions between the polluted and a neutral third party, such as a bottled water supplier. By forcing even "involuntary" risks—risks not subjected to these kinds of market conversations—into cost-benefit analysis, economists and other analysts have contrived an unrealistic market where none realistically can exist.

Finally, and equally important, cost-benefit analysis also tends to ignore, and therefore to reinforce, patterns of economic and social inequality. Cost-benefit analysis consists of adding up all the costs and benefits of a policy and comparing the totals. Implicit in this innocuous-sounding procedure is the assumption that it doesn't matter who gets the benefits and who pays the costs. Both benefits and costs are measured simply as dollar totals; those totals are silent on questions of equity and distribution of resources. If pollution trading reduces the total cost of pollution reduction, it increases efficiency as economists define the term, regardless of whether it also makes the dirtiest areas even dirtier. Yet concerns about equity frequently do and should enter into debates over public policy.

It is no coincidence that pollution so often accompanies poverty. Imagine a cost-benefit analysis of siting an undesirable facility, such as a landfill or incinerator. Benefits are often measured by willingness to pay for environmental improvement. Wealthy communities are able and willing to pay more for the benefit of not having the facility in their backyards; thus when measured this way the net benefits to society as a whole will be maximized by putting the facility in a low-income area.

Wealthy communities do not actually have to pay for the benefit of avoiding the facility; the analysis depends only on the fact that they are willing to pay. This kind of logic was made infamous in a 1991 memo circulated by Lawrence Summers (who later became Treasury secretary and later still president of Harvard University) when he was the chief economist at the World Bank. Discussing the migration of "dirty industries" to developing countries, Summers's memo explained:

> The measurements of the costs of health-impairing pollution depend on the foregone earnings from increased morbidity and mortality. From this point of view a given amount of health-impairing pollution should be done in the country with the lowest cost, which will be the country with the lowest wages. I think the economic logic behind dumping a load of toxic waste in the lowest-wage country is impeccable and we should face up to that.

After this memo became public, Brazil's then–secretary of the environment Jose Lutzenburger wrote to Summers: "Your reasoning is perfectly logical but totally insane. . . . Your thoughts [provide] a concrete example of the unbelievable alienation, reductionist thinking, social ruthlessness and the arrogant ignorance of many conventional 'economists' concerning the nature of the world we live in."

If decisions were based strictly on cost-benefit analysis and willingness to pay, most environmental burdens would end up being imposed on the countries, communities, and individuals with the least resources. This theoretical pattern bears an uncomfortably close resemblance to reality. Economic theory should not be blamed for existing patterns of environmental injustice; we suspect that pollution is typically dumped on the poor without waiting for formal analysis. Still, cost-benefit analysis rationalizes and reinforces the problem, allowing environmental burdens to flow downhill along the income gradients of an unequal world. It is hard to see this as part of an economically optimal or politically objective method of decision making.

When risks are reduced to numbers alone, funny things happen. Uncertainty collapses into a precise—which is not to say accurate—estimate of future hazards. Inequity is covered up by a market framework that is silent about the distribution of costs and benefits, and silently makes that distribution less equitable.

The context of risk, the fairness of burdens and benefits—all these characteristics, which are all-important in real decisions—are priceless. They cannot be forgotten in making effective public policy, but they cannot be remembered with a number.

Adapted from Priceless: On Knowing the Price of Everything and the Value of Nothing.

A DIFFERENT KIND OF EPIDEMIC

Ernest Drucker

A subtle but significant factor in inequality is America's use of long prison sentences for nonviolent crimes, which has hit black Americans especially hard. A prominent epidemiologist explains this as a new kind of public health problem.

Beginning in the 1970s, a new epidemic occurred in our nation—affecting tens of millions of Americans over the course of more than three decades. Yet despite its huge scale and powerful effects on our population, almost no one noticed it. Here are some of the things we know about this new epidemic:

- The population involved is diverse: men and women, adults and children, different social classes.
- The onset was very rapid: in thirty-five years the population directly affected by this epidemic increased tenfold, from 250,000 in 1970 to 2.3 million by 2009.
- The effects of the epidemic extend beyond the actual cases: over 30 million have been affected in the last thirty years.
- Young minority men have been affected most severely: although they make up only 3 percent of the U.S.

population, young black and Hispanic men constitute over 30 percent of the cases.

- While this epidemic is nationwide, most cases have occurred in the poorest neighborhoods of America's urban areas—in some communities, over 90 percent of families have afflicted members.
- Individuals who are afflicted are also socially marginalized and often become incapacitated for life—unable to find decent work, get proper housing, participate in the political system, or have a normal family life.
- The children of families affected by this new epidemic have lower life expectancy and are six to seven times more likely to acquire it themselves than the children of families not affected.

Like the sinking of the *Titanic*, this new event is a disaster—but it is no accident. Indeed, it is the result of laws and deliberate public policies, fueled by the expenditure of trillions of dollars of public funds, and supported by powerful political and economic interests. Although no known biological agent is involved, as with cholera and AIDS, this new epidemic exhibits all the characteristics of an infectious disease—spreading most rapidly by proximity and exposure to prior cases.

This new epidemic is mass incarceration—a plague of prisons.

Mass incarceration? The term seems out of place for America—a nation premised on individual rights and freedom. It conjures up images of brutal foreign tyrannies and totalitarian despots—widespread oppression and domination of individuals under regimes of state power built upon fear, terror, and the absence of effective legal protection. When we think of large-scale systems of imprisonment throughout history, we think of great crimes against humanity—Hitler's network of diabolical concentration camps or the vast hopelessness of Stalin's archipelago of slave-labor prison camps. Stalin's system established a model for mass incarceration whose effects penetrated every corner of Russian society, shaping the experience of millions beyond those in the camps—most immediately the prisoners' families. More broadly, it created an entire population living under the threat of arrest and arbitrary detention. This model seems foreign to life in our democratic society—a product of different times and faraway places.

The facts about current-day American incarceration are stark. Today, a total of 7.3 million individuals are under the control of the U.S. criminal-justice system: 2.2 million prisoners behind bars, 800,000 parolees, and another 4.2 million people on probation. If this population had their own city, it would be the second largest in the country.

The U.S. prison population grew apace with the general population (averaging about 125 prisoners per 100,000 population) until 1975, when there were about 250,000 people in jails and prisons. Then it climbed sharply, reaching over 2 million prisoners by 2006—a historic peak rate of nearly 750 per 100,000. That is six times the historic rate.

This huge system of imprisonment and the criminal-justice system's control of millions of Americans is fueled by even more millions of arrests—an average of 10 million per year for each of the last twenty-five years. There were 14 million arrests in 2008 alone. These arrests, together with the use of longer prison sentences, keep state and federal prisons filled with new inmates: over 600,000 enter prison each year, with an average sentence of four to six years. This means that many also exit the system each year. In 2009, 700,000 individuals were discharged from prisons, most reentering the communities from which they came.

But most are also destined to be reincarcerated. Circulating through the infamous revolving door of the system, 67 percent of discharged prisoners will be back inside within three years of their release. A decade after violent crime began to decline sharply nationwide (reaching historic lows in 2006), the growth of the prison system continued. Each week in 2006 saw one thousand prison beds added. In 2007 and 2008, another 100,000 prison beds were added across the nation. Only in 2010, after thirty-five years of relentless growth, did we see the first decline in the U.S. prison population—a sign that this phase of the epidemic may have peaked. The total population of state and federal prisons was 2.2 million in 2011.

Having described the unprecedented scale of imprisonment in America, we may still ask: is America's use of imprisonment really a justifiable (and effective) solution to an epidemic of crime? Indeed, with crime rates at historic lows, one might even conclude that all this imprisonment is a good thing. Or is it a problem in its own right? How can we assess the significance of mass incarceration in America?

Here is where the tools of epidemiology can help. By looking more closely at the data on imprisonment in the United States through the lens of public health, we can begin to parse the prison epidemic. Is crime really the source of epidemic-level imprisonment, or is something else driving this phenomenon? As is always the goal in public health, can we also understand enough about mass incarceration to learn how to contain and eradicate this modern plague?

DEFINING MASS INCARCERATION

Incarceration—punishment by imprisonment—is based on a set of laws established by a state or nation to ensure public safety by the separation and isolation of criminals from society.

By contrast, mass incarceration results from policies that support the large-scale use of imprisonment on a sustained basis for political or social purposes that have little to do with law enforcement. Hitler, Stalin, and Pol Pot all employed mass imprisonment, each presiding over a process that arrested and incarcerated millions. Such systems are often part of massive programs of slave labor or forced resettlement, in which high death rates are a typical by-product. And some examples of mass incarceration are explicitly part of a program of ethnic cleansing or genocide—a tool of policy that intends the extermination of entire populations. But now, for the first time, we see mass incarceration in a democratic society.

The judicial mechanisms that states employ to accomplish programs of mass incarceration include laws and strategies of enforcement explicitly designed to imprison large populations. Methods include expansion of the list of criminal offenses punishable by prison terms, as well as harsher sentencing practices that impose long prison terms for crimes not previously prosecuted at all: being Jewish in Nazi Germany, or being an enemy of the state in Stalin's Russia.

This expansion of the use of incarceration (creating a vastly larger prison system) is almost always accompanied by worsened prison conditions, with more dangers to inmates' health and safety. In addition, the rapid growth of a larger prison system creates an expanded and more powerful system of "correctional" administration, which tends to have self-perpetuating features. These systems then add more and larger prisons, with better-endowed and more powerful correctional, police, and prosecutorial agencies at every level of government.

THE EPIDEMIOLOGICAL CHARACTERISTICS OF MASS INCARCERATION

What makes all epidemics important to public health is their large scale and the great loss of life or disabilities that are left in their wake. As we saw with the sinking of the *Titanic*, cholera in London, and AIDS in the Bronx, understanding epidemics includes understanding the many nonbiological, social factors that frequently determine who lives and who dies. These can be issues of social convention ("women and children first"), of moralistic and punitive attitudes (defining drug use as a moral issue and resisting framing addiction as a public health issue), or of turning a blind eye to social policies gone awry (as in the case of the consequences of the war on drugs).

Failure to identify and address these underlying factors stands in the way of letting us cope effectively with any preventable disease and reduce the death and suffering it causes. Indeed, in the case of AIDS and drug addiction, we see matters worsen, with the epidemic expanding to new populations even as we develop effective medical treatments for individual cases.

Normally, imprisonment is not seen as a disease, or even a serious problem for anyone but the inmate. Yet an epidemiological analysis of mass incarceration reveals that it meets all the important criteria for being an epidemic, a collective phenomenon that is more than the sum of its individual cases. These criteria include its rapid growth rate, large scale, and self-sustaining properties.

RAPID GROWTH RATE

Mass incarceration easily meets the first criterion for status as an epidemic—the rapid growth of new cases (increased incidence) over a short period of time. In the past thirty-five years, the United States has increased its incarcerated population tenfold. For almost a hundred years, from 1880 to 1975, the rate of imprisonment stayed flat, averaging 100–150 individuals imprisoned for every 100,000 members of the population. Beginning in the 1970s, laws and enforcement policies were put in place that caused the rate to multiply five times over the course of thirty years, to more than 750 individuals imprisoned for every 100,000 members of the population today. This growth rate is unprecedented in our nation's history.

LARGE MAGNITUDE

The very large scale of incarceration in America defines its great public health significance, with tens of millions affected. The magnitude of our prison system has effectively made this country the world champion of incarceration. Today, the United States has the highest rate of imprisonment of any nation in the world—possibly the highest rate in the history of any nation. By comparison, European countries average less than one-fifth of the American rate, and many average only one-tenth of it. The U.S. rate of incarceration is the highest in the world—about 750 per 100,000—a rate more than seven times that of European Union countries and greater than that of Russia or South Africa.

The number affected by long-term incarceration in state and federal prisons is dwarfed by the number of those arrested and held, even briefly, in local jails—another 14 million each year. In total since 1975, about 35 million Americans have been arrested and jailed or imprisoned, probably more than all Americans incarcerated for all offenses in the previous hundred years.

In addition there is the "collateral damage" of mass incarceration: the children, wives, parents, siblings, and other family members of those incarcerated over the course of the last thirty-five years. In 1960, a school-age child in Harlem or in the South Bronx had a 2 percent to 4 percent chance of having a parent imprisoned before reaching age eighteen. Today, that chance is more than 25 percent in many communities. Though innocent of any crime, the children of prisoners are also punished by the far-reaching effects of our system of mass incarceration, just as surely as if they themselves had been convicted.

With an average of about two children for about half of all inmates, over 25 million American children have by now been directly exposed to parental incarceration. Concentrated in the mostly urban neighborhoods targeted for mass arrests, they are the residents of the prison system's "feeder communities," where parents, siblings, uncles, aunts, cousins, close friends, and neighbors have all been incarcerated. In these communities, the epidemic of incarceration affects everyone—more damaging than the drugs that were the original rationale for so many of the arrests. In these communities, incarceration has become the norm, spawning successive generations of prison orphans and gang members.

It is no secret these feeder communities are largely black and Hispanic. An estimated 50 percent of all the extended black and Hispanic families in the United States by now have had a member incarcerated in the last thirty-five years; for the poorest in both groups, that number approaches 100 percent. For example, in Washington, D.C., more than 95 percent of African American men have been in prison at some point.

PERSISTENCE AND SELF-SUSTAINING CAPABILITIES

Another hallmark of any epidemic is its persistence, due to factors that allow it to sustain its large scale and grow ever larger. Mass incarceration has shown this ability to reproduce itself (as infectious or communicable diseases do) by several mechanisms that keep people "infected" and create new cases in a way that has sustained its heightened prevalence over many years. Part of this is related to the vast apparatus created to administer the criminal-justice system; part is related to the new laws that mandate longer sentences and keep the prisons full of older inmates for longer periods; part is due to the rules governing release and reentry—parole policies that lower the threshold for violations and ensure recidivism; and part is the result of lasting damage done to the families and the social fabric of the communities from which most prisoners are drawn.

Over the past thirty years, the nation's prison industry has grown exponentially to accommodate a growing prison population. Currently the prison industry supports one full-time employee for every one of the 2.3 million people behind bars.

Not surprisingly, this huge American "industry" has huge political clout—with the expansion of prosecutorial and correctional workers' power, the growing number of lobbyists for these groups, and the many vendors who build and service prisons. Add in the financial dependence of many communities on prison industries in their localities and prison budgets are hard to touch.

Despite studies showing that there are, in fact, few long-term economic benefits of this "industry" for the localities that host them, prisons are often seen as an economic lifeline, especially in poor rural communities that have lost many industries to globalization over the last two decades. In New York State, for instance, fully half of the state's prison beds were once located in the upstate home districts of three powerful Republican state senators. In California, the correction officers' union in 2008 helped defeat a bill that would have moved $1 billion from the prison system to drug treatment, paying for rehabilitation and relapse-prevention programs rather than prison time. The enormous and powerful prison-industrial complex that America has created is a growth industry, and it fights to sustain its "market share," always bringing new "services" under its auspices—most significantly, mandated drug treatment.

In recent years, budget crises in many states have led to the first decline in incarcerations in thirty years, via the early release of some nonviolent offenders and a politically mandated drop in arrests. In New York, this has resulted in a 20 percent decline in the prison population. But many of the sentencing policies that first built and filled these prisons continue unabated (fourteen states increased prison populations in 2010), with the focus of law enforcement increasingly shifting to lower-level offenses (e.g., marijuana arrests are up 5,000 percent in the last decade).

U.S. prison budgets are also unprecedented in American history, representing the diversion of public treasure from other great needs—education, health care, Social Security for the aged. Averaging over $25,000 per inmate or about $60 billion annually, most of the money comes from state budgets. With several billion more to build all these prisons, we have created a large privatized "correctional industry," which, among other offensive aspects, offers new investment opportunities on Wall Street for operating "for-profit" prisons. With so many vested interests in maintaining the prison-industrial complex, it is no wonder the system has become self-perpetuating.

Another way in which the plague of prisons has become self-sustaining, according to new, cutting-edge research by criminologists including Todd Clear, is by destabilizing communities. Clear has documented that crime rates in Florida communities with high incarceration rates can be traced directly to increases in imprisonment. In other words, what started out as a punishment for crime—prison—has now become a source of the very crime it seeks to control.

Clear argues that massive levels of arrest and imprisonment concentrated in certain communities damage the social bonds that sustain life, especially for poor communities. By corroding or destroying this most common basis of social capital, mass incarceration sets up a perverse relationship: punishment leads to increased crime, as it replaces the moral mechanisms of family and community. These are the forces that normally function to assert social control, over young males especially, by the use of noncoercive means involving family and community.

Furthermore, because so much money is diverted to incarceration, other public services that might play a role in keeping down crime in these communities are defunded in favor of funding to build and maintain more prisons. Programs including health care, job training, retirement benefits, housing, and community development have all suffered a loss of public revenues, even as funding allocated for mass incarceration has grown exponentially.

All these are worsened by the economic downturn that began in 2008 and which further restricts ex-prisoners' options.

Longer sentences also build incarceration rates and create a chronic condition of social incapacitation for those imprisoned, as they face severe restrictions on their rights and opportunities after release from prison. Individuals who enter prison and become a case in the criminal-justice system today have a 50 percent or more chance of remaining under the system's control for life with recurrent arrests and periods of incarceration.

Like the story of global warming and climate change, this epidemic of mass imprisonment includes many "inconvenient truths"—critical realities we do not care to know about—such as its sheer size, huge social disparities, and monumental costs. But unlike climate change, the scale and consequences of mass incarceration derive from relatively recent events and a deliberate set of public policies that continue to be defended as being in the public interest. Unlike many other afflictions, a deadly new virus or bacteria did not cause this epidemic. It is self-inflicted and has required the expenditure of a great fortune, more than $1 trillion in public funds over its thirty-five-year course.

Paradoxically, despite its enormity and great significance for tens of millions of our citizens, America's mass incarceration remains largely invisible. Denial is the norm for the public at large, even in the face of the profound effects imprisonment has on the lives of so many American families.

Compared to the burning issues of the present day—the economy, health care, overseas wars, and the threat of terrorism—imprisonment, even mass imprisonment, is only a marginal political issue at best. Via constant exploitation in the media—with scores of TV shows about crime and punishment aired each week—we by and large maintain the ability to look the other way, actively evading any moral responsibility for this system's existence. Perhaps that is because the story is almost always about "public safety," protecting us and our families, not the far more consequential and damaging epidemic of punishment we sponsor.

A public-health approach to mass incarceration offers a new way to examine this phenomenon and the role of the laws and public policies that with or without intention, now sustain our vast and socially damaging system of prisons and prisoners.

Adapted from A Plague of Prisons: The Epidemiology of Mass Incarceration in America

PRISON'S DILEMMA

Glenn C. Loury

America has less than 5 percent of world population but more than
a fifth of all prisoners. A Brown University professor shows how high
incarceration rates decimate the economics of African American
communities, harming many more than just those locked up.

Over the past four decades, the United States has become a
vastly punitive nation, without historical precedent or international parallel. With roughly 5 percent of the world's population, the United States currently confines about one-quarter of the
world's prison inmates. In 2008, one in a hundred American adults
was behind bars. Just what manner of people does our prison policy
reveal us to be?

America, with great armies deployed abroad under a banner
of freedom, nevertheless harbors the largest infrastructure for
the mass deprivation of liberty on the planet. We imprison nearly
as great a fraction of our population to a lifetime in jail (around
seventy people for every hundred thousand residents) as Sweden,
Denmark, and Norway imprison for any duration whatsoever.

That America's prisoners are mainly minorities, particularly
African Americans, who come from the most disadvantaged cor-
ners of our unequal society, cannot be ignored. In 2006, one in nine
black men between the ages of twenty and thirty-four was serving

time. The role of race in this drama is subtle and important, and the racial breakdown is not incidental: prisons both reflect and exacerbate existing racial and class inequalities.

Why are there so many African Americans in prison? It is my belief that such racial disparity is not mainly due to overt discriminatory practices by the courts or the police. But that hardly exhausts the moral discussion. To begin with, let's remember the fact that the very definition of crime is socially constructed: as graphically illustrated by the so-called war on drugs, much of what is criminal today was not criminal in the past and may not be tomorrow.

Let us also frankly admit that a massive, malign indifference to people of color is at work. I suspect strongly, though it is impossible to prove to the econometrician's satisfaction, that our criminal and penal policies would never have been allowed to expand to the extent that they have if most of the Americans being executed or locked away were white.

We must also frankly ask why so many African American men are committing crimes. Many of the so-called root causes have long been acknowledged. Disorganized childhoods, inadequate educations, child abuse, limited employability, and delinquent peers are just a few of the factors involved. In America, criminal justice policies have become a second line of defense, if you will, against individuals whose development has not been adequately fostered by other societal institutions, like welfare, education, employment and job training, mental-health programs, and other social initiatives. As a result, it is an arena in which social stratification, social stigmas, and uniquely American social and racial dramas are reinforced.

We should also remember that punishment and inequality are intimately linked—that the causality runs in both directions. Disparities in punishment reflect socioeconomic inequalities, but they also help produce and reinforce them.

Is it not true, for example, that prisons create criminals? As the Rutgers criminologist Todd Clear concluded after a review of evidence, the ubiquity of the prison experience in some poor urban neighborhoods has had the effect of eliminating the stigma of serving time. On any given day, as many as one in five adult men in these neighborhoods is behind bars, and as Clear has written, "cycling of these young men through the prison system has become a central factor determining the social ecology of poor neighbor-hoods, where there is hardly a family without a son, an uncle or a father who has done time in prison."

For people who go to prison, time behind bars almost always also diminishes their odds of living crime-free lives when they get out, by lowering employability, severing ties to healthy communal sup-ports, and hardening their own attitudes. When such individuals return to their communities, they join many others with the same harsh life experience, often forming or joining gangs. This, in turn, further diminishes the opportunities that law-abiding residents in those same neighborhoods have to escape poverty or preserve the (often meager) value of their property.

Huge racial disparities in the incidence of incarceration should therefore come as no surprise. The subordinate status of black ghetto dwellers—their social deprivation and spatial isolation in America's cities—puts them at greater risk of embracing dysfunc-tional behaviors that lead to incarceration, and then incarceration itself leads to more dysfunction.

Put it all together and look at what we have wrought. We have established what looks to the entire world like a racial caste sys-tem that leaves millions stigmatized as pariahs, living either behind bars or in conditions of concentrated crime and poverty that breed still more criminality. Why are we doing this?

The present American regime of hyperincarceration is said to be necessary in order to secure public safety. But this is not a compel-ling argument. It is easy to overestimate how much crime is pre-vented by locking away a large fraction of the population. Often those who are incarcerated, particularly for selling drugs, are sim-ply replaced by others. There is no shortage of people vying to enter illicit trades, particularly given how few legal paths to upward mo-bility exist for many young black males.

A key empirical conclusion of the academic literature is that increasing the severity of punishment has little, if any, effect in deterring crime. But there is strong evidence that increasing the *certainty* of punishment has a large deterrent effect. One policy-relevant inference is that lengthy prison sentences, particularly in the form of mandatory minimum-type statutes such as California's Three Strikes Law, are difficult to justify.

The ideological justification for the present American prison system also ignores the fact that the broader society is implicated in the existence of these damaged, neglected, feared, and despised communities. People who live in these places are aware that outsiders view them with suspicion and contempt. (I know whereof I speak in this regard, because I am myself a child of the black ghetto, connected intimately to ghetto dwellers by the bond of social and psychic affiliation. While in general I am not much given to advertising this fact, it seems appropriate to do so here.)

The plain historical truth of the matter is that neighborhoods like North Philadelphia, the West Side of Chicago, the East Side of Detroit, and South Central Los Angeles did not come into being by an accident of nature. As the sociologist Loïc Wacquant has argued, these ghettos are man-made, coming into existence and then persisting because the concentration of their residents in such urban enclaves serves the interests of others. As such, the desperate and vile behaviors of some ghetto dwellers reflect not merely their personal moral deviance, but also the shortcomings of our society as a whole. "Justice" operates at multiple levels, both individual and social.

Defenders of the current regime put the onus on lawbreakers: "If they didn't do the crimes, they wouldn't have to do the time." Yet a pure ethic of personal responsibility does not and could never justify the current situation. Missing from such an argument is any acknowledgment of social responsibility—even for the wrongful acts freely chosen by individual persons.

I am not saying that a criminal has no agency in his behavior. Rather, I am arguing that the larger society is implicated in a criminal's choices because we have acquiesced to social arrangements that work to our benefit and to his detriment—that shape his consciousness and his sense of identity in a way that the choices he makes (and that we must condemn) are nevertheless compelling to him.

Put simply, the structure of our cities with their massive ghettos is a causal factor in the deviancy among those living there. Recognition of this fact has far-reaching implications for the conduct of public policy. What goals are our prisons trying to achieve, and how should we weigh the enormous costs they impose on our fellow, innocent citizens?

In short, we must think of justice as a complex feedback loop. The way in which we distribute justice—putting people in prison— has consequences, which raise more questions of justice, like how to deal with convicts' families and communities, who are also punished, though they themselves have done nothing wrong. Even if every sentence handed out to every prisoner were itself perfectly fair (an eminently dubious proposition), the morality of our system would still be in doubt, because it punishes innocents. Those who claim on principled arguments that "a man deserves his punishment" are missing the larger picture. A million criminal cases, each rightly decided—each distributing justice to a man who deserves his sentence—still add up to a great and historic wrong.

This article originally appeared in the Washington Monthly *of January–February 2013.*

FAMILY

MEN AND THEIR UNDERPAID WOMEN

David Cay Johnston

Not only do women make less than men, but a study of similarly positioned executives at similarly sized organizations showed that men make more and hold a greater share of the top jobs at larger organizations.

Data on U.S. incomes, poverty, pensions, and philanthropy all show a common economic reality: women are still getting shortchanged. Do men care?

Before *Ms.* magazine was a gleam in Gloria Steinem's eye, men had quite a deal. Married middle-class men often controlled the purse while enjoying the pleasures of a full-time homemaker, who might work a few hours here and there for "pin money" they could spend on themselves. Mothers of small children seldom worked full-time.

When it comes to incomes from all sources, including investments, men still make out better than women. Men's median income in 2010 was $1.54 for each dollar women received, my analysis of census data shows. The median income—half make more, half less—for men was $32,137, but for women just $20,831.

Ignoring investment income, the pattern still holds. In 2010, men averaged $1.29 to the dollar earned by women. Men averaged $47,715 a year, women $36,931, a difference of $10,784 for the year.

That's $207 per week less for women workers. A married opposite-sex couple with each partner at the average would make 12.4 percent more money—the equivalent of more than six weeks of extra pay—if both husband and wife earned the male average.

The pattern of more pay for men is not just because men may choose more lucrative occupations or not take time off to bear children. Data disclosed by nonprofit organizations in their annual reports to the Internal Revenue Service (on Form 990) show that among executives and managers men make much more than women.

Women run a majority of nonprofit organizations with budgets under $1 million. But as budgets grow, the ranks of women shrink. At nonprofits with budgets of $50 million or more, only one in six is run by a woman. The few women who run these biggest are paid 25 percent less than men, according to the eleventh annual nonprofit pay study by Guidestar, a salary survey I urged its founder to make a core part of its operations before the organization launched in the mid-1990s.

All of this raises a question: why do men, especially married men, put up with this? Why aren't men in the vanguard of demanding equal pay for women?

It is unfair that the women they love work for less. Viewed in purely selfish terms, men should see gender pay discrimination as severe limits on a family's resources. And what about fringe benefits? Many couples lose the value of a second health or other benefit plan because plans designed in a one-income era are often incompatible with one another. Men could agitate for more cafeteria-style fringe-benefit packages, so one spouse could get health care benefits and the other extra retirement money or longer vacations or some other benefit.

We have been through two generations since women began to break out of the narrow list of white-collar occupations readily open to them—teacher, nurse, librarian, secretary—all of them usually expected to be temporary until the job title became wife or wife and mother. Some women now work in better-paid blue-collar jobs, because what had been a 100 percent male quota is now history for such occupations as machinist, mechanic, and stevedore.

The first women who fought to become street cops are now retired, some with granddaughters patrolling the streets. Women to-day captain jetliners, while men serve coffee to passengers. My wife runs a quarter-billion-dollar charitable endowment, the kind of job she was bluntly told, three decades ago, that a woman would never hold. While the pay gap has narrowed some, the official data still show that whether they are sales clerks or CEOs, servers or surgeons, women overall make less than men doing the same work.

Women are still more likely than men to be poor, especially in old age, census data show. Among single women, one in nine lives in extreme poverty, which means annual income is less than half of the poverty line.

Married couples with children in 2009 worked 492 more hours than in 1979, a 15 percent increase, census data analyzed by the Economic Policy Institute show. The extra money comes at a price: less time for the joys of parenting, coupling, and community engagement.

Why have men quietly given up all those perks, and the power that goes along with being sole breadwinner, for three-quarters of an extra paycheck? For fathers, that can mean half an extra paycheck or less once child-care costs are covered.

Since most men's wages have been flat to falling, it takes two incomes to get by. IRS data show that average income in 2009 was back at the 1997 level when inflation was taken into account. In 2010 median household income fell again, new census data show. It fell again in 2011.

The women's movement encouraged self-reliance—not being dependent on the goodwill and good health of a husband—as well as self-realization. Equal pay for equal work was central.

The price of pay discrimination stalks retirement, too, since less pay means a smaller check in old age. Among baby boomers, the youngest of whom turn fifty in 2014, single women have a retirement-savings shortfall nearly twice that of single men, the Employee Benefits Research Institute estimated.

Among men age sixty-five or older, median income in 2009 was $25,409, two-thirds more than the $15,209 median for women, the Congressional Joint Economic Committee reported in April. Retired men averaged nearly twice as much from pensions as women.

Married men and fathers can help close these economic chasms. Will self-interest motivate us to challenge enduring economic discrimination against our wives and sisters, our mothers and daughters? Or will the gender income and pay gaps still be around two generations from now?

RACE, GENDER, FAMILY STRUCTURE, AND POVERTY

Peter Edelman

Poverty is linked to family structure, with two-income couples doing better than single mothers. But it is also deeply connected to institutional ways that race and gender are handled in America.

Regardless of the reasons, the growth in the number of female-headed families with children is a significant cause of the increase in child poverty. The combination of low-wage work with the changes in family composition has been highly detrimental. A family with only one wage earner—especially a woman, who still earns 77 percent of what a man earns—is going to have a difficult time. And, although with many individual exceptions, the statistics leave no doubt that children of single parents—for economic reasons, if nothing else—face longer odds for the future.

Working on issues of poverty in the mid-1960s, I saw the prospects for progress in the context of that era. We were still riding the wave of postwar prosperity despite the Vietnam War and the competition between guns and butter. We could still feel the wind of the civil rights movement at our back despite the civil unrest in our cities. We thought Richard Nixon was finished politically after he was defeated in his run for governor of California in 1962. To us, Watergate was merely a garish real estate development on the Potomac. The 1960s turned into a tough decade as it wore on, but we were still confident. Few, if any, foresaw the profound changes in both the economy and the structure of the American family that would greatly complicate the fight against poverty. I certainly did not.

Discussing such metamorphoses in the American family gets into muddy political waters. The changes have been sensationalized and used to blame the poor and especially women of color. But they are big and important, with major policy implications.

Between 1970 and 2009, the percentage of families headed by women with children under eighteen doubled—from 12.7 percent to 25.4 percent. For African American families the numbers rose from 37.1 percent in 1971 (the first year the statistics were broken down by race) to 52.7 percent in 2009. Most of these increases occurred during the 1970s.

Reflecting these changes—and coupled with the increase in low-wage jobs and consequent difficulty for a single mother to support her family—the proportion of poor children under eighteen who lived in female-headed families rose from 24.1 percent in 1959 to 55 percent in 2010.

UNMARRIED WHITE AND HISPANIC MOTHERS

Paralleling the increase in the number of female-headed families has been the increase over the last seventy years in births to unmarried mothers of all races and ethnicities. The rate of births to unmarried women in the United States rose from under ten per thousand women in 1940 to more than fifty per thousand in 2006. The changes cut across lines of race and ethnicity, although the increase occurred almost entirely among women who did not have a college degree.

The pattern is similar across most of the developed world. From 1980 to 2007 in the United States, the percentage of births to unmarried women went from 18 percent to 40 percent. The United Kingdom's percentage went up much more, from 12 percent to 44 percent; the Netherlands' from 4 percent to 40 percent; France's from 11 to 50 percent; Iceland's, with the highest numbers in both years, from 40 to 66 percent; Japan's from 1 percent to 2 percent.

In 2007, the United States ranked seventh out of fourteen countries examined by the National Bureau of Health Statistics, which suggests that the changes were certainly not the unique result of American social policy. On the other hand, unmarried mothers in other countries are more likely to be living with the fathers of their children than is the case in the United States.

The numbers are much higher historically in the African American community, and consequently discussion of this issue has always had a racial component. But however surprising to some, the unmarried birth rate among African American women has actually decreased since 1970, from ninety-five per thousand women to seventy-two by 2006.

White rates went from about fifteen per thousand women in 1970 to almost forty in 1998. The white rate went to under thirty in 1989, when Hispanics were first counted separately. Unmarried birth rates among Hispanic women, counted separately since 1989, went from about 90 per thousand women to 106 in 2006. Thus the growth in the rate of unmarried births in the United States over the past thirty years is almost entirely attributable to changes among whites and Hispanics.

TEEN BIRTHS DECLINE

The overall trend in teen out-of-wedlock births has been downward since 1991, when it was 61.8 per thousand. It hit 34.3 per thousand in 2010 and is now at the lowest level ever recorded. There were 409,840 teen births in 2009. Teenagers accounted for 23 percent of nonmarital births in 2007, down from 50 percent in 1970. The percentage drop since 1990 has been largest among African Americans, from one hundred per thousand unmarried African American teens to fifty-four per thousand in 2010.

Trends in the percentage of births that are out of wedlock are a significant and telling way to look at the problem. By 2007, 39.7 percent of all births were to unmarried women. Again, the increased incidence of nonmarital births cuts across lines of race and ethnicity, and should be a matter of concern regardless of race. Nonetheless, the percentage of births to unmarried African American women remains a particular concern. In 2009, 72.3 percent of African American children were born outside of marriage, compared to

24 percent in 1965. The trend among Hispanics was from 37 percent to 42 percent over the same period, and among whites was from 6 percent to 24 percent.

Why the number of out-of-wedlock births was—and still is—so much higher in the African American community is not definitively answered by research. The allegation that low-income African American women have children in order to get on welfare or to get an increased welfare payment is hard to maintain in light of the declining level of welfare payments from the early 1970s onward. At the same time as births outside marriage were increasing, beginning in the 1970s, welfare benefits went down steadily relative to inflation in nearly all states. And the increase in the benefit that came from having another child was in almost every state so small that it only threw the family into deeper poverty.

A partial explanation that makes sense to me is William Julius Wilson's "marriageable male" hypothesis, one which applies especially to people living in neighborhoods of concentrated poverty (including high-rise public housing). Beginning in 1973, with deindustrialization occurring in the broader economy and affecting workers across the board, employment and wages of African American men, numbers which had been on the rise since 1945, took a nosedive; at the same time, the disproportionate incarceration of African American men began its steep climb. Women kept having children, but because the economic prospects of the children's fathers were so bleak, they did not marry nearly as often.

One reason why so many African American women are coping on their own in raising their children is what the criminal-justice system does to the men of the community, especially in the inner city. The massive and unnecessary imprisonment of African American men is preventing two-parent families from forming and destroying others on a large scale. Prison time takes away what could be productive and parental years by putting men behind bars with long sentences, and it jeopardizes the future because it blemishes their employment prospects so severely. In fact, poverty rates would be considerably higher if incarcerated men were counted for purposes of poverty. Ex-offenders, with their high rates of unemployment, drive up the current poverty number.

When compared to the trend since 2000, what happened in the

late 1990s is particularly interesting. The last half of the 1990s was the only time since the early 1970s when there was noticeable real growth in both employment and real wages among lower-income families. Unmarried births declined among African American and Latino women during that period.

That was also a time when welfare became less available due to the effects of the 1996 law. Some argue that the decline in unmarried births was due to the decline in the availability of welfare, whereas others credited the improved employment climate. The events of the past decade support the argument that variations in employment are the most important factor. Unmarried birth rates went up again during the middle of the past decade, but welfare did not become more available. The variables that did change were the availability of jobs and the level of wages.

Analysis of the research literature tells us that there is no clear explanation why unmarried birth rates among African Americans have historically been higher than those among whites, but the impaired economic situation of African American men since the mid-1970s is an especially noteworthy variable in the statistics.

Regardless of the explanation for the disparity, it is imperative that the issue be addressed. Conservatives say it is entirely a matter of personal responsibility. Some liberals seem to be in denial that there is actually an issue at all. But the consequences are undeniably troubling.

The solutions are not simple. The aim is to postpone childbearing until the partners marry or establish a long-term commitment to each other and have a realistic economic approach to making it work. Hackneyed slogans, shibboleths, or bumper-sticker simplicities will not suffice: improved educational and employment opportunities are critical, as are criminal-justice reform and strategies to build healthy neighborhoods. But programs at the community level that stress postponing parenthood and that support responsible parenthood should it still occur are essential as well, although, granted, messages about the wisdom of delaying parenthood are more likely to be heeded in a world in which there are viable escape routes out of poverty.

Issues of race and gender are at the heart of the public debate about poverty. Such subjects are not new, but they appeared in new form over the last four decades in the use of welfare and the criminal-justice system as race-related political issues.

MOST POOR PEOPLE ARE WHITE

The fact that the largest number of poor people are white is almost never mentioned. Ronald Reagan's fictional anecdote about a Cadillac-driving "welfare queen" pervades and pollutes our political culture. Everyone knew he was talking about African American women. Millions of Americans instinctively associate "poverty" with "black." This matters. The white majority is less likely to support safety-net programs if they think only or primarily blacks will benefit.

Here resides the hot button. It is of course true that there is a disproportionate number of African Americans and Latinos in poverty. The question is, "Why?" The debate divides, roughly speaking, into two camps. One says the problem is basically structural: a paucity of good jobs, terrible schools, the cradle-to-prison pipeline that disproportionately incarcerates poor minorities, race and gender discrimination. The other postulates that the overriding problem is with individual behavior and failure to take responsibility—attributable to "bad parenting" and ensuing individual failure, wrongheaded public policy, or both.

Because it is the image many have of American poverty in general, the continuing concentrated poverty in our inner cities is at the heart of the debate. Comparatively speaking, the numbers for urban venues are not large, encompassing perhaps 10 to 12 percent of the poor. But because these ghettos are even more disproportionately black and brown than poverty in general and because it is associated with media images of crime and children born to unmarried women, it shapes political debate and impedes efforts to craft broader solutions.

There is no question about the behaviors and the statistics. They include not only out-of-wedlock births and street crime, but also dropping out of school, gang violence and violence in the home, and drug and alcohol abuse, as well as the drug trade. The late senator Daniel Patrick Moynihan pointed to the "breakdown of the black family" in his famous (to many, infamous) report of 1965, eliciting a fusillade of unremitting flack. The result was that respected researchers steered a wide berth away from research on inner-city behaviors for more than two decades, until William Julius Wilson tackled the issue in his 1987 book *The Truly Disadvantaged*.

Wilson and others (including me) argue that the basic facts are the result of too many poor people living in the same place—concentrated poverty. The increase in concentrated urban poverty resulted from the migration out of most middle-class residents, sparked by the unrest of the 1960s and the new protections against housing discrimination in the Fair Housing Act of 1968 and played out against the broader tableau of the growing scourge of low-wage work. Public policy, too, played a significant role, in both what it failed to do and what it did all too well. The failures were neglect of schools, lapses in helping people prepare for and find work, and lack of support for neighborhood-revitalization strategies. What public policy did all too well was to lock up the men of the community. What it did about welfare (before 1996) was a mixed bag. It did provide income to families that had no other source of support, but it failed to help (and push) recipients to get and keep jobs.

RACIAL POLITICS

The new racialization of the politics of poverty coincided with the 1968 election of President Richard Nixon. He supported and signed important legislation expanding food stamps and creating housing vouchers and Supplemental Security Income, and also proposed a guaranteed minimum income. But, important as all these were, his overriding political focus concerning race was in a different direction, one that had significant implications for poverty.

The real focus of the Republican Party with regard to race appeared in its "southern strategy" to capture the South. The new political reality was that overtly antiracial policies like those of George Wallace and his ilk had become unacceptable. As a result, Republicans needed strategies that would communicate their racial slant without speaking in racial terms. Criminal justice and welfare were perfect vehicles.

The GOP appealed to white southerners (and others around the country) by advocating law-enforcement policies that would disproportionately lock up black (and Latino) men and by harping on welfare. We have only to remember Reagan's "welfare queen" and the Willie Horton commercial that was run to discredit Governor Michael Dukakis during his 1988 presidential campaign against George H.W. Bush. (For those readers who don't remember or who weren't yet born, in 1988 Willie Horton absconded from a prison furlough in Massachusetts and committed assault, armed robbery, and rape. Lee Atwater, the brilliant political operative of then–vice president Bush, produced a political advertisement attacking Dukakis's furlough policy and showing Horton's picture. Horton was African American, and the racial message was not lost on voters: a vote for Dukakis would endorse not only being soft on crime but also a look-the-other-way posture toward the specter of violent black men preying on white communities. Three years later, when Atwater was dying of brain cancer, he apologized to Dukakis for the "naked cruelty" of the 1988 campaign.)

With regard to criminal justice, street crime, in fact, was on the rise, and it had a visible racial element. I was youth corrections commissioner in New York State in the mid- to late 1970s, and I saw it firsthand. My theory was that the containment of the inner-city unrest of the 1960s had plugged the outlets young people had for political protest, and that with no channels to express grievances, especially against the police, the continuing anger had erupted into sometimes-violent street crime.

As noted earlier, the number of people receiving welfare benefits had increased greatly in the 1960s and become an important lifeline for inner-city mothers and children in the 1970s and thereafter. The increased presence of African American women and children on the welfare rolls served up juicy political fodder.

The response to street crime was to lock up African American and Latino men for longer and longer periods of time—including the thousands of men who committed low-level drug offenses—and to engage in the politics that went along with all of that. And it was clear that at every stage, from arrest through sentencing, African American and Latino men were (and still are) treated more harshly than were whites committing identical crimes.

The history of welfare is intertwined with that of criminal justice. The men were locked up, and the women subsisted on welfare. Attacks on welfare and tough rhetoric on crime were staples of Republican political campaigns from the 1970s on.

Criminal-justice policy changed greatly over those years, whereas welfare—though it was a favorite target for attack by President Reagan and also was the subject of numerous welfare-to-work initiatives at the state level in the 1980s, as well as a modest federal reform in 1988—had remained substantially unchanged when President Clinton took office in 1993. By then, there were 14.3 million people on welfare—disproportionately women of color and their children. With the changes in welfare embraced by Clinton, the rolls shrank by 2007 to well under five million people, but most former recipients did not escape poverty. Single mothers who neither have a job nor receive welfare assistance now constitute, with their children, a substantial percentage of those in extreme poverty.

SIMPLISTIC APPROACH

The mantra of the Right is, at best, simplistic. Single mothers, they say, should have jobs and/or get married. It is true that getting a job without getting married is possible for most people in good times, but even then, the problem is getting a job that at the very least gets the family out of poverty, especially if the woman has not graduated from high school (and, increasingly, even if she has). "So," the mantra continues, "they should get married." The point seems to be that then there will be two possible income earners and everything will be hunky-dory.

We do want to make marriage more feasible. Children tend to do better when two parents are under one roof, and two wage earners do make things easier, but it shouldn't be the case that the only route out of poverty is to get married to someone who also has a job.

Jobs should pay enough so a single parent can support a family with two or three children on one job, a daunting challenge when a quarter of the jobs in the country pay less than $11 an hour. Single mothers work, in large numbers. The biggest problem is that the jobs don't pay enough to get them out of poverty. Besides, there is a rather serious problem of where to find a marriageable man. So many men are in jail or are ex-offenders who face almost insurmountable barriers to finding remunerative work. Marriage—which is a basic human instinct for most people—is not always achievable.

Welfare receded as a political issue after the 1996 law was enacted, but the hostility against it still lurks just below the surface. It is time to recognize the racialization of welfare and criminal-justice policies for what they are doing to impede progress against poverty. The story of our economy and its negative effects on people of all races must take center stage, but the institutional racism embedded in our welfare, criminal-justice, and education systems needs frontal attention as well if we are going to make real progress in reducing poverty and creating the kind of society we say we want.

Adapted from So Rich, So Poor: Why It's So Hard to End Poverty in America.

EMPLOYED PARENTS WHO CAN'T
MAKE A LIVING
Lisa Dodson

*Even with two incomes, not all parents can make enough to provide
a decent life for their children because of government policies that affect earnings and benefits, as these touching stories reveal.*

Do we have any responsibility for what happens to them?
> —*Ellen, a manager in a company employing many low-wage*
> *workers (2002)*

Ellen raised this question during a community conversation with
other employers from a variety of businesses in the Milwaukee
area. They had been talking about common problems they faced
with "entry-level" employees. Together they came up with a list of
inconveniences and disruptions that come with people "who are
disorganized" and bring that disarray to the workplace. They are
absent too much, come to work late, get calls that distract them, or
leave early, and they are often just "not focused on the job." They
said that there always seems to be some problem going on that
complicates getting work done; their lives "just aren't organized"
or "they don't have that work ethic."

Most of the employers at this meeting supervised workers
who were mothers, and they spoke at length about "family problems." Eventually, their description of these troubles turned into a

discussion about how inconvenient it was that these workers had families at all, because raising children is so time demanding. With some honesty, members of this group acknowledged that if you make $18,000—even $30,000—a year and have kids, "family life is going to create a problem" for those who employ you. Frequently, employers who discussed such issues were raising families themselves and had intimate knowledge of how much time—or, in lieu of time, money—it takes to keep kids on a schedule; manage all their schooling, extracurricular, and emotional needs; and just keep a stable family routine. If you can't be home to make sure all this is taken care of and you can't buy substitute care, well, "it's just a mess," said one young manager, herself a mother of two.

On this day, the five men and two women started examining an idea that reemerged in employer conversations over the years that followed. They raised the notion that if you pay people wages that guarantee they can't really "keep things organized at home" and then, because of that, the flow of work is disrupted, well, is that only the employee's problem? Or is it just built into this labor market? And if it is wired into America's jobs, as Ellen, a middle-aged white woman, asked the others, "do we have any responsibility for what happens to them?" Over the course of hundreds of interviews and discussions this question was often at the center.

INEQUALITY AT WORK

During the 1990s and into the first part of the first decade of the millennium, the United States saw a surge in wealth among the richest Americans. But that decade of economic gain was largely limited to those at the very top. Today, one in four U.S. workers earns less than $9 an hour—about $19,000 per year; 39 percent of the nation's children live in low-income households. The Economic Policy Institute reported that in 2005, minimum-wage workers earned only 32 percent of the average hourly wage. And African American and Latino families are much more likely to be poor or low income and are less likely to have assets or home equity to offset low wages. Furthermore, the living standards for households in the middle relative to the previous decade have seen a decline, particularly "working-age households," those headed by at least one adult of working age. Thus the nation increasingly became divided into acutely different ways of life: millions of working families—the economic bottom third—that cannot make a living, millions in the middle clinging to their standard of living, and the very top economic tier of ever-greater wealth.

This America is not lost on ordinary people. As a midwestern father of two who drives a "big rig" across states for a living said, "That money [gained by the richest people] came from somewhere, didn't it? It came out of my pocket and my kids' mouths." While most busy working people don't sit down to study the macroeconomy, many understand the rippling effects that shake their world.

At the university where I teach about poverty issues, I always ask students if they think that it matters if wealth increases for a few while others lose ground. For example, does it matter if that dad, driving his truck eighteen hours a day and seldom seeing his family, is able to buy less now than he could five years ago, when his days were shorter? Yes, of course it matters to him, his spouse, and his children. But does it matter beyond their private world? And always students point out that "maybe he's not driving as well" after eighteen hours. Thus, certainly with many jobs, there is a danger effect of low wages and overwork, causing damage that can spread. But a fair number of other students ponder harm beyond self-interest and even our public interest in avoiding a forty-ton truck slamming down the highway with a sleepy driver. Do losses to a family, probably an extended family, maybe even a community eroded by mounting poverty-induced problems—does all that matter in a larger way? Even assuming that we can avoid all those trucks, is America harmed when our workers and their families are ground down by an economy that has been funneling wealth to only a few?

There is always a range of responses to this challenge to the way the economy distributes its resources. Many young people particularly believe that we can do better, and they are ready to get on board. In every class that I have ever taught, some students speak of wanting the chance to devote real time—years, not just term breaks—to working for another kind of democracy. They are part of a deep, still untapped well of commitment to an economically just society—not the only source by any means, but a very valuable one. As young people have pointed out, this is the world they will take on and they should make it a more equitable one.

Alongside that sentiment, some young people point out that there is also a sound business-management argument that doing better by our lower-wage workers means that we all gain, because both the society and businesses do better. This "high road" argument counsels investing in better wages, decent schedules, and benefits for low-wage workers because, ultimately, this pays off for companies and the nation. Others also point out that investing in lower-income families will mean that millions of children are better prepared for school, are healthier, and have more stable families, all of which build the nation. Essentially, this is the argument that other nations use to invest public funding in families raising children and guarantee a minimum family income. So there is a defensible set of arguments—albeit not a winning one in the United States, but a compelling one—that we ought to pay people a decent income because it takes care of our people, serves productivity, and upholds the nation as a whole.

Yet, talking with employers, students, and many others, I found another public impulse largely left outside most economic debate. Sometimes middle-class people talked about a sense of obligation—a social obligation—at the core of their individual identity and their understanding of being part of this country. And many talked about their jobs—the work they do each day—as key to fulfilling the sense of being part of something bigger.

This idea of work was almost always explained to me personally, not as a philosophical stand. Middle-income people would describe relationships with others at work whose earnings were so low that if you decided to think about it, you knew there was no way they could support a family. Managers, business owners, and other professionals told me about getting to know certain people who seemed to be doing everything they possibly could, but that wasn't enough. And so all kinds of personal and family troubles would mount up, spill over, and eventually turn up at work. I heard about how when you hire, supervise, or even just work next to working-poor people—and, like it or not, get close to them—the harms they live with can start leaking into your world too.

A question would be raised: do we have some responsibility for people to whom we are connected through our jobs and economic role in their daily lives and, indirectly, the families that count on

them? Do we have some obligation to others—not just our family, but those who are co-workers, neighbors, part of our society,
and who are being diminished? I found nothing near a consensus.
But a wide array of people diverse in background, religion, profession, race, ethnicity, and geography spoke of this reflection as part
of their workaday lives, where they are connected to those who are
working hard but living poor.

As a young mother who was a sales clerk in Denver in 2001 put
it, "This took everything . . . just to keep this job. You know, you're a
single mother, you're not born with a silver spoon in your mouth. . . .
My child keeps calling me [while the child is home alone] and begging me to quit. . . . This is my responsibility."

"I COULDN'T HELP FEELING LIKE I WAS ALMOST TO BLAME"

Bea was a fortyish white woman in a flowery blouse and pink slacks;
she wore a square plastic badge that read "Bea, Floor Manager." In
2004 she agreed to talk to me over a cup of coffee near the store
where she was a manager of "about thirty-five" employees. It was a
well-known low-end retail chain, a "big box." She had worked there
for five years. She described the workforce as largely local people,
and that meant "almost all white, mostly women, and with maybe
high school diplomas, for the most part." Bea herself had lived in
that general area of Maine all her life.

After many interviews, my questions had been honed for gathering information about how it is to manage a workforce and what, if
any, conflicts arise. Bea quickly focused on the dilemma of "knowing too much" about the personal lives of the people who worked
for her and how that contrasted poorly with what she understood
as the model of how a professional manager behaves: "Some of what
they teach you in this business is to learn to think of them as part
of the job . . . the way to try to get the job done. That means being friendly [to the workers], learning everybody's name; that's very
important. But you keep people . . . it's important to keep a distance.
You do that to keep it professional. But I think . . . it is also how to
keep it clean."

"What does that mean?" I asked.

"It can get messy quickly," she said, "if you start encouraging
people to tell you what is going on, because they all have these

problems. They have child care problems, problems with someone is sick . . . there's domestic abuse. They have a lot of crises. It's better not to ask because it opens the door to all that and then you have to tell them they have to stay late or you have to cut hours or someone wants a raise . . . all of that other comes up in your mind."

"And that makes it hard to . . . ?" I said.

"That makes it hard to flip back into the business mode," she said. "I have to keep in mind my job is to serve the business, which is serving the public. We serve the public." This phrase, often repeated among the managers I met, seemed like a mooring, something to grab on to when human matters started to rock the boat.

"And . . . these people . . . aren't really . . . the public?" I asked.

"No," she said, "in business the public is the people who pay. . . . It isn't the public, really, it is the customer, the paying public."

"So . . . how does this work, for you?" I asked.

Bea's capitulation was immediate: "Not very well really. I actually break my rules all the time. I know a lot more about a lot of people than I should. I get involved more than I should. I am that kind of person; my husband is always telling me that. Not that he really blames me; he does the same thing at [a local lumber business]. But, like before . . . when we were talking about what they pay . . . ?" Bea and I had discussed the company wages of $6–$8 an hour. "I know that when someone asks for a raise, they really need it." At that point Bea started reciting the needs of many of these workers. Clearly she had annihilated her dictate to "keep it clean."

Here is just one of the stories that she told: "'Nancy' has two kids, her husband's on disability, and she couldn't buy her daughter a prom dress. This kid has worked very, very hard to graduate." Apparently Nancy's daughter had been employed throughout most of her high school years to help the family. "I'm like, 'How is it fair that this family can't buy her a prom dress?'"

Bea looked away, out the window. She disconnected from me for a few seconds as though recalling and applying manager rules. But it didn't work. When she looked back at me, she was teary. And she seemed a little angry too: "I remember how much my prom meant to me. I don't know about where you live, but around here, it's a big deal. The girls . . . we all hope for a big wedding someday but your high school graduation, that's something you have earned.

You want to look glamorous—not just good, but runway good. No way was Edy going to have the dress, the hair, the manicure. And I couldn't help but feeling that I was almost to blame, or partly. Nancy doesn't make what she deserves. . . . I am not saying they all work that hard, but . . . really, many do."

Bea was quiet for a while, and I began to think that was the end of the story. I tried to think of how to draw out what was being said, to hear more about this balance of roles and rules and Bea's conflict. She had started with her manager badge. But then she moved along a spectrum of moral thinking that I was to hear about many times. Bea put it simply: "Actually, we sell prom dresses in this store. . . . Did you see them?" I had not.

Again Bea was silent and she looked at my tape recorder. I asked, "You want me to turn it off?"

Bea said, "No, that's okay. . . . Well, let's just say . . . we made some mistakes with our prom dress orders last year. Too many were ordered, some went back. It got pretty confusing."

When Bea looked me in the eye this time, there were no tears and no apology.

I thought I knew my line: "So . . . Edy looked good at her prom?" Bea laughed, with a touch of gratitude I thought. "She knocked them dead," she said.

Over this and another conversation, Bea talked about how she could not make up for even a small part of what the workforce was lacking, because their wages meant they could not make their bills, never mind buy prom dresses, a fan for hot days, a child's plastic pool. So she found small ways to help out, subsidize poor wages, and try to make jobs move workers an inch closer to a decent life.

Adapted from The Moral Underground: How Ordinary Americans Subvert an Unfair Economy.

CONTRIBUTORS

Frank Ackerman (1946–) is a senior economist at Synapse Energy Economics in Cambridge, MA, known for his work on environmental economics. He is the author of *Can We Afford the Future? Economics for a Warming World* and is co-founder of *Dollars and Sense* magazine.

Nancy Altman (1950–) is a lawyer and co-director of Social Security Works, who taught at Harvard University's Kennedy School of Government in the 1980s and served as Alan Greenspan's assistant when he chaired the National Commission on Social Security Reform that developed the 1983 Social Security amendments.

Moshe Adler (1948–) teaches economics at Columbia University and the Harry Van Arsdale Jr. Center for Labor Studies at Empire State College. He is the author of *Economics for the Rest of Us* (The New Press, 2010).

Jared Bernstein (1955–) is a senior fellow at the Center on Budget and Policy Priorities in Washington. From 2009 to 2011, Bernstein was the chief economist and economic adviser to Vice President Joseph Biden in the Obama administration.

Stephen Bezruchka (1943–) is with the faculty of the Departments of Health Services and Global Health at the University of Washington. He worked as an emergency physician for thirty years and has spent much of his career studying and teaching about social and economic determinants of health.

Kim Bobo (1954–) is the founding executive director of Interfaith Worker Justice in Chicago. The *Utne Reader* listed her as one of "50 Visionaries Who Are Changing Your World."

Olveen Carrasquillo (1967–) is chief of the internal medicine division and an assistant professor at the University of Miami Miller School of Medicine.

Chuck Collins (1959–) is a co-founder of United for a Fair Economy and Responsible Wealth.

Donna Cooper (1958–) is a senior fellow with the Center for American Progress.

Linda Darling-Hammond (1951–) is the Charles E. Ducommun Professor of Education at the Stanford Graduate School of Education and the author of more than a dozen books on education policy and practice. She was an adviser to Barack Obama's presidential campaign.

Neil deMause (1965–) is the contributing economics editor at *City Limits* magazine and a contributing writer for Fairness and Accuracy in Reporting's magazine *Extra!* He also runs the sports-stadium news website fieldofschemes.com, as well as co-authoring the book of the same name. For seven years he wrote questions for the board game Trivial Pursuit.

Lisa Dodson (1958–) is a professor of sociology at Boston College. Previously, she was on the faculty at Harvard University and was a policy fellow at the Radcliffe Public Policy Center.

Ernest Drucker (1940–), a licensed clinical psychologist, is professor emeritus in the Family and Social Medicine at Montefiore Medical Center/Albert Einstein College of Medicine, adjunct professor of Epidemiology at Columbia University's Mailman School of Public Health, and senior research associate and scholar in residence at John Jay College of Criminal Justice of the City University of New York.

Peter Edelman (1938–) is a professor at Georgetown University Law Center with a long history of working on issues of poverty, welfare, juvenile justice, and constitutional law.

Editorial Projects of Education Research Center is the research arm of the nonprofit organization that publishes Education Week.

Barbara Ehrenreich (1941–), who earned her doctoral degree in cellular immunology, is a journalist who worked undercover in low-paid jobs for her widely acclaimed book *Nickel and Dimed: On (Not) Getting By in America.*

Robert H. Frank (1945–) is a professor of economics at the Samuel Curtis Johnson Graduate School of Management at Cornell University. His "Economic View" column appears monthly in the *New York Times.* He is a distinguished senior fellow at Demos.

Leo W. Gerard (1947–) is a Canadian steelworker who first won election in 2001 as president of the United Steelworkers Union, which represents 1.2 million active and retired aluminum, chemical, forestry, glass, paper, refining, rubber, steel, and other industrial workers in the United States, Canada, and the Caribbean.

Lisa Heinzerling (1961–) is professor of law at Georgetown University whose specialties include environmental and natural-resources law. She served as senior climate-policy counsel to the Environmental Protection Agency administrator in 2009 and then for eighteen months as associate administrator of EPA's Office of Policy.

Glenn Howatt (1957–) is the *Minneapolis Star Tribune*'s computer-assisted reporting editor.

Thomas L. Hungerford (1953–) is an economist at Economic Policy Institute who earned his doctoral in economics at the University of Michigan and for twenty-two years was an economic policy adviser to Congress and executive branch agencies.

Christopher Jencks (1936–) is the Malcolm Wiener Professor of Social Policy at the Kennedy School of Government at Harvard University. He has taught at Harvard, Northwestern, the University of Chicago, and the University of California, Santa Barbara.

David Cay Johnston (1948–) is the author of *Perfectly Legal, Free Lunch,* and *The Fine Print,* a trilogy based on his Pulitzer Prize–winning investigative reporting for the *New York Times.* He now teaches the regulatory and tax law of the ancient world at Syracuse University College of Law and is board president of the 4,800-member Investigative Reporters and Editors.

Eric Kingson (1946–), co-director of Social Security Works, is a professor at Syracuse University's School of Social Work and was a policy adviser to the National Commission on Social Security Reform and the 1994 Commission on Entitlement and Tax Reform.

Paul Krugman (1953–), Princeton University economist and *New York Times* columnist, won the 2008 Nobel Memorial Prize in Economic Sciences.

Robert Kuttner (1943–) is co-founder and co-editor of the *American Prospect*, "an authoritative magazine of liberal ideas," who for two decades wrote a column for *Business Week*. He is also a founder of the Economic Policy Institute and a distinguished senior fellow at Demos, a research institute.

Glenn C. Loury (1948–) is the Merton P. Stoltz Professor of the Social Sciences and Professor of Economics at Brown University. He is the author of, among other works, *Race, Incarceration, and American Values: The Tanner Lectures.*

Barack Obama (1961–) is the forty-fourth president of the United States. He was the junior senator from Illinois and an Illinois state senator. He attended Occidental College in Los Angeles and graduated from Columbia University. At Harvard Law School he was elected president of the *Harvard Law Review*, widely regarded as the most eminent position for any law student in America.

Mary E. O'Brien (1952–) is a primary-care internist at Columbia University Health Services and a faculty member at Columbia College of Physicians and Surgeons. She is on the board of the New York metro chapter of Physicians for a National Health Program.

Stephen Pimpare (1965–) has taught American politics, public policy, and the history of social work and social welfare at Columbia University, New York University, the City University of New York, and Yeshiva University.

sean f. reardon (1964–) is a professor at Stanford University whose research examines the patterns and trends in racial and socioeconomic inequality in American education.

Gary Rivlin (1958–) is a former *New York Times* reporter and the author of five books, including *BROKE, USA: From Pawnshops to Poverty, Inc.—How the Working Poor Became Big Business* (Harper Business, 2010).

Mike Rose (1944–) is on the faculty of the UCLA Graduate School of Education and Information Studies and is the author of a number of books about education, work, and social class including *The Mind at Work: Valuing the Intelligence of the American Worker.*

Chris Serres (1970–) was an investigative reporter covering business for the *Minneapolis Star Tribune*, who now works for the union UNITE HERE, which represents culinary, hotel, and casino workers.

Elizabeth Setren (1988–) is an assistant economist at the Federal Reserve Bank of New York.

Donald S. Shepard (1947–), an internationally respected health economist, is a professor at the Heller School, Brandeis University.

Beth Shulman (1949–2010) was a Washington labor consultant and former vice president of the United Food and Commercial Workers Union, who was co-chair of the Fairness Initiative on Low-Wage Work and a senior fellow at Demos. She died in 2010 at age sixty.

Adam Smith (1723–1790) was a Scottish moral philosopher who was the first to figure out market economics. He is known as the father of capitalism and of modern economics. His books include *An Inquiry into the Nature and Causes of the Wealth of Nations* and *The Theory of Moral Sentiments.*

Joseph E. Stiglitz (1943–), a 2001 Nobel laureate in economics, is a professor at Columbia University. He is a former chairman of the Council of Economic Advisers and chief economist for the World Bank, whose books include *The Price of Inequality.*

Studs Terkel (1912–2008) was an author, radio broadcaster, and historian best known for his oral histories of ordinary Americans. He was awarded the Pulitzer Prize in 1985 for his book *The Good War.*

Jaime Torres (1957–) founded Latinos for National Health Insurance, which advocates for single-payer lifelong health insurance for every person living in the United States.

Elizabeth Warren (1949–) is the senior United States senator from Massachusetts. Before her election in 2012, she was the Leo Gottlieb Professor of Law at Harvard Law School and was widely regarded as America's leading authority on individual bankruptcy.

Richard Wilkinson (1943–) is professor emeritus of social epidemiology at the University of Nottingham, honorary professor of epidemiology and public health at University College, London, and visiting professor at University of York.

Edward N. Wolff (1946–) is a professor of economics at New York University known for his work on the concentration of economic gains at the top. He is the author of thirteen books, including *Top Heavy*, a study of increasing inequality first published in 1995.

Felice Yeskel (1953–2011) founded the Stonewall Center at the University of Massachusetts.

ADDITIONAL READING

Gar Alperovitz and Lew Daly, *Unjust Deserts: How the Rich Are Taking Our Common Inheritance* (New York: The New Press, 2008)

Dean Baker, *The Conservative Nanny State: How the Wealthy Use the Government to Stay Rich and Get Richer* (New York: Center for Economic and Policy Research, 2006)

Robert Frank, *Richistan: A Journey Through the American Wealth Boom and the Lives of the New Rich* (New York: Crown, 2007)

Jacob S. Hacker and Paul Pierson, *Winner-Take-All Politics: How Washington Made the Rich Richer—and Turned Its Back on the Middle Class* (New York: Simon & Schuster, 2010)

Robert Kuttner, *The Squandering of America: How the Failure of Our Politics Undermines Our Prosperity* (New York: Alfred A. Knopf, 2007)

Les Leopold, *The Looting of America: How Wall Street's Game of Fantasy Finance Destroyed Our Jobs, Pensions, and Prosperity* (White River Junction, VT: Chelsea Green, 2009)

Meizhu Lui, Barbara Robles, Betsy Leondar-Wright, Rose Brewer, and Rebecca Adamson, *The Color of Wealth: The Story Behind the U.S. Racial Wealth Divide* (New York: The New Press, 2005)

Ferdinand Lundberg, *America's 60 Families* (New York: Vanguard, 1937)

Ferdinand Lundberg, *The Rich and the Super-Rich: A Study in the Power of Money Today* (Lyle Stuart, 1968)

Timothy Noah, *The Great Divergence: America's Growing Inequality Crisis and What We Can Do About It* (New York: Bloomsbury, 2012)

Sam Pizzigati, *Greed and Good: Understanding and Overcoming the Inequality That Limits Our Lives* (New York: Apex, 2004)

Joseph Stiglitz, *The Price of Inequality* (New York: Penguin, 2012)

Edward N. Wolff, *Top Heavy: A Study of the Increasing Inequality of Wealth in America and What Can Be Done About It* (New York: The New Press, 1996)

INFLATION ADJUSTER

Readers who want to convert any dollar figures in these pages to the values for any other year can do so easily by going to the Bureau of Labor Statistics Consumer Price Index adjustment website, http://data.bls.gov/cgi-bin/cpicalc.pl

PERMISSIONS

"The Vanishing Middle Class" by Elizabeth Warren is adapted with permission from *Ending Poverty in America: How to Restore the American Dream*, ed. Senator John Edwards, Marion Crane, and Arne L. Kalleberg (New York: The New Press, 2007).

"How Gains at the Top Injure the Middle Class" by Robert H. Frank, "Why Do So Many Jobs Pay So Badly?" by Christopher Jencks, and "Don't Drink the Kool-Aid" by Robert Kuttner are adapted with permission from *Inequality Matters: The Growing Economic Divide in America and Its Poisonous Consequences*, ed. James Lardner and David A. Smith (New York: The New Press, 2005).

"Inequality Is Holding Back Recovery" by Joseph E. Stiglitz is adapted with permission from an article published in the *New York Times*, January 19, 2013.

"Wage Theft" by Kim Bobo is adapted with permission from *Wage Theft: Why Millions of Working Americans Are Not Getting Paid—And What We Can Do About It* (New York: The New Press, 2009).

"Home Depot's CEO-Size Tip" by Barbara Ehrenreich is excerpted from *The Land Is Their Land: Reports from a Divided Nation*. Copyright 2008 by Barbara Ehrenreich. Permission granted by Henry Holt and Company, LLC. All rights reserved.

"In the Heart of Our Economy and Our Lives" by Beth Shulman is adapted with permission from *The Betrayal of Work: How Low-Wage Jobs Fail 30 Million Americans* (New York: The New Press, 2003).

"Household Wealth Inequality" by Edward N. Wolff is adapted with permission from *Top Heavy: The Increasing Inequality of Wealth in America and What Can Be Done About It* (New York: The New Press, 2002).

"Inequality Across Generations" by Jared Bernstein and "Educational Quality and Equality" by Linda Darling-Hammond are adapted with permission from *All Things Being Equal: Instigating Opportunity in an Inequitable Time*, ed. Brian D. Smedley and Alan Jenkins (New York: The New Press, 2007).

"'I Didn't Do It Alone'" by Chuck Collins and Felice Yeskel is adapted with permission from *Economic Apartheid: A Primer on Economic Inequality and Insecurity* (New York: The New Press, 2000).

"Arthur A. Robertson and the 1929 Crash" by Studs Terkel is adapted from *Hard Times: An Oral History of the Great Depression* (New York: The New Press, 2000).

"Graduates v. Oligarchs" by Paul Krugman is adapted with permission from an article published in the *New York Times,* November 1, 2011.

"No Rich Child Left Behind" by Sean F. Reardon is adapted with permission from an article published in the *New York Times*, April 27, 2013.

"Achievement Gap" by the Editorial Projects of the Education Research Center was adapted with permission from an article published in *Education Week*, July 7, 2011.

"Back to School" by Mike Rose is adapted with permission from *Back to School: Why Everyone Deserves a Second Chance at Education* (New York: The New Press, 2012).

"Health and Income Inequalities Are Linked" by Richard Wilkinson is adapted with permission from *The Impact of Inequality: How to Make Sick Societies Healthier* (New York: The New Press, 2005).

"Unequal Quality of Care" by Mary E. O'Brien, "Reducing Health Care Disparites" by Olveen Carrasquillo and Jaime Torres, and

"Universal Health Care" by Leo W. Gerard are adapted with permission from *10 Excellent Reasons for National Health Care*, ed. Mary O'Brien and Martha Livingston (New York: The New Press, 2008).

"Jailed for Being in Debt" by Chris Serres and Glenn Howatt is adapted with permission from an article published in the *Minneapolis Star Tribune*, June 6, 2010.

"America's Poverty 'Tax'" by Gary Rivlin is adapted with permission from *Broke, USA: From Pawnshops to Poverty, Inc.—How the Working Poor Became Big Business* (New York: HarperBusiness, 2010).

"Hunger in America" by Donald S. Shepard, Elizabeth Setren, and Donna Cooper is adapted with permission from *Hunger in America: Suffering We All Pay For* (2011) by the Center for American Progress, published on the center's website.

"Georgia's Hunger Games" by Neil deMause is adapted with permission from an article published on *Slate*, December 26, 2012.

"Living Down to Expectations" by Stephen Pimpare is adapted with permission from *A People's History of Poverty in America* (New York: The New Press, 2008).

"How Economics Is Biased Toward the Rich" by Moshe Adler is adapted with permission from *Economics for the Rest of Us: Debunking the Science That Makes Life Dismal* (New York: The New Press, 2010).

"Inequality of Hazard" by Frank Ackerman and Lisa Heinzerling is adapted with permission from *Priceless: On Knowing the Price of Everything and the Value of Nothing* (New York: The New Press, 2003).

"A Different Kind of Epidemic" by Ernest Drucker is adapted with permission from *A Plague of Prisons: The Epidemiology of Mass Incarceration in America* (New York: The New Press 2011).

"Prison's Dilemma" by Glenn C. Loury is adapted with permission from an article published in the *Washington Monthly*, January–February 2013.

"Race, Gender, Family Structure, and Poverty" by Peter Edelman is adapted with permission from *So Rich, So Poor: Why It's So Hard to End Poverty in America* (New York: The New Press, 2012).

PUBLISHING IN THE PUBLIC INTEREST

Thank you for reading this book published by The New Press. The New Press is a nonprofit, public interest publisher. New Press books and authors play a crucial role in sparking conversations about the key political and social issues of our day.

We hope you enjoyed this book and that you will stay in touch with The New Press. Here are a few ways to stay up to date with our books, events, and the issues we cover:

- Sign up at www.thenewpress.com/subscribe to receive updates on New Press authors and issues and to be notified about local events
- Like us on Facebook: www.facebook.com/newpressbooks
- Follow us on Twitter: www.twitter.com/thenewpress

Please consider buying New Press books for yourself; for friends and family; or to donate to schools, libraries, community centers, prison libraries, and other organizations involved with the issues our authors write about.

The New Press is a 501(c)(3) nonprofit organization. You can also support our work with a tax-deductible gift by visiting www.thenewpress.com/donate.